The Paradigm Shift to Multimodality in Contemporary Computer Interfaces

Synthesis Lectures on Human-Centered Informatics

Editor
John M. Carroll, *Penn State University*

Human-Centered Informatics (HCI) is the intersection of the cultural, the social, the cognitive, and the aesthetic with computing and information technology. It encompasses a huge range of issues, theories, technologies, designs, tools, environments, and human experiences in knowledge work, recreation and leisure activity, teaching and learning, and the potpourri of everyday life. The series publishes state-of-the-art syntheses, case studies, and tutorials in key areas. It shares the focus of leading international conferences in HCI.

The Paradigm Shift to Multimodality in Contemporary Computer Interfaces
Sharon Oviatt and Philip R. Cohen
April 2015

Multitasking in the Digital Age
Gloria Mark
April 2015

The Design of Implicit Interactions
Wendy Ju
March 2015

Core-Task Design: A Practice-Theory Approach to Human Factors
Leena Norros, Paula Savioja, and Hanna Koskinen
March 2015

An Anthropology of Services: Toward a Practice Approach to Designing Services
Jeanette Blomberg and Chuck Darrah
February 2015

Proxemic Interactions: From Theory to Practice
Nicolai Marquardt and Saul Greenberg
February 2015

The Paradigm Shift to Multimodality in Contemporary Computer Interfaces
Sharon Oviatt and Philip R. Cohen

ISBN: 978-3-031-01085-9 print
ISBN: 978-3-031-02213-5 ebook

DOI 10.1007/978-3-031-02213-5

A Publication in the Springer series
SYNTHESIS LECTURES ON HUMAN-CENTERED INFORMATICS #30
Series Editor: John M. Carroll, Penn State University

Series ISSN 1946-7680 Print 1946-7699 Electronic

The Paradigm Shift to Multimodality in Contemporary Computer Interfaces

Sharon Oviatt
Incaa Designs

Philip R. Cohen
VoiceBox Technologies

SYNTHESIS LECTURES ON HUMAN-CENTERED INFORMATICS #30

ABSTRACT

During the last decade, cell phones with multimodal interfaces based on combined new media have become the dominant computer interface worldwide. Multimodal interfaces support mobility and expand the expressive power of human input to computers. They have shifted the fulcrum of human-computer interaction much closer to the human. This book explains the foundation of human-centered multimodal interaction and interface design, based on the cognitive and neurosciences, as well as the major benefits of multimodal interfaces for human cognition and performance. It describes the data-intensive methodologies used to envision, prototype, and evaluate new multimodal interfaces. From a system development viewpoint, this book outlines major approaches for multimodal signal processing, fusion, architectures, and techniques for robustly interpreting users' meaning. Multimodal interfaces have been commercialized extensively for field and mobile applications during the last decade. Research also is growing rapidly in areas like multimodal data analytics, affect recognition, accessible interfaces, embedded and robotic interfaces, machine learning and new hybrid processing approaches, and similar topics. The expansion of multimodal interfaces is part of the long-term evolution of more expressively powerful input to computers, a trend that will substantially improve support for human cognition and performance.

KEYWORDS

multimodal interface, multimodal-multisensor interface, new media, mobility, expressive power, human-centered, communication interfaces, cognition and performance, multisensory perception, design prototyping, data-intensive systems, signal processing, semantic integration, time-sensitive processing, hybrid architectures, commercialization, smart phones and mobile devices, wearable technology, technology paradigm shift, theoretical foundations

Dedication

In memory of Harriet

Contents

Preface: Intended Audience and Teaching with this Book

This book is intended as a primary introductory text for courses on multimodal and mobile interfaces, including upper division undergraduate and graduate classes. It explains the basic concepts and terminology required to understand the rapidly expanding literature on multimodal interaction and interface design. This includes the main types of multimodal interface, and their current role in supporting the global expansion of mobile devices like cell phones. It introduces multimodal system processing at the signal and language levels, and current approaches to building multimodal system architectures. From a design perspective, students are introduced to prototyping techniques for envisioning and realizing new multimodal systems. They also learn the dominant multimodal application areas and their commercialization status. From a usability standpoint, this book describes how multimodal interface design has been informed by theory and the cognitive science literature on multisensory processing, as well as the different performance advantages of using a multimodal interface.

We recommend assigning this text at the beginning of a quarter or semester course, after which supplementary readings can be added to expand students' understanding of different subtopics. For example, a projects-based course could assign additional readings on prototyping and data collection methods, which students could exercise to develop and test their own multimodal interfaces for cell phones and other mobile devices. A computationally oriented course might instead focus on assigning further readings on language processing, signal fusion techniques, and alternative approaches to developing multimodal architectures. In contrast, a multidisciplinary course with cognitive and learning science students could assign primary readings on foundational theory, as well as hands-on projects that involve user testing of multimodal interfaces to evaluate aspects of performance improvement.

This book also is intended as an introductory text for general courses on human-computer interaction and computer interface design. Although new media and combined multimodal interfaces on mobile devices are now the dominant interface worldwide, we are not aware of other textbooks that summarize the foundational topics in this growing area. As part of such a course, it is recommended that this book be read after a general HCI textbook. In this context, it provides a coherent update on the more advanced interfaces that exist today. Since most students use multimodal interfaces daily on cell phones, this book bridges the gap between their own experience of using computer interfaces and the course topic they must master. It also prepares students for corporate internships where they may be expected to design, develop, and evaluate multimodal interfaces based on new media.

The content of this book is relevant to students studying technology and human-computer interfaces, education and learning sciences, cognitive science and psychology, linguistics and communication sciences, design, and many multidisciplinary majors (e.g., Science, Technology and Society, Symbolic Systems). Apart from students, this book is highly recommended for anyone who wants to understand the future directions of computer technology, including the major paradigm shift toward new media and multimodal interfaces on mobile devices. This book will help readers to understand the impact of these new interfaces on their own performance and society at large.

Acknowledgments

Support for writing this book was provided by Incaa Designs (http://www.incaadesigns.org/). We would especially like to thank Diane Cerra, Executive Editor at Morgan & Claypool Publishers, for her expert advice, responsiveness, and flexibility throughout this project. Special thanks also to Jack Carroll, editor of the *Human-centered Informatics Synthesis* book series, and to the three reviewers for many insightful comments that led to improvements in the final draft. We also thank the large number of students and colleagues who collaborated with us over the past two decades on different aspects of multimodal interface and system design. Without their enthusiasm, insights, and friendship, we could never have developed the expertise needed to write this book.

Introduction

"Multimodal systems... initially will supplement, and eventually replace, the standard GUIs of today's computers for many applications."

-Oviatt and Cohen, 2000, p. 52

During the last decade, mobile devices with multimodal user interfaces (MUIs) based on combined new media have eclipsed keyboard-based graphical user interfaces (GUIs) as the dominant computational interface worldwide. This proliferation of *multimodal interfaces*, and their increasingly sophisticated design and implementation, has been driven largely by the rise in cell phones. On a global scale, this trend toward expanded development of multimodal interfaces is accelerating with the adoption of smart phones and other mobile devices in developing regions.

In addition to support for mobility, multimodal interfaces have been an important key to shifting the fulcrum of human-computer interaction much closer to the human. Their emergence is part of the long-term evolution of more expressively powerful user input to computers. As described in Section 3.7 and Chapter 11, expressively powerful interfaces can substantially facilitate human cognition and the design of computer interfaces as more effective "thinking tools" (Oviatt, 2013a). From a communications perspective, Figure I.1 illustrates that expressively powerful interfaces are ones that support expression of information involving different modalities, representations, and linguistic codes.

In this book, Chapters 1 and 2 discuss the different types of multimodal interface, the history and status of their development, and how factors such as mobility and globalization are driving their expansion. Chapter 3 explains the major advantages of multimodal interfaces, which have motivated their development, functionality, and commercial success. To support a deeper understanding of their documented performance advantages for users, Chapters 4 and 5 summarize the evolutionary, neuroscience, cognitive science, and theoretical foundations of multimodal interface design. At the center of this discussion is an overview of human multisensory processing, a body of scientific research that has matured in parallel with multimodal technology.

From a process-oriented viewpoint, chapter 6 describes human-centered design strategies. It presents high-fidelity simulation methods for iterative prototyping and evaluation of new multimodal interfaces. These critical tools provide support for the design of complex, data-intensive multimodal systems, including ones capable of guiding the development of collaborative multimodal user input, language, interaction patterns, and error resolution.

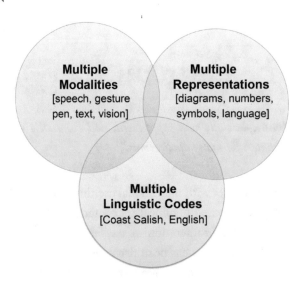

Figure I.1: Richly expressive communication interfaces that support multiple modalities, representations, and linguistic codes. From Oviatt (2012). Copyright © 2012 Lawrence Erlbaum Assoc. Used with permission.

From a systems perspective, Chapters 7 and 8 summarize how multimodal systems process information at the signal and language level, how they accomplish fusion and are integrated architecturally, and principles for strategizing multimodal integration. With the proliferation of new input modes and sensors, especially on cell phone platforms, there now are numerous opportunities for strategically fusing information in different ways to improve system performance. Chapter 9 describes the dominant application areas for which multimodal interfaces most often have been commercialized. Chapter 10 then discusses examples of rapidly emerging multimodal research topics and application areas, including multimodal analytics, affect recognition, robotic interfaces, virtual assistants, accessible interfaces, and many types of ubiquitous and wearable interfaces.

Chapters 11 and 12 analyze future directions for improving multimodal systems in major ways. Chapter 11 summarizes design principles for guiding the development of more expressively powerful computer interfaces. It also discusses the expansion of multimodality to better support 80% of global users whose native language is not Roman alphabetic (e.g., Mandarin, Hindi). During the next decade, mobility, multi-functionality, and global communication requirements are factors that will continue to transform multimodal interfaces and the technology industry more generally.

CHAPTER 1

Definition and Types of Multimodal Interface

Multimodal interfaces support user input and processing of two or more modalities—such as speech, pen, touch and multi-touch, gestures, gaze, and virtual keyboard. These input modalities may coexist together on an interface, but be used either simultaneously or alternately. The input may involve recognition-based technologies (e.g., speech, gesture), simpler discrete input (e.g., keyboard, touch), or sensor-based information. Some of these modalities may be capable of expressing semantically rich information and creating new content (e.g., speech, writing, keyboard), while others are limited to making discrete selections and controlling the system display (e.g., touching a URL to open it, pinching to shrink a visual display). As will be discussed in this chapter, there are numerous types of multimodal interface with different characteristics that have proliferated during the past decade. This general trend toward multimodal interfaces aims to support more natural, flexible, and expressively powerful user input to computers, compared with past keyboard-and-mouse interfaces that are limited to discrete input.

This book focuses on interfaces involving multimodal user input capabilities, as distinct from the complementary and large body of literature on multimedia system output from a signal processing, circuits, networking, algorithms and software design viewpoint (Chen, 2015; Steinmetz, 2015; Steinmetz and Nahrstedt, 2004). It also is distinct from treatments of intelligent multimedia systems that emphasize presentation planning and application of artificial intelligence techniques to system processing and output (Maybury, 1993). Our treatment of multimodal input addresses the human-centered design of system capabilities available to users for accessing and interacting with computational devices, rather than the development of system output capabilities. Although it is common to do so, a multimodal interface may or may not be combined with multimedia system output to the user.

Throughout this book, we distinguish between keyboard-and-mouse interfaces that combine two relatively simple and discrete forms of input, from multimodal interfaces that expand the expressive power, flexibility, and naturalness of interfaces by incorporating recognition- and sensor-based information sources. In a multimodal interface, some modalities may involve active user input to a system (e.g., semantic content of speech, writing, or typing), while others process passively tracked continuous information that the user may not intend specifically as system input (e.g., visual processing of facial expressions, gaze location). Passively tracked information also can include paralinguistic or low-level signal dimensions of input modalities like speech and writing, such as speech pitch or volume that can reveal energy level and emotional state.

This distinction between active input modes and *passive input modes* depends on whether the user is consciously deploying their actions with the intent of providing input to a computer system. Passive input modes and sensors can provide information to a multimodal system more unobtrusively and transparently to facilitate interactions, and their use is expanding rapidly. However, unless carefully designed, systems that process sensors and passive input modes can result in higher false alarms and be less intuitive to users. As will be discussed in Chapter 12, continuous monitoring of user behavior also risks violation of privacy, commercial exploitation, government surveillance, and other concerns that our society is struggling with today. See Table 1.1 for terms.

The most advanced multimodal interfaces are *fusion-based* ones that co-process two or more combined user input modes that can be entered simultaneously, such as speech and pen input, speech and lip movements, or speech and manual gesturing. They process meaning from two recognition-based technologies to fuse an overall interpretation based on joint meaning fragments from the two signal streams (see Chapter 8 for details). At the signal level, recognition technologies process continuous input streams (e.g., acoustic speech, digital ink trace) that contain high-bandwidth and often semantically rich information, which can be used for *content creation*—or to create and interact with a system's application content. Fusion-based multimodal interfaces have been developed and commercialized in recent years (see Chapters 7-9), and their interfaces have been designed and optimized to support a specific range of tasks. See Table 1.1 for italicized terminology.

At the other end of the spectrum, the simplest multimodal interfaces have input options that are used as *alternative modes,* rather than being co-processed. These rudimentary multimodal interfaces have been widely commercialized, for example on cell phones. They often offer more input options than a fusion-based multimodal system, such as speech, touch and multi-touch, gestures (e.g., pinching, flicking), stylus, keyboard,[1] and sensor-based controls (e.g., proximity for system activation, tilt for direction of screen display). In this regard, their interfaces typically involve a more "kitchen-sink" modality combination, which is less optimized for any specific set of modalities. These interfaces often include modes limited to *controlling the system display*, such as touching a URL to open a web page or pinching the screen to shrink its size. When input modes capable of

---

[1] New hybrid virtual keyboards on cell phones are becoming more flexible, multi-lingual, intelligent, and even multimodal. For example, some products such as Swype (Nuance, 2015a) support (1) four different interaction modes: tapping to type, gestural swiping of letters, handwriting letters, or spoken dictated letters; (2) choice of input language; (3) choice of level of recognition (stroke, character, sentence). Users can enable predictive input of subsequent letters. They also can enable data collection from certain applications, so the system learns and improves recognition. Some systems also support flexible shifting of languages during input, such as active use of "Hinglish" by Indian users who code mix. In this book, we distinguish between traditional tap-to-type keyboard interfaces, and these new hybrid virtual "keyboards" on mobile devices.

content creation are included in an alternative-mode multimodal interface (e.g., speech), recognizers may be used to process them but they are not processed jointly with another mode.

On mobile devices, some multimodal interfaces actually are *multimodal-multisensor* ones (see Table 1.1). These interfaces combine multimodal user input with one or more forms of sensor control involving contextual cues. For example, proximity of a cell phone to the user's ear may turn it on, or the angle of holding a phone may orient its display. When a user says or types, "Where are the nearest Italian restaurants?" sensor information about the user's location can constrain the listings and display them on a map. Users do not necessarily need to consciously engage sensor controls, although they may learn their contingencies over time and begin to do so. Multimodal-multisensor interfaces aim to transparently facilitate user interaction, especially while they are in mobile settings. This type of interface already has been commercialized widely on cell phones, wearables, in-vehicle interfaces, and other mobile devices.

On current multimodal interfaces, true alternative-mode interfaces actually are increasingly rare. For example, cell phone interfaces typically only process speech after a user presses to talk, which then engages speech processing. In other cases, speech input queries are not processed in isolation, but rather fused with sensor-based information (e.g., location) as illustrated in the above restaurant search example. In this respect, the simplest types of multimodal interface today typically use one mode or sensor to either engage or constrain a second modality.

Temporally cascaded multimodal interfaces process a combination of modalities that tend to be sequenced in a particular order, such as gaze directed at an object followed by speaking about it. When a temporally predictable sequence of modalities is present in users' behavior, the system can use partial information supplied by the earlier modality (e.g., gaze, touch) to constrain interpretation of information presented in the later-arriving mode (e.g., speech). Systems of this type potentially could process meaningful information trimodally, for example processing a user's gaze, then touch or pointing, followed by speech. Temporally cascaded multimodal interfaces potentially can powerfully constrain meaning interpretation, but they have been under-exploited.

As illustrated in the above example, some multimodal interfaces fuse information from more than two sources. However, this processing does not necessarily always assume a fixed temporal sequence. In multi-biometric interfaces, for which highly reliable person identification is imperative, three or more information sources processed jointly can achieve highly reliable identification that rules out imposters. Such systems emphasize fusing a larger number of information sources, uncorrelated information sources, and passively tracked behaviors or physical characteristics that are difficult to spoof (e.g., iris pattern, fingerprints, face recognition, gait, speech quality). To further improve reliable identification, this type of multimodal system often includes a multi-algorithm or parallel fusion approach (Ross and Poh, 2009). Commercial multi-biometric systems are described further in Chapter 9.

The long-term trend has been expansion in the number and type of information sources represented in multimodal interfaces, which has been especially noteworthy on current smart phones. This has included both active and passive recognition-based input modes. It also has involved rapid incorporation of new sensors, increasing the prevalence of multimodal-multisensor interfaces. One impact of these trends has been to multiply the strategies observed for effectively fusing information among sensors and modes in order to create new functionality. While new functionality often simply controls the interface display, increasingly it also is expanding the system's ability to interpret users' meaning more accurately. This may include processing that extends beyond handling individual input, to refining the accuracy of interpretation during interactive dialogues with follow-up queries. Figure 1.1 illustrates the progression of increasingly more powerful types of multimodal interface.

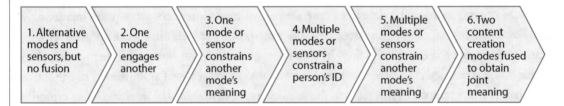

Figure 1.1: Different types of multimodal interface, which have been developed to support increasing complexity and expressive power, from: (1) alternative modes and sensors on the interface, but no fusion among them; (2) one modality used to engage another, such as touch to talk; (3) one mode or sensor constrains another's meaning interpretation, such as location while mobile determining what "nearby" means in a spoken query about restaurants; (4) multiple modes or sensors retrieve person identification from a database, as in multi-biometric systems; (5) multiple modes or sensors constrain another mode's meaning, such as GPS location, direction of movement, and pointing at a highway route to disambiguate the meaning of a spoken query about "gas stations up ahead"; and (6) two content creation modes are fused to produce a joint meaning interpretation, such as writing to encircle an area while speaking "show real estate." Beyond level 6 fusion systems, there are opportunities to increase expressive power in a number of ways. For example, interactive dialogue capabilities could be added to progressively constrain or correct information (see Section 2.3 examples). In addition, passively-tracked information (e.g., facial expressions, voice quality) could be added to provide further information about a user's attitude, emotional state, personality, and so forth, thereby resulting in a system with multiple content creation and passively tracked modes. From Oviatt (2012). Copyright © 2012 Lawrence Erlbaum Assoc. Used with permission.

Table 1.1: Definition and types of multimodal interface

Multimodal Interfaces support input and processing of two or more modalities, such as speech, pen, touch and multi-touch, gestures, gaze, and virtual keyboard, which may be used simultaneously or alternately. User input modes can involve recognition-based technologies (e.g., speech) or discrete input (e.g., keyboard, touch). Some modes may express semantically rich information (e.g., pen, speech, keyboard), while others are limited to simple selection and manipulation actions that control the system display (e.g., gestures, touch, sensors).

Fusion-based Multimodal Interfaces co-process information from two or more input modalities. They aim to recognize naturally occurring forms of human language and behavior, which incorporate one or more recognition-based technologies (e.g., speech, pen, vision). More advanced ones process meaning from two modes involving recognition-based technologies, such as speech and gestures, to produce an overall meaning interpretation (see chapter 8). Simpler ones jointly process information from one mode or sensor (e.g., pointing/touching an object, location while mobile) to constrain the interpretation of another recognition-based mode (e.g., speech).

Alternative-Mode Multimodal Interfaces provide an interface with two or more input options, but users enter information with one modality at a time and the system processes each input individually.

Multimodal Interfaces for Content Creation incorporate high-bandwidth or semantically rich modes, which can be used to create, modify, and interact with system application content (e.g., drawing lake on a map). They typically involve a recognition-based technology.

Multimodal Interfaces for Controlling the System Display incorporate input modes limited to controlling the system or its display, such as zooming or turning the system on, rather than creating or interacting with application content. Examples include touch and multi-touch (e.g., for selection), gestures (e.g., flicking to paginate), and sensor-based controls (e.g., tilt for angle of screen display).

Active Input Modes are ones that are deployed by the user intentionally as explicit input to a computer system (e.g., speaking, writing, typing, gesturing, pointing).

Passive Input Modes refer to naturally occurring user behavior or actions that are recognized and processed by the system (e.g., facial expressions, gaze, physiological or brain wave patterns, sensor input such as location). They involve user or contextual input that is unobtrusively and passively monitored, without requiring any explicit user command to a computer.

Temporally Cascaded Multimodal Interfaces are ones that process two or more user modalities that tend to be sequenced in a particular temporal order (e.g., gaze, gesture, speech), such that partial information supplied by recognition of an earlier mode (e.g., gaze) constrains interpretation of a later one (e.g., manual selection), which then may jointly constrain interpretation of a third mode (e.g., speech). Such interfaces may combine active input modes, passive ones, or blend both types of input.

Multimodal-Multisensor Interfaces combine one or more user input modalities with sensor information that involves passive input from contextual cues (e.g., location, acceleration, proximity, tilt) that a user does not need to consciously engage. They aim to incorporate passively-tracked sensor input to transparently facilitate user interaction, which may be combined with an active input mode (e.g., speech) or a passive one (e.g., facial expression). The type and number of sensors incorporated into multimodal interfaces has been expanding rapidly on cell phones, in cars, robots, and other applications—resulting in explosive growth of multimodal-multisensor interfaces (see Chapter 9).

Visemes refer to the classification of visible lip movements that correspond with audible phonemes during continuous articulated speech. Many audio-visual speech recognition systems co-process these two sources of information multimodally to enhance the robustness of recognition.

CHAPTER 2

History of Paradigm Shift from Graphical to Multimodal Interfaces

The paradigm shift in computer interface design from keyboard-and-mouse graphical interfaces (GUIs) to multimodal interfaces (MUIs) has taken place over a period of 40-50 years, following Engelbart's demonstration of the oN-Line System and invention of the mouse in the 1960s, and the Xerox 8010 Star's mouse-driven graphical user interface in the 1970s and early 1980s (Card et al., 1978; Engelbart, 1962; Kay, 1977; Smith et al., 1982; Thacker et al., 1982). Graphical interfaces dominated commercial computer interfaces from the time personal computers first became available in the 1980s. However, by the 1980s research on combined multimodal interfaces for recognizing speech and pointing and speech and lip movements already was underway (Bolt, 1980; Brooke and Petajan, 1986; Kobsa et al., 1986; Petajan, 1984). For example, early work examined the integration of speech and lip movements, for which *visemes* and phonemes were co-processed. Visemes refer to the detailed classification of visible lip movements that correspond with audible phonemes for consonants and vowels during continuous articulated speech. This work aimed to improve intelligibility over unimodal speech alone, especially in noisy environments. It also aimed to create a more natural synthesis of media for supporting realistic animated characters (Brooke and Petajan, 1986; Cassell et al., 2000; Cohen and Massaro, 1993; Stork and Hennecke, 1995). Other seminal work designed multimodal speech and pen interfaces for transmitting complex information during remote collaboration as part of the FreeStyle system[2] (Wang, 1990).

Perhaps surprisingly, work on recognition technologies that later became components of multimodal interfaces were invented in the 1800s. In fact, the first U.S. patent on an electronic tablet with a stylus for handwritten input was granted in 1888 (Gray, 1888). Very early patents also were filed for recognition of handwritten characters on a pen interface (Goldberg, 1914), a touch screen for handwritten input (Moodey, 1942), and stylus input on a tablet computer for pointing and handwritten text recognition (Dimond, 1957). In 1952, researchers at Bell Labs built a system for isolated digit recognition for a single speaker, guided by acoustic-prosodic theory (Davis et al., 1952; Juang and Rabiner, 2005). All of these developments substantially predated the first graphical interfaces.

Early multimodal interfaces were inspired heavily by parallel cognitive science research on multisensory perception and the integration of modalities in both humans and animals (Brooke and Petajan, 1986; Kendon, 1980; McGrath and Summerfield, 1985; McGurk and MacDonald,

---

2   For a videotape of the Wang FreeStyle system, see: http://www.youtube.com/watch?v=FRKzmFH7-cM.

1976; McLeod and Summerfield, 1987; Sumby and Pollack, 1954). Historically, psychological research on sensory perception was dominated by a focus on individual modes of sensory perception, such as vision and audition. In the 1980s, systematic research began to examine interaction among different sensory modalities, both behaviorally and at the neuronal level. By the end of the 1990s, the multidisciplinary field of multisensory processes had consolidated and was flourishing. It has now radically changed scientific views on sensory perception (Calvert et al., 2004; Stein, 2012). Section 4.2 describes key developments in multisensory processes, which provides a foundation for understanding the usability advantages of multimodal interfaces.

2.1   EARLY MULTIMODAL INTERFACES

Multimodal systems developed rapidly during the 1990s and beyond (Benoit et al., 2000; Oviatt et al., 2000). Major developments occurred in the hardware and software required to support critical component technologies incorporated in multimodal systems, as well as in techniques for integrating parallel input streams. Multimodal systems also diversified to include new modality combinations, such as speech and manual gesturing, speech and writing, gaze and typing, and other combinations (Benoit and Le Goff, 1998; Cohen et al., 1997; Salisbury et al., 1990; Stork and Hennecke, 1995; Turk and Robertson, 2000; Zhai et al., 1999). In addition, the array of multimodal applications expanded rapidly, including multimodal interfaces for map systems, simulations, virtual reality systems, web browsers and web-based transaction systems, in-vehicle controls, person identification/verification systems, robotics, medical systems, education systems, personal information management, mobile cell phones, and other areas (Cohen and McGee, 2004; Iyengar et al., 2003; McGee, 2003; McGee et al., 2000; Neti et al., 2000; Oviatt, 2003; Oviatt et al., 2000, 2004b; Oviatt and Lunsford, 2005; Pankanti et al., 2000; Reithinger et al., 2003; Waibel et al., 1997).

In one of the earliest concept demonstrations, Bolt had users sit in front of a projection of "Dataland" in "the Media Room" (Negroponte, 1978). Using the "Put That There" interface (Bolt, 1980), they could use speech and pointing on a touchpad to create and move objects on a 2-D large screen display. For example, the user could issue a command to "Create a blue square there," with the location of "there" indicated by a 2-D cursor on the screen. Semantic processing was based on spoken input, and the meaning of the deictic "there" was resolved by processing the x,y coordinate indicated by the cursor at the time "there" was spoken.

Early multimodal systems frequently supported speech input as part of a keyboard-and-mouse graphical interface. The focus of these systems was on providing richer natural language processing and expressive power for users when they were manipulating complex visuals or engaging in information extraction. As speech recognition technology matured during the late 1980s and 1990s, numerous early multimodal-multimedia map systems were developed to which a user could speak or type and point with a mouse to extract tourist information or engage in military simulations.

Among the many examples of this type of multimodal interface are CUBRICON, Georal, Galaxy, XTRA, Shoptalk and Miltalk (Cohen et al., 1989; Kobsa et al., 1986; Neal and Shapiro, 1991; Seneff et al., 1996; Siroux et al., 1995; Wahlster, 1991).

For example, using the CUBRICON system users could point to an object on a map and ask:

"Is this <point> an air base?"

CUBRICON was an expert system with extensive domain knowledge, as well as natural language processing that included referent identification and dialogue tracking (Neal and Shapiro, 1991). With the Georal system, users could query a tourist information system to plan travel routes using spoken input and pointing using a touch screen (Siroux et al., 1995). The Shoptalk system permitted users to interact with graphics representing a factory production flow for chip manufacturing (Cohen et al., 1989). Users could point to a specific machine in the production layout and say:

"Show me all the times when this machine was down."

After the system delivered its answer as a list of times, users could click on one to ask the follow-up question:

"What chips were waiting in the queue then, and were any of them hot lots?"

Multimedia system feedback provided text answers, and users also could click on graphics such as a particular machine to view an exploded diagram of queue contents.

2.2   LATER ADVANCED MULTIMODAL INTERFACES

Since the mid 1990s, multimodal systems have been designed that can co-process two parallel input streams containing rich semantic information. These multimodal systems can recognize two natural forms of human language and behavior, for which two recognition-based technologies are incorporated within a more powerful bimodal user interface. Systems that combine either speech and pen input (Oviatt and Cohen, 2000) or speech and lip movements (Benoit, et al, 2000; Stork and Hennecke, 1995; Rubin et al., 1998; Potamianos et al., 2003) became the most mature areas within multimodal research. In these new interfaces, the keyboard and mouse were abandoned. In multimodal speech and pen systems, spoken language was processed along with complex pen-based gestural input involving hundreds of different symbols (Oviatt et al., 2000). For multimodal speech and lip movement systems, spoken language was processed along with corresponding human lip movements during natural audio-visual spoken interaction. In both of these areas, considerable work addressed quantitative modeling of the integration and synchronization characteristics of the two input modes being processed. Innovative *time-sensitive architectures* also were developed to process these patterns in a robust manner, which departed radically from the architectures required for graphical interfaces (see Chapter 7). See Table 7.1 for italicized terms.

Historically, multimodal speech and lip movement research was driven by cognitive science interest in intersensory audio-visual perception and the coordination of speech output with lip and facial movements (Benoit and Le Goff, 1998; Bernstein and Benoit, 1996; Cohen and Massaro, 1993; Massaro and Stork, 1998; McGrath and Summerfield, 1985; McGurk and MacDonald, 1976; McLeod and Summerfield, 1987; Robert-Ribes et al., 1998; Sumby and Pollack, 1954; Summerfield, 1992; Vatikiotis-Bateson et al., 1996). Among the many contributions of this literature was a detailed classification of human lip movements (*visemes*) and the viseme-phoneme mappings that occur during articulated speech. Existing systems that have processed combined speech and lip movements include the classic work by Petajan (1984), Brooke and Petajan (1986), and others (Adjoudani and Benoit, 1995; Bregler and Konig, 1994; Silsbee and Su, 1996; Tomlinson et al., 1996). Additional examples of speech and lip movement systems, applications, and relevant cognitive science research have been detailed elsewhere (Benoit et al., 2000).

Research on multimodal speech and lip movement systems actively explored adaptive techniques for improving system robustness, especially in noisy environmental contexts (Dupont and Luettin, 2000; Meier et al., 1996; Potamianos et al., 2003; Rogozan and Deglise, 1998). With respect to applications, quantitative modeling of synchronized phoneme/viseme patterns eventually led to the development of realistic animated characters capable of generating text-to-speech output with coordinated lip movements for television and the movie industry. With respect to interface design, animated characters also have been used extensively in the design of multimodal virtual agents and educational systems (See Chapter 9; Cassell et al., 2000; Cohen and Massaro, 1993).

Multimodal systems that recognize speech and pen-based gestures first were prototyped and studied in the early 1990s (Oviatt et al., 1992). The seminal QuickSet system prototype was built in 1994. Systems such as this were designed using high-fidelity prototyping techniques and empirical studies (see Section 6.1), which helped to ensure that they could process users' actual language and behavior accurately. The QuickSet system was an agent-based collaborative multimodal system that ran on a hand-held PC (Cohen et al., 1997). With QuickSet, users could combine speech and pen input to place the correct number, length, and orientation (e.g., SW, NE) of aircraft landing strips on a map by speaking and drawing the following multimodal command:

"Airstrips... facing this way <draws arrow>, and facing this way <draws arrow>"

Compared with graphical interfaces, multimodal interfaces such as this were particularly adept at handling spatial content. RASA was the first tangible multimodal system, which extended the QuickSet multimodal interface to include digital paper and pen technology (McGee et al., 2000).

Other research systems of this type also were built in the late 1990s. Examples include the Human-centric Word Processor, Portable Voice Assistant, QuickDoc and MVIEWS (Bers et al., 1998; Cheyer, 1998; Oviatt et al., 2000; Waibel et al., 1997). These systems represented a variety of different multimodal interface features, applications, information fusion, and linguistic process-ing techniques. In most cases, these multimodal systems jointly interpreted speech and pen input based on a late frame-based information fusion approach. In contrast, QuickSet used a unification process (Johnston, 1998; Johnston et al., 1997), and a hybrid symbolic/statistical architecture (Wu et al., 1999). Since then, other mobile systems have adopted unification-based multimodal fusion and a hybrid architecture approach for processing multimodal input (Denecke and Yang, 2000; Pfleger, 2004; Wahlster, 2001), and even multimodal output (Kopp et al., 2004). See Chapters 7 and 8 for a discussion of the main multimodal signal and language processing techniques, as well as types of architecture.

By the late 1990s, multimodal systems that process speech and manual gesturing also were developed (Encarnacao and Hettinger, 2003; Flanagan and Huang, 2003; Sharma et al., 1998; Pavlovic et al., 1997). These systems required segmenting and interpreting continuous three-dimen-sional manual movements, which was a more difficult technical challenge than processing a stream of two-dimensional x,y ink coordinates for speech and pen input. Significant cognitive science research on human gestures was used to guide the design of this new type of multimodal interface (Condon, 1988; Kendon, 1980; McNeill, 1992). Among the first multimodal systems to process manual gesturing combined with speech were those developed by Koons et al. (1993), Sharma et al. (1996), Poddar et al. (1998), and Duncan et al. (1999).

During the past 15 years, multimodal interfaces that incorporate vision-based technologies for diverse purposes also have been developed, including for recognition of gaze, facial expressions, head nodding, and large body movements (Flanagan and Huang, 2003; Morency et al., 2005; Morimoto et al., 1999; Pavlovic et al., 1997; Turk and Robertson, 2000; Zhai, et al., 1999). Many such systems have been commercialized, as described in Section 9.7. These technologies unobtru-sively or passively monitor users' natural behaviors in context, and need not require explicit user commands to a computer. Some of these systems expanded beyond bimodal ones to incorporate three or more input modes, for example within biometrics research (see Section 9.5). Biometrics combined behavioral input modes (e.g., voice, handwriting) with physical or physiological ones (e.g., retinal scans, fingerprints) to achieve reliable person identification and verification in chal-lenging field conditions (Choudhury et al., 1999; Jain et al., 1999; Jain and Ross, 2002; Pankanti et al., 2000). The combination of active and passive input modes was designed to capitalize on the strengths of each type of input. While passive modes may be "attentive" and less obtrusive, active ones generally are more reliable indicators of user intent.

Related to passive multimodal interfaces and biometrics, considerable international multi-modal research has focused on the collection and automatic analysis of audio-visual activity pat-terns during collaborative group meetings. This work included hardware, software, and interface research to improve the robustness of information capture and interpretation using a combination of multimodal techniques and machine learning. These projects included CALO in North America (http://www.ai.sri.com/project/CALO), the IM2 (http://www.im2.ch/) and AMIDA (http://www.amiproject.org/) projects in Europe, and others. While much of this research was aimed at engineering advances in detection and analysis of human activity patterns related to surveillance and similar applications, other aspects were focused on designing computational meeting assistants for in-person and remote interactions (Oviatt et al., 2008), multimodal meeting browsers and information retrieval systems (Lalanne et al., 2005, 2008; Lisowska, 2007; Popescu-Belis and Georgescul, 2006; Popescu-Belis et al., 2008; Whittaker et al., 2005), and adaptive human-centered interfaces for collaborative work, problem-solving, and educational exchanges (Oviatt et al., 2008). During the past decade, research on group multimodal activity patterns has established new approaches for detecting floor control, agreement, decision-making, personality, and other interaction dynamics during conversation (Chen and Harper, 2009; Gatica-Perez et al., 2005; Germesin, 2009; Hsueh and Moore, 2007).

Many of the multimodal interfaces described above were designed with an emphasis on mobility and field use, for which they were uniquely suitable. The next section discusses expansion of this trend during the design of multimodal interfaces for increasingly small mobile devices—especially commercial cell phones. Chapter 9 discusses the many multimodal systems that have been commercialized, and Chapter 10 introduces actively emerging multimodal research areas.

2.3   RECENT MOBILE DEVICES WITH MULTIMODAL INTERFACES

During the last decade, cell phones and other mobile devices with multimodal interfaces have eclipsed keyboard-and-mouse graphical interfaces as the dominant computer interface worldwide. While the array of mobile devices includes tablets, in-vehicle interfaces (See Section 9.1), robotics (see Sections 9.4 and 10.5), tangible and wearable interfaces (see Sections 9.6 and 10.1), ubiquitous interfaces supported by Kinect and similar tools (see Sections 9.7, 9.9, and 10.1), cell phones and other platforms, this section will highlight the dramatic changes that have occurred in cell phone interfaces in particular. To date, it is the relatively innovative and sophisticated changes in cell phone interfaces that have largely driven the paradigm shift toward new input modes and multimodal interfaces. One clear reason for this is their sheer commercial volume and continued rate of expansion, which is outlined below.

The first commercially available cell phone was introduced in 1983, the Motorola DynaTAC 8000X, after the Federal Communications Commission allocated analog frequencies for a new mobile telephone network. Cell phones have exploded in adoption during the last 30 years, transitioning to over six billion mobile cell phone subscriptions for seven billion people worldwide (DeGusta, 2012; ITU World Telecommunications, 2013). During the past 10-15 years, cellular 3G and 4G capabilities have enabled higher data rates, more powerful streaming media (e.g., video calls, ultra-broadband internet access, mobile TV), and the proliferation of smart phones that blend PDA with mobile phone functionality (Rainie and Poushter, 2014). Approximately one-third of the six billion cell phone subscriptions worldwide now include mobile broadband, with 75% penetration in developed regions and 20% in developing ones (ITU World Telecommunications, 2013). However, penetration currently is changing fast in developing regions like India, where the number of cheap smart phone users doubled in the 18 months before 2015 (McLean, 2015). These developments have directly enabled the widespread commercialization of multimodal interfaces.

Business projections estimate that by 2020 smart phones with mobile broadband will increase from two to six billion, resulting in two-to-three times more smart phones in use than PCs (Evans, 2014). One impact is that new multimodal-multisensor interfaces will be required to support a vastly expanded ecosystem of smart phone applications within the next five years. Consistent with the ubiquitous computing trend, this will include new application directions in which smart phones become the preferred platform to control distant physical objects via the Internet (see Section 10.1), to interact with virtual agents and robots (see Section 10.5), to control in-vehicle systems (see Section 9.1), to support everyday functions for disabled users (see Section 10.4), to monitor learning during education (see Section 10.3) as well as personal health and medical care, and other rapidly emerging areas discussed in Chapter 10. Arguably, mobile devices and their use not only have remade the dominant human interface, but at a deeper level they are rapidly transforming the entire technology industry (Evans, 2014).

This proliferation of multimodal interfaces on cell phones has gradually expanded user options for input, which initially included simple tap-to-type virtual keyboards, touch, and speech. Newer input modalities on smart phones now also include multi-touch, gestures, images and eye movements, stylus, and a multitude of sensors. The content of users' intended input involving speech, gestures, stylus, images, gaze, and sensors can be processed using recognition technologies. Most cell phone applications still process this information individually, rather than fusing it for a joint interpretation. However, touch input for engaging a speech recognizer, or for selecting a location or input field before speaking, is commonly available. Pointing and selection actions serve to constrain the interpretation of subsequent speech. For example, in a T-Mobile multimodal interface that supports speech and stylus input for personal information management, a user can simultaneously tap on a music selection and say "Play this song" (Englert and Glass, 2006). Based on the summary of types of multimodal interface shown in Figure 1.1, this is an example of a level 3 multimodal interface.

As discussed in Chapter 1, the proliferation of new input modes and sensors on mobile devices such as cell phones is generating new opportunities and strategies for fusing information to improve recognition and also deliver new functionality. An AT&T mobile multimodal interface called MATCH (Multimodal Access to City Help) can process pen input that involves gesturing fused with speech, and also linguistic content (Bangalore and Johnston, 2009). For example, users can retrieve urban restaurant and subway information by circling a neighborhood on a map and saying: "Show cheap Italian restaurants in this neighborhood." If the environment is noisy, the user also can circle the area and write: "cheap" and "Italian." That is, this system flexibly accepts input that is either multimodal or unimodal, depending on mobile usage conditions. As feedback, the system responds with both synthetic speech and graphical output (Bangalore and Johnston, 2009). This multimodal interface has been optimized for expected modality usage patterns involving speech and pen input. Based on Figure 1.1, it is an example of a level 6 multimodal interface.

To further expand expressive power, some multimodal interface applications on cell phones also track dialogue context, so a user can follow up on, refine, or correct a system response (Apple, 2014; Ehlen and Johnston, 2013; Google, 2015a; Microsoft, 2015a). In recent years, mobile conversational interfaces with interactive dialogue capabilities have been widely commercialized, such as Siri on the Apple iPhone (Apple, 2015a), Microsoft's Cortana (Microsoft, 2015a), and Google Now voice search (Google, 2015a). Siri is based on a simple multimodal interface in which a user touches and speaks each utterance, and system feedback is provided with text-to-speech and graphical output. It is designed to provide eyes-free personal information management for a multi-functional array of applications, most notably information retrieval, voice dialing, scheduling, personal reminders, and related functions. Siri is multilingual, and uses location-based contextual information to provide adaptive support. Siri also can use the VoiceOver screen reader to speak textual information to visually impaired or eyes-busy cell phone users.

The AT&T mobile multimodal interface capabilities for co-processing speech and pen-based gestures also have been extended to handle dialogue context. In an application called Speak4it, users can search for and retrieve information on local businesses (Ehlen and Johnston, 2013). For example, a mobile user in the car might say "gas stations" while tracing a highway route to search choices where they will be arriving soon. As a follow-up, the user could point to a nearer town along the route and say, "And how about here?" Compared with Siri, Cortana, and Google Now, AT&T's multimodal interface fuses more expressively powerful gesturing along with speech and pointing, supporting them with dialogue context. However, the other commercially available virtual assistants integrate more sources of data, and they support a wider array of personal information management functions. The multimodal fusion, language processing, and virtual assistants that are required to develop these types of multimodal interface, which are now so popular on cell phones, are described further in Chapters 7-10.

The availability of commercial cell phone platforms with multimodal input has substantially expanded the development of applications and adaptive multimodal interfaces (Evans, 2014; Oviatt and Lunsford, 2005). It also has promoted the current multi-functionality of cell phones, as originally predicted by Oviatt and Cohen:

"In the area of mobile computing, multimodal interfaces will promote… the multi-functionality of small devices, in part due to the portability and expressive power of input modes."

—Oviatt and Cohen, 2000, p. 52

Guidelines for mobile multimodal interface design now emphasize the central importance of adaptive capabilities:

"Multimodal interfaces should adapt to the needs and abilities of different users, as well as different contexts of use. Dynamic adaptivity enables the interface to degrade gracefully by leveraging complementary and supplementary modalities according to changes in task and context."

—Reeves et al., 2004, p. 59

In the past, developers of multimodal cell phone applications adopted the approach that mobile users should "choose the most appropriate input and output channel according to the specific usage situation and the actual usage goals" (Englert and Glass, 2006). However, mobile multimodal interfaces for cell phones could benefit from more thoughtfully designed interfaces that reduce demands on users' attention when interacting with applications. One major way to accomplish this is to select an appropriate modality combination that generally alleviates mobile attentional demands. A second avenue is to exploit context awareness so mobile multimodal interfaces can be adapted to the physical context, task, and important aspects of users' status (e.g., affect, cognitive load, activity; Dumas et al., 2013; Reeves et al., 2004). Future adaptation of this kind will depend largely on more effective incorporation of sensors and passively tracked input within multimodal interfaces. This could expand the available types of multimodal interface beyond level 6, as shown in Figure 1.1, to ones that are capable of fusing multiple content creation and passively tracked modes.

In extreme cases where user safety is an issue, adaptivity could include turning a device off, as required by law when driving in many U.S. states. In fact, some approaches to selecting an appropriate modality combination for a particular mobile application advocate enabling and disabling different subsets of modalities from the larger collection on a cell phone platform (Dumas et al., 2013). This could either be accomplished with software, or by swapping in customized hardware components that support different interface modalities. In fact, Google's Project Ara (Google, 2015b) currently is developing a smart phone prototype with modular components, which permits customizing the phone's features and functionality for different users and applications. For example, a user might select a particular camera for their smart phone. This new concept of a smart phone with customizable components is driven largely by the expectation of an expansion in cell phone applications, leading to extreme demands on multi-functionality.

In summary, cell phone interfaces have been the high-impact mobile platform that has driven the paradigm shift to new input modes and multimodal-multisensor interfaces. Their explosive adoption and commercial success supported the innovative change, sophistication, and increased expressive power in computer interfaces today. This shift to new input modes and multimodal interfaces is continuing to evolve on a wide array of mobile devices that will be discussed further in Chapters 9 and 10, including in-vehicle interfaces, robotics, tangible interfaces, wearable interfaces, ubiquitous interfaces, tablets, and cell phone interfaces. The next chapter describes the major advantages of multimodal interfaces, which motivate the development of the systems outlined in this book.

CHAPTER 3

Aims and Advantages of Multimodal Interfaces

Multimodal interface design has been inspired largely by the goal of supporting more expressively powerful, flexible, natural, and transparent means of interacting with computers. It can reduce cognitive load, stimulate cognition, and improve performance in a variety of tasks. As discussed earlier, multimodal interfaces are uniquely well suited for mobile use, including during multi-tasking and adverse or changing conditions. They also are adept at accommodating individual differences among users, and therefore can provide *universal access* to computation. See Table 4.2 for terms. Past research indicates that users have a strong preference to interact multimodally for many applications. Multimodal systems also have been demonstrated to function in a more robust and stable manner than unimodal recognition systems that process speech, writing, gaze, or images. During system development, all of these advantages potentially can be realized, assuming the system that is designed is a well integrated one.[3] In this section, we summarize the main motivations and advantages for developing multimodal interfaces.

3.1 USER PREFERENCE AND NATURAL INTERACTION PATTERNS

A large literature has documented that multimodal interfaces satisfy higher levels of user preference than keyboard-based graphical or unimodal interfaces. Users have a strong preference to interact multimodally, rather than unimodally, across a variety of different application domains, although this preference is most pronounced in spatial ones (Hauptmann, 1989; Oviatt, 1997). For example, 95%–100% of users preferred to interact multimodally when they were free to use either speech or pen input in a map-based spatial domain (Oviatt, 1997). Parallel studies have shown that 71% of users preferred to interact multimodally using combined speech and manual gestures, rather than only one input mode, when manipulating graphic objects on a CRT screen (Hauptmann, 1989).

In research that conducted a task analysis on user input, it was discovered that the type of action users had to perform determined whether they expressed information multimodally. Figure 3.1 illustrates that users communicated multimodally 86% of the time when they had to describe spatial information about the location, number, size, orientation, or shape of an object (Oviatt et

---

[3] It is always possible to design a poorly integrated system interface, or a "kitchen-sink" one with too many alternatives that are poorly chosen and with no attempt to integrate them. If a multimodal interface is not well integrated, it cannot be expected to fully realize the advantages discussed in this chapter.

al., 1997). They were moderately likely to communicate multimodally when simply selecting an object from an array, which only required location information. However, when performing general actions without any spatial component, users expressed themselves multimodally less than 1% of the time. This study involved speech and pen input during a map task.

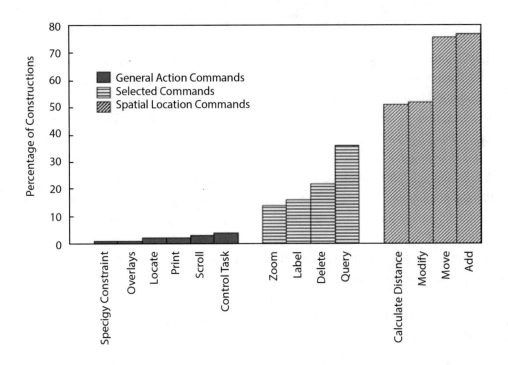

Figure 3.1: Percentage of all constructions that users expressed multimodally as a function of the type of action command, with spatial commands on the right, selection in the middle, and general actions on the left. Based on Oviatt et al. (1997). Copyright © 1997 ACM. Used with permission.

Other analyses indicate that users prefer speech input for describing objects and events, sets and subsets of objects, out-of-view objects, conjoined information, past and future temporal states, and issuing commands for actions or iterative actions (Cohen and Oviatt, 1995; Oviatt and Cohen, 1991). In contrast, they prefer pen input when conveying digits, symbols, graphic content, and the location or shape of spatial information on a graphic display such as a map (Oviatt and Olsen, 1994; Oviatt, 1997; Suhm, 1998). Task analysis of the functions for which people prefer to use a particular mode can reveal opportunities for combining modes synergistically into a more robust multimodal interface.

3.2   FLEXIBLE INTERACTION PATTERNS

Unlike a keyboard-based or unimodal interface, multimodal interfaces support flexible use of input modes. This includes the choice of which modality to use for conveying different types of information, to use input modes together, or to alternate among modes at any time during changing conditions. Since input modalities are well suited for some situations, but less ideal or even inappropriate for others, modality choice is an important design issue in a multimodal system. As systems become more complex and multi-functional, a single modality simply does not permit all users to interact effectively across all tasks and environments.

Importantly, multimodal interfaces provide the adaptability required to accommodate the continuously changing conditions of mobile use. For example, systems involving speech, gesture, touch, or written input are suitable for different mobile tasks. When combined, users can shift among these modalities from moment to moment as environmental conditions change (Holzman, 1999; Oviatt, 2000b, 2000c). In a certain respect, mobility can induce a state of temporary disability, such that a person is unable to use a particular input mode for some period of time. For example, the user of an in-vehicle application may frequently be unable to use manual or gaze input, although speech is available. In this respect, a multimodal interface supports selecting and switching among modalities as needed during the changing circumstances typical of field use.

3.3   ACCOMMODATION OF INDIVIDUAL DIFFERENCES

Since there are large individual differences in ability and preference to use different modes of communication, a multimodal interface supports diverse users in controlling how they interact with the computer. In this respect, multimodal interfaces have the potential to accommodate a broader range of users than traditional interfaces, including users of different ages, skill levels, native language status, cognitive styles, sensory impairments, and other temporary illnesses or permanent handicaps. For example, a visually impaired user or one with repetitive stress injury may prefer speech input and text-to-speech output. In contrast, a user with a hearing impairment or accented speech may prefer touch, gesture, or pen input. The natural alternation between modes supported by a multimodal interface can also prevent overuse and physical damage to any individual modality, especially during extended periods of computer use (Markinson, 1993).

3.4   EFFICIENCY

During the early design of multimodal systems, it was assumed that efficiency gains would be the main advantage of designing an interface multimodally, and that this advantage would be due to processing input modes in parallel. It is true that multimodal interfaces can support improved efficiency, especially when manipulating spatial information. In simulation research comparing speech-only with multimodal speech and pen interaction, multimodal interaction yielded 10% faster task completion during visual-spatial tasks, but no efficiency advantage during verbal or quantitative ones (Oviatt, 1997; Oviatt et al., 1994). Likewise, efficiency improved when users combined speech and manual gestures multimodally to manipulate objects, compared with unimodal input (Hauptmann, 1989). In another study, multimodal speech and mouse input improved efficiency during a drawing task (Leatherby and Pausch, 1992). In studies comparing task completion time when using a keyboard-based graphical interface vs. a multimodal speech and pen one, the multimodal interface sped up creation of complex simulation scenarios on a map by a factor of between 2.4-to-4-fold (Cohen et al., 2000; Cohen et al., 2015). These latter studies were based on testing fully functional multimodal systems, rather than simulations. The multimodal speed advantage also included time to correct recognition errors.

3.5   SUPERIOR ERROR HANDLING

One particularly advantageous feature of multimodal interface design is its superior error handling, both in terms of error avoidance and recovery from errors (Oviatt and van Gent, 1996; Oviatt et al., 1999; Oviatt, 1999a; Rudnicky and Hauptmann, 1992; Suhm, 1998; Tomlinson et al., 1996). There are both user-centered and system-centered reasons why multimodal interfaces facilitate error recovery, compared with unimodal interfaces. First, users typically select the input mode that they judge to be less error prone for particular lexical content, which leads to error avoidance (Oviatt and van Gent, 1996). They may prefer speedy speech input, but will switch to pen input to communicate a foreign name. Second, users' language input often is simplified when interacting multimodally, which can substantially reduce the complexity of language processing and associated recognition errors (Oviatt and Kuhn, 1998). Third, users typically will switch modalities after system recognition errors, which improves error recovery when interacting with recognition-based technologies. This error resolution occurs because the confusion matrices differ for specific lexical content when using different recognition technologies (Oviatt et al., 1999; Oviatt, 2002).

In addition, there are system-centered reasons for superior error handling. A well-designed multimodal system with two semantically rich input modes can support mutual disambiguation of input signals. For example, if a user says "ditches" but the speech recognizer confirms the singular "ditch" as its best guess, then parallel recognition of several graphic marks can result in recovery of the correct plural interpretation. This recovery can occur in a multimodal system even though the speech recognizer initially ranked the plural interpretation "ditches" as a less preferred choice on its *n-best list*. Mutual disambiguation involves recovery from unimodal recognition errors within a multimodal architecture, because semantic information from each mode supplies partial disambiguation of the other, thereby leading to more stable and robust system performance (see Chapter 8; Oviatt, 1999a, 2000a, 2002). Another example of mutual disambiguation is shown in Figure 3.2.

To achieve optimal error handling, a multimodal interface ideally should be designed to include complementary input modes. See Tables 7.1 and 8.3 for terms.

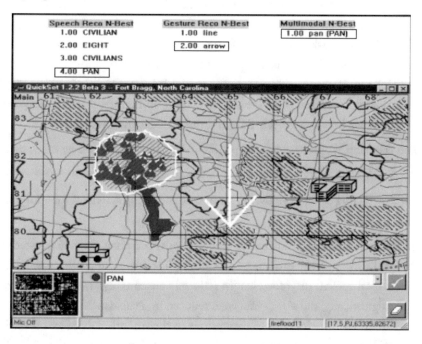

Figure 3.2: Multimodal command to "pan" the map, which illustrates mutual disambiguation occurring between incoming speech and gesture information, such that lexical hypotheses were pulled up on both n-best lists to produce a correct final multimodal interpretation. From Oviatt (1999a). Copyright © 1999 ACM. Used with permission.

In two studies involving over 4,600 multimodal commands, a multimodal system supported mutual disambiguation and error suppression ranging between 19 and 41% (Oviatt, 1999a, 2000a, 2002). Improved robustness was greater for challenging user groups (e.g., accented ones, rather than native speakers) and also usage contexts (e.g., mobile field use, rather than stationary use). These results show that a well-designed multimodal system not only can perform more robustly than a unimodal system, but also in a more stable way across varied users and contexts. For further details, see Section 8.3. During audio-visual perception of speech and lip movements, improved speech recognition also has been demonstrated for both human listeners (McLeod and Summerfield, 1987) and multimodal systems (Adjoudani and Benoit, 1995; Tomlinson et al., 1996).

3.6 MINIMIZATION OF COGNITIVE LOAD

From a cognitive viewpoint, multimodal interfaces can substantially minimize users' cognitive load and improve performance. In one study, people who interacted multimodally using speech and pen during visual-spatial map tasks made 36% fewer task-critical errors, compared with interacting using speech alone (Oviatt, 1997). During tasks of this kind, users' cognitive load is increased when they have to engage in utterance planning about spatial information. The need to specify relative directional information (e.g., east, west) is especially taxing and error-prone. The following example illustrates the difference between speech-only and multimodal communication:

> When speaking, a user says to a map system: "*Add six solar panels on the north end of, on the north part of [pause] the far roof, north.*"

> When interacting multimodally, the same user encircles an area on the roof and says: "*Six solar panels.*"

When people in research studies used a multimodal interface, they eliminated locative descriptions entirely by using the pen to convey locations, lines, areas, and other spatial information. As a result, their total spoken utterance length reduced substantially, their sentence constructions were simplified linguistically, and *disfluencies* were reduced by a substantial 50% (Oviatt, 1997; Oviatt and Kuhn, 1998). Disfluencies refer to disruptions to the smooth flow of an otherwise coherent spoken utterance. They can involve pausing, or non-lexical fillers such as "uh" or "ah." Disfluencies are a major cause of recognition failure in unimodal speech systems. Since utterance planning is well known to increase users' cognitive load sharply, designing a multimodal interface is an effective way to minimize this burden so users can focus on their task. This is reflected in the large reduction in both disfluencies and task errors. See Table 8.3 for term.

Disfluencies are an especially sensitive index for predicting cognitive load (Oviatt, 1995). In previous work involving spatial tasks, disfluencies, inter-sentential pausing, fragmented sentences, and slower speech rate all increased when users were subjected to time pressure or navigational obstacles that elevated their cognitive load (Müller et al., 2001). Data also shows that users' spoken disfluency rate is higher on utterance constituents that contain locative information, compared with non-locative content (Oviatt, 1997). This is illustrated in the following utterance that a user spoke to a map-based real estate application (locative constituent italicized, disfluency bold):

> "*Show me all of the homes for sale under $600,000 west,* **uh, no** *east of May Lake in Nevada City.*"

In research with elementary school children and adults, active manual gesturing was demonstrated to reduce cognitive load and improve memory during a task that required explaining math solutions. During more difficult tasks, this impact of gesturing on reducing cognitive load increased (Goldin-Meadow et al., 2001). The physical activity of manual or pen-based gesturing is believed to play a particularly important role in organizing and facilitating people's spatial information processing, which has been shown to reduce cognitive load on tasks involving geometry, maps, and similar areas (Alibali et al., 2000; Oviatt, 1997)

As task complexity increases, users self manage their working memory limits by distributing information across multiple modalities. This effectively enhances their performance during both perception and production tasks (Calvert et al., 2004; Mousavi et al., 1995; Oviatt, 1997; Oviatt et al., 2004a; Tang et al., 2005). In one study, users' ratio of multimodal interaction increased as tasks became more difficult, from 59.2% during low-difficulty tasks, to 65.5% during moderate difficulty, 68.2% during high difficulty, and 75.0% on very high difficulty ones. As illustrated in Figure 3.3 (right), this represented an overall relative increase of +27% (Oviatt et al., 2004a).

Working Memory theory (Baddeley, 1992) maintains that modality-specific information is processed in different areas of the brain that function largely independently, which enables the effective size of memory to expand when interacting multimodally (Baddeley, 2003). The inherent flexibility of a multimodal interface permits users to "upshift" to interacting multimodally as tasks become difficult, but also "downshift" to interacting unimodally when they are easy. In this regard, multimodal interfaces support users in adapting their interaction to perform well, while also conserving energy whenever possible. They are especially well suited for accommodating the high and changing load conditions that are typical of mobile use. A more detailed discussion of the theoretical foundations of multimodal interface design is presented in Chapter 5.

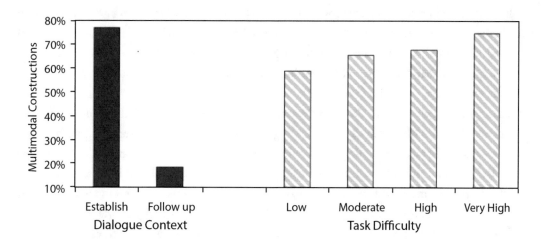

Figure 3.3: Percentage of multimodal constructions as a function of establishing dialogue context vs. following up on it (left) and during increased task difficulty during a map task (right). Based on Oviatt et al. (2004a). Copyright© 2004 ACM. Used with permission.

3.7   EXPRESSIVE POWER AND STIMULATION OF COGNITION

Recent findings have revealed that more expressively powerful interfaces (e.g., digital pen, multi-modal) can substantially stimulate cognition beyond the level supported by either keyboard interfaces or analogous non-digital tools. The magnitude of improvement in appropriate idea generation, correct problem solving, and accurate inferential reasoning in different studies ranges from 9–38% in native English speakers. These results generalize widely across different user populations (e.g., ages, ability levels), content domains (e.g., science, math, everyday reasoning), types of cognition, computer hardware, and evaluation metrics (Oviatt et al., 2012; Oviatt, 2013a).

Pen input is a rich content creation modality that can be used to express all types of representation (i.e., linguistic, symbolic, numeric, diagrammatic). It also can be used to shift rapidly and flexibly among representations while focusing on a task (Oviatt and Cohen, 2010b; Oviatt et al., 2012). Recent studies show that pen interfaces elicit more nonlinguistic communication (e.g., diagrams, symbols, numbers), whereas the same users completing the same type of tasks with a keyboard interface produce more linguistic content. In one study, high school students working on biology hypothesis-generation tasks expressed more nonlinguistic content when using pen interfaces (Figure 3.4, left). When using the pen interfaces, their ideational fluency also increased a substantial 38.5%, which involved producing appropriate biology hypotheses. Regression analyses revealed that knowing a student's level of *nonlinguistic fluency* predicted their ideational fluency (Figure 3.5, left; Oviatt et al., 2012).

In contrast, when the same students switched to using keyboard input to complete the same science hypothesis-generation tasks, they now expressed more *linguistic fluency* (Figure 3.4, right). They typed more total words, rather than nonlinguistic content, and composed full sentences. In this case, regression analyses indicated that an increase in linguistic fluency instead suppressed ideational fluency (Figure 3.5, right; Oviatt et al., 2012). See Table 8.3 for terms.

These results demonstrate the direct relation between language and thought, an Activity theory theme discussed further in Section 5.6. Vygotskian Activity theory asserts that what people communicate directly mediates, guides, and refines their thoughts about the content they are expressing. These results also demonstrate that using a particular input tool that is more expressively powerful (i.e., pen, or multimodal interface incorporating it) can facilitate thinking and reasoning substantially. This topic is described in further detail in Chapter 11, which summarizes additional research and explanatory theory. Chapter 11 also discusses the need for future studies with speakers of world languages that are not Roman alphabetic ones.

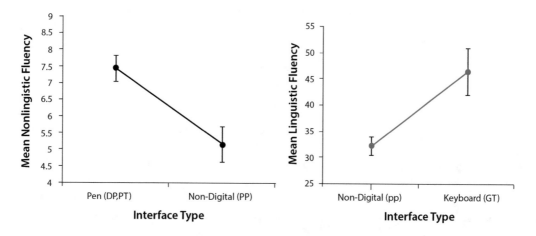

Figure 3.4: Total nonlinguistic communicative fluency during hypothesis generation tasks when using pen interfaces (digital pen and paper, DP; pen tablet, PT), compared with non-digital pencil and paper, PP (left); total linguistic communicative fluency during hypothesis generation tasks when using keyboard interface on a graphical tablet (GT), compared with non-digital pencil and paper, PP (right). From Oviatt et al. (2012). Copyright© 2012. Used with permission.

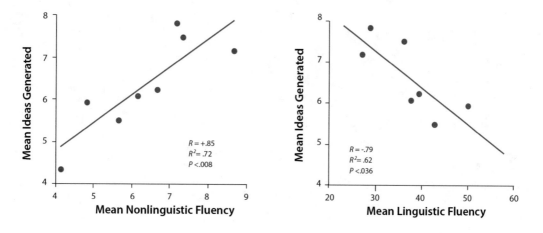

Figure 3.5: Regression analysis showing positive relation between nonlinguistic communicative fluency and ideational fluency (left); regression showing negative relation between linguistic communicative fluency and ideational fluency (right). From Oviatt et al. (2012). Copyright© 2012. Used with permission.

CHAPTER   4

Evolutionary, Neuroscience, and Cognitive Foundations of Multimodal Interfaces

This chapter focuses on the foundations of human-centered multimodal interface design in experimental cognitive psychology and neuroscience. Research from these perspectives has informed our understanding of human multisensory processing, including perception and communication. This chapter also describes research results collected during human-computer multimodal interaction. This latter work has revealed when users typically interact multimodally, what semantic content they express when using different modes, and how they synchronize their multimodal input temporally and semantically. This has provided the basic information needed to design and implement new multimodal interfaces. To set the context for this discussion, we begin by providing brief background on the evolution of human multimodal perceptual and communication abilities.

4.1   EVOLUTION OF MULTIMODAL PERCEPTUAL AND COMMUNICATION ABILITIES

During the transition to homo erectus, the hands were freed for continuous engagement in many critical new functions, including gestural communication (Arbib, 2003; Corballis, 2003). Subsequent brain and anatomical evolution enabled oral speech, which became more dominant during the past 170,000–500,000 years (Arbib, 2003; Corballis, 2003; Dunbar, 2003; Pinker and Bloom, 1990). The transition from exclusive manual gesturing to combining speech with gestures represented a major evolutionary expansion toward modern multimodal communication. In an upright en-face position, human multimodal communication with other humans was stimulated to begin combining facial expressions, speech, and gesturing in the patterns we observe today. Evolution of the neurological substrates that enabled these gradual changes is described elsewhere (Oviatt, 2013a).

The expansion of flexible multimodal communication opened up additional critical functionality for humans, and it expanded the contexts in which people could communicate. In particular, the recruitment of speech as part of multimodal communication enabled people to communicate while walking, in darkness, from a distance, and while demonstrating an action and simultaneously explaining it (Corballis, 2002, 2003; Darwin, 1896). These evolutionary adaptations enhanced people's ability to survive in the wild, to collaborate socially, and to learn from one another by observing an action while hearing an explanation. Multimodal communication also provided the flexibility to use one of several modalities, which made communication more robust against human disability involving any single mode.

From a communications perspective, the advent of multimodal abilities increased the intelligibility, information throughput, abstractness, and flexibility of communication (Lindblom, 1990; Zipf, 1935; Corballis, 2002, 2003). Multisensory convergence directly supports the enhanced intelligibility of a communication by reducing its signal variability, which is especially valuable for improving robustness in adverse field conditions (Calvert et al., 2004; Oviatt, 2000c, 2012). The recruitment of speech as part of multimodal communication also improved humans' ability to communicate more briefly and rapidly, as discussed in Section 3.6. These changes are consistent with the trend for all human communication systems to progress toward greater simplicity and reduced length and effort, including spoken, signed, and written languages.

One important impact of this evolutionary transition to multimodal communication was to enable reduced cognitive load associated with communicating per se, which freed up human's mental resources for performing their primary tasks (Oviatt, 2013a; Oviatt et al., 2004a). As early hominids expanded their range of habitats and social contacts, improved multimodal communication and intelligibility helped them to adapt and thrive in a wide range of contexts.

4.2   NEUROSCIENCE AND BEHAVIORAL RESEARCH ON MULTISENSORY PROCESSES

During the past three decades in biology, experimental psychology, and cognitive neuroscience, a rapidly growing literature has clarified that brain processing fundamentally involves multisensory perception and integration (Calvert et al., 2004; Stein, 2012), which cannot be predicted by studying the senses in isolation. When individual modalities are merged during normal processing, nonlinear interaction effects and illusions dominate, leading to qualitatively distinct perceptual blends (Stein and Meredith, 1993). Multisensory processing and communication are supported by multimodal neurons and multisensory convergence regions, which are a fundamental design feature of the human brain. Multisensory processing has evolved to exert extensive control over human perception, attention, language, memory, learning, and other behaviors (Calvert et al., 2004; Schroeder and Foxe, 2004; Stein and Meredith, 1993). In both animals and humans, it functions to achieve remarkable accuracy through fusion of different and complementary information sources, a major evolutionary advantage (Massaro and Stork, 1998; McGrath and Summerfield, 1985; McLeod and Summerfield, 1987; Murphy, 1996; Pick and Saltzman, 1978; Robert-Ribes et al., 1998; Stein and Meredith, 1993; Sumby and Pollack, 1954). Integrated multisensory processing effects now are viewed as fundamental and pervasive, rather than constituting a specialized or infrequent phenomenon that is an exception to the rule.

The *mirror neuron system* is arguably the most important behavioral neuroscience discovery of the past century. This multimodal system includes both visual components (*mirror neurons*) and auditory ones (*echo neurons*), which jointly support action understanding, flexible multimodal language processing, and learning by social imitation (Kohler et al., 2002; Rizzolatti and Craighero, 2004). See Section 5.3 for further description. There is evidence that speech and gesture are inextricably coordinated as a single communication system in one brain region. For example, blind people gesture when they speak, as do speakers on the telephone (Iverson and Goldin-Meadow, 1998). There also is a high degree of co-timing between speech and gesture during interpersonal and human-computer communication. This co-timing has been documented in different communication contexts, such as exchanges involving error resolution (Kendon, 1980; McNeill, 1992; Oviatt et al., 2003, 1998). See Table 4.1 for italicized terms.

One of the earliest and most widely cited multisensory processing phenomena is the *McGurk effect*, which elegantly demonstrates that human speech perception involves a multimodal blend between audition and vision. For example, the viseme "ga" and phoneme "ba" typically is perceived as "da," a multimodal blend that is qualitatively distinct from perception of either individual sensory input (McGurk and MacDonald, 1976). Since this initial discovery, a wide range of additional findings now thoroughly document the brain's integrated processing of modalities. These include *spatial ventriloquism effects* (Bertelson and deGelder, 2004), *temporal ventriloquism effects* (Morein-Zamir et al., 2003; Recanzone, 2003), *modality dominance effects* (Welch et al., 1986), and cross-modal matching on pitch, loudness, brightness, and other features (Marks, 1989). Table 4.1 lists examples of empirical effects related to multisensory binding of signals.

The above effects emphasize that there is a strong bias to perceive multisensory synchrony when two stimuli arrive from the same location and co-occur within a specified time window, which results in an integrated percept. See *spatial and temporal rules*, Table 4.1. In fact, a relatively wide temporal window exists for perceiving simultaneity between signals (Spence and Squire, 2003), which has been documented in human audio-visual perception of complex events (Dixon and Spitz, 1980).[4] It also has been demonstrated at the cellular level for simple stimuli within the superior colliculus (King and Palmer, 1985; Meredith et al., 1987). Sugita and Suzuki (Sugita and Suzuki, 2003) have clarified that the magnitude of humans' bias to perceive synchrony between related auditory and visual stimuli depends on their distance from the person, up to about 10 m, which constitutes a "moveable window" for perceiving temporal synchrony. Morein-Zamir and colleagues (2003) also have demonstrated that a temporal ventriloquism effect can correct for asynchronous auditory and visual input by effectively binding an earlier visual stimulus into temporal alignment

---

[4]   Approximately a 250 ms lag is required between speech and corresponding lip movements before asynchrony is perceived.

with a subsequent auditory one. Similarly, Recanzone (2003) has shown that the perceived rate of a visual event can be modulated by that observed for a concurrent auditory stream. In contrast, in the spatial ventriloquism effect it is the perceived location of a sound that becomes bound perceptually to that of a concurrent visual stimulus (Bertelson and deGelder, 2004). These collective findings support the modality appropriateness account of sensory dominance (Welch et al., 1986), which states that the modality providing the greatest acuity and most appropriate information dominates the total perceptual experience (e.g., audition for temporal information, vision for spatial).

Large individual differences but substantial intra-subject stability have been observed in the conditions that trigger a person's perception of multisensory synchrony (Mollon and Perkins, 1996; Stone et al., 2001). This is especially true for stimulus precedence effects, and the magnitude of audio-visual stimulus temporal discrepancy before an individual's perception of synchrony breaks down. These substantial individual differences in multisensory perception have been called the "personal equation" (Mollon and Perkins, 1996). They are remarkably parallel to the individual differences discussed in Section 4.3.3 in users' integration patterns during multimodal input to a computer.

Neurons in the deep superior colliculus now are well known to exhibit multisensory enhancement in their firing patterns, or *super-additivity*, which can produce responses larger than the sum of the two modality-specific sources of input. Figure 4.1 illustrates this enhancement (Bernstein and Benoit, 1996; Anastasio and Patton, 2004). The human brain can increase the reliability of a percept through multisensory integration, which reduces the variance associated with correct object recognition (Ernst and Bulthoff, 2004). Remarkably, the brain optimizes its process of sensory integration by weighting more heavily the modality that provides the most appropriate information for determining an accurate multimodal percept (see Table 4.1, *maximum-likelihood estimation principle of multisensory fusion*). This includes a bias toward heavier weighting of audition for accurate temporal information, but vision for spatial content (Ernst and Banks, 2002; Ernst and Bulthoff, 2004; Welch et al., 1986). This capacity improves the speed and accuracy of people's responsiveness to objects and events, an evolutionary adaptation that has directly supported human survival in many situations. See Table 4.1 for terms.

Multimodal communication is distinct in that it involves briefer but more intense bursts of activity by a combination of modalities. More intense and extensive activity during multimodal interaction reflects widely distributed engagement of the brain's neurological substrates, which involves long-distance connections. This higher activity level typically occurs because a person perceives that a situation is more difficult, and they are in a higher state of arousal. At a behavioral level, more extensive neural activity stimulates elaborated learning, improved retention and retrieval, and greater transfer of learning. These facilitatory effects of multisensory processing have been widely documented in studies on attention, perception, memory, and learning (Calvert et al., 2004). They also provide a promising basis for designing future educational interfaces (Oviatt, 2013a).

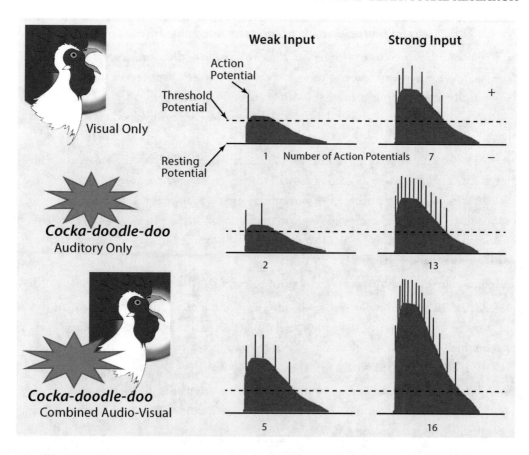

Figure 4.1: Individual auditory and visual action potentials combine to produce super-additive multi-sensory enhancement, which facilitates adaptive responding in humans and animals.

Table 4.1: Terminology for neuroscience and multisensory integration effects

Activity- and Experience-Dependent Neural Plasticity refers to the brain's capacity for dynamic change in structure and basic processing as a function of sensory experience and physical and communicative activity. Brain adaptations can be extensive, persistent, and occur throughout the lifespan. However, massive neural adaptations occur during sensitive periods early in development.

Mirror Neurons activate when an animal acts, and also when it observes the same action in others. Both visual and auditory stimuli associated with an observed action thereby prepare an animal to act as part of a behavioral "perception-action loop" (see echo neurons). As such, mirror neurons provide the neurological substrate for action understanding, both at the level of physical and communicative actions. They have been documented in various species, including humans, primates and birds.

Echo Neurons are the auditory analogue of mirror neurons.

Super-Additivity refers to multisensory enhancement of the neural firing pattern when two sensory systems (e.g., auditory and visual) are both activated during a perceptual event. This can produce a total response larger than the sum of the two modality-specific inputs, which improves the reliability of the signal.

Spatial Rule specifies that multisensory integration of two signals is more likely, and demonstrates a stronger effect, when the signals are in the same location or close physical proximity to one another (Stein and Meredith, 1993).

Temporal Rule specifies that multisensory integration of two signals is more likely, and demonstrates a stronger effect, when the signals occur simultaneously or within a given window of time (Stein and Meredith, 1993).

Modality Dominance Effects demonstrate that the brain optimizes the integration of sensory signals by more heavily weighting a modality that provides greater reliability and acuity in identifying a percept. For example, usually visual and tactile signals are weighted more than auditory ones during spatial judgments, but in most contexts auditory signals receive greater weighting during temporal judgments (Welch et al., 1986).

Maximum-Likelihood Estimation Principle of Multisensory Fusion refers to the principle of Bayesian maximum-likelihood estimation, which determines the degree to which one modality dominates another during signal fusion. This principle is designed to minimize variance in a final estimate, or maximize accuracy of the multimodal percept. For example, during visual-haptic fusion, visual dominance occurs when the variance associated with visual estimation is lower than that for haptic estimation (Ernst and Banks, 2002).

McGurk Effect demonstrates that speech perception is a multimodal blend between audition and vision, in which a perceived sound can be distinct from either individual sensory input. For example, the viseme "ga" and phoneme "ba" often is perceived as "da" (McGurk and MacDonald, 1976).

Spatial Ventriloquism Effects demonstrates that auditory location perception can be shifted toward a corresponding visual cue (Bertelson and deGelder, 2004).

Temporal Ventriloquism Effects demonstrate the temporal analogue of the spatial ventriloquism effect, in which visual perception can be influenced by auditory cues. For example, a preceding sound that occurs within a given temporal window can influence the perception of lights in a visual temporal order task (Morein-Zamir et al., 2003).

The findings discussed above offer dynamic models of multimodal timing, and fertile grounds for building the theoretical foundation that will be needed to design future adaptive multimodal interfaces with greater flexibility, generality, and power. More specifically, results of this kind have the potential to define what it means to build a "well integrated" multimodal interface, including the circumstances under which super-additivity effects can be expected rather than interference between modalities (Spence and Driver, 1999). In addition, the striking individual differences in both multisensory perception and multimodal production warrant further research. Together, they underscore that user-adaptive multimodal processing is a fertile direction for new system development. They also suggest that future research should explore whether individuals' multimodal integration patterns may provide a useful behavioral signature for biometric purposes, especially since multi-biometric patterns are known to have anti-spoofing and other performance advantages (Jain and Ross, 2004).

4.3   COGNITIVE SCIENCE AND MULTIMODAL HUMAN-COMPUTER INTERACTION RESEARCH

This section discusses cognitive science and human-computer interaction research on multimodal exchanges. Given the complex nature of users' multimodal interaction, cognitive science has and will continue to play an essential role in guiding the design of multimodal systems. Their design depends on knowing the properties of different modes and the information content they carry, the unique characteristics of users' multimodal language and its processability, and the integration and synchronization characteristics that typify users' multimodal interaction. To design fusion-based multimodal architectures (see Chapters 7 and 8), information on the order of users' input modes and the average time lag between modes is needed to establish temporal thresholds for fusion of input. It also is needed to determine the likelihood that an utterance is a multimodal vs. unimodal one before interpreting its meaning. The design of multimodal systems also relies on accurate prediction of when users are likely to interact multimodally at all, and how alike users are in their integration patterns. The cognitive science literature on these topics is extensive. As a result, this section will be limited to introducing the main cognitive science themes and findings relevant to common types of multimodal system, with an emphasis on advanced fusion-based multimodal interfaces.

4.3.1   FREQUENCY AND OCCURRENCE OF MULTIMODAL INTERACTION

During natural interpersonal communication, people are always interacting multimodally. The modality information sources that a communication partner has available to monitor is extensive. This also is true of multimodal systems that track passive user input modalities, such as their gaze or facial expressions, because passive visual processing of such information is continuous. From the system's viewpoint, users of such a system always are interacting multimodally. The primary technical challenge in such multimodal systems is segmentation and interpretation of users' continuous input streams to extract meaningful information upon which the system can act. For example, the cognitive science literature has contributed to segmenting and classifying human lip movements (visemes), and identifying synchronized viseme-phoneme mappings that occur during articulated speech. This information has provided a basis for designing related multimodal systems that can accurately interpret users' audio-visual speech.

In contrast, other multimodal systems process active user input modes, like speech and writing. Each type of user input occurs only intermittently, as does their combination. As a result, the multimodal system must be designed to process and interpret either unimodal speech, unimodal writing, or combined speech and writing. Although users have a strong preference to interact multimodally, there is no guarantee that they will always do so when interacting with this type of multimodal interface. In fact, users typically intermix unimodal with multimodal input. Furthermore, their ratio of multimodal interaction can vary widely depending on task content, what actions are being performed, their difficulty level, and other factors. In a variety of studies, users' frequency of interacting multimodally has varied from 20-70%, compared with entering information unimodally (Oviatt et al., 1997, 2005; Oviatt, 1999b). These findings emphasize that multimodal systems with active input modes need to distinguish when users are and are not communicating multimodally, so accurate decisions can be made about when parallel input streams should be interpreted jointly.

4.3.2   MULTIMODAL INTEGRATION AND SYNCHRONIZATION PATTERNS

The cognitive science literature has provided information on the integration patterns that typify people's speech, lip, and facial movements (Benoit et al., 1996; Ekman, 1992; Ekman and Friesen, 1978; Fridlund, 1994; Hadar et al., 1983; Massaro and Cohen, 1990; Stork and Hennecke, 1995; Vatikiotis-Bateson et al., 1996), speech with pen input, and speech with manual gestures (Kendon,

1980; McNeill, 1992; Oviatt et al., 1997). Early work on multimodal systems focused exclusively on processing point-and-speak integration patterns during selection actions. However, this exercised a very limited use of multimodal capabilities. In fact, studies of users' speech and writing during human-computer interaction indicate that a speak-and-point pattern comprises only 14% of all spontaneous multimodal combinations (Oviatt et al., 1997). Linguistic analysis of manual gesturing during speech also shows that simple pointing accounts for less than 20% of all gestures (McNeill, 1992). This research highlights that any multimodal system designed exclusively to process point-and-speak will fail to provide users with much useful functionality. Most integration patterns span a broader range of functionality. They also require segmenting and interpreting richer meaning contained within two or more signal streams. For example, pen input can create graphics, symbols, digits, gestural marks, lexical content, and other information besides simply pointing.

In addition, it also was naively assumed that all multimodal signals co-occur temporally, such that temporal overlap would determine which signals to combine during system processing. For example, Bolt's original system assumed that a point gesture would co-occur precisely when a user uttered "that square," so that it would identify the intended referent. However, empirical studies indicate that users often do not speak deictic terms like "that" at all. When they do, the deictic term frequently is not overlapped in time with the corresponding pointing gesture that would be needed to disambiguate it. One study estimated that as few as 25% of users' commands actually contain a spoken deictic that overlaps with the pointing needed to disambiguate its meaning (Oviatt et al., 1997).

Apart from point-and-speak, studies have shown that users' input during more complex multimodal constructions frequently does not overlap at all (Oviatt, 1999b; Oviatt et al., 2003, 2005; Xiao et al., 2002, 2003). Although two input modes may be highly interdependent and synchronized during multimodal interaction, synchrony does not imply simultaneity. Therefore, multimodal system designers cannot necessarily count on conveniently overlapped signals to achieve successful processing in the multimodal systems they build. The next section describes typical multimodal integration patterns, and pervasive individual differences among users in these patterns.

4.3.3   INDIVIDUAL AND CROSS-CULTURAL DIFFERENCES IN INTEGRATION PATTERNS

There are large individual differences in users' multimodal interaction patterns, including their preference to interact unimodally vs. multimodally, and which modes they more strongly prefer (e.g., speaking vs. writing; Oviatt et al., 2004a). In research on speech and pen multimodal input to a computer, two distinct types of user integration patterns have been identified—*simultaneous integrators*, and sequential ones (see Figure 4.2). A user who habitually integrates her speech and pen input in a simultaneous manner overlaps them temporally, whereas a *sequential integrator* finishes one mode before beginning the second. These two types of user integration pattern occur across the lifespan from children through the elderly (Oviatt et al., 2005; Xiao et al., 2002, 2003).[5] A given user's dominant signal integration pattern can be detected almost immediately during multimodal interaction, usually on the very first input. Her habitual pattern remains strikingly consistent during a session, as well as resistant to change following explicit instructions or attempts at training (Oviatt et al., 2003, 2005). This bimodal distribution of user integration patterns has been observed in different task domains (e.g., map-based real estate selection, crisis management, educational applications with animated characters), when using different types of interface (e.g., conversational, command style), and during both human-computer and human-human interaction (Darves and Oviatt, 2004; Oviatt, 1999b; Xiao et al., 2002, 2003). In summary, empirical studies have demonstrated that this bimodal distinction in user integration pattern occurs across different age groups, task domains, and types of interface. For terms, see Table 4.2.

The two multimodal integration patterns described above have been attributed to fundamental differences among user groups in reflective-impulsive cognitive style, the most pervasive dimension of individual differences identified in the psychological literature (Messer, 1976; Oviatt et al., 2005). Research has shown that simultaneous integrators demonstrate a more impulsive style, whereas sequential integrators have a more reflective one. For example, *impulsive individuals* have shorter attention spans and weaker impulse control, but *reflective individuals* study information for longer periods and show greater self restraint (Messer, 1976). The reflective individuals who are sequential integrators articulate more precisely, and their speech is less disfluent. They also use more direct command-style language with a smaller and less varied vocabulary, which would help them to achieve error-free communication (Oviatt et al., 2005). In general, they adopt strategies aimed at ensuring error-free interaction (Oviatt et al., 2005). Table 4.2 summarizes terms.

One interesting discovery in recent work is a phenomenon called *multimodal hypertiming*. This refers to the fact that both sequential and simultaneous integrators accentuate their habitual multimodal integration pattern further during system error handling and also during increasingly difficult tasks. As illustrated in Figures 4.3 and 4.4, sequential integrators increase their intermodal lag more between signals, whereas simultaneous integrators have the opposite pattern of increasing their overlap between signals. Studies have shown that users will progressively increase their degree of entrenchment by 18% as system errors rise, and by 59% as task difficulty increases (Oviatt et al., 2003). Multimodal hypertiming is another example of a counter-intuitive modality interaction effect, similar to those described in Section 4.2 on multisensory perception. See Table 4.2 for terms.

---

[5] In a series of studies "extreme seniors," who were healthy and mobile but 80–100 years old, were given a multimodal interface to use that permitted speaking and writing to a map system. In addition to identifying their multimodal integration patterns, seniors who had never used a computer before began using the multimodal interface with no training. In one case during a session, a 100-year-old woman paused and asked, "Am I using a computer now?"

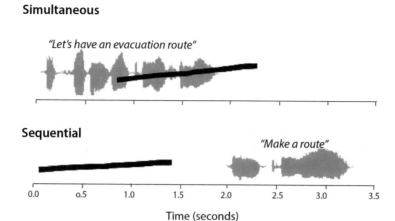

Figure 4.2: Model of average temporal integration pattern for simultaneous and sequential integrators' typical constructions. From Oviatt et al. (2005). Copyright© 2005 ACM. Used with permission.

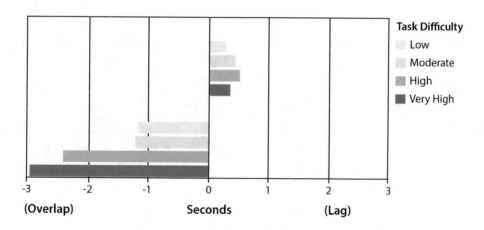

Figure 4.3: Average increased signal overlap in seconds for simultaneous integrators (left) but increased lag for sequential integrators (right) as they handle tasks increasing in difficulty.

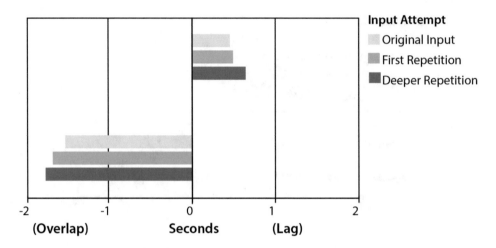

Figure 4.4: Average increased signal overlap for simultaneous integrators in seconds (left) but increased lag for sequential integrators (right) as they handle an increased number of system errors.

Table 4.2: Terminology for individual differences in system design
Simultaneous Integrators are users of a multimodal system whose input signals overlap temporally when expressing an utterance.
Sequential Integrators are users of a multimodal system whose input signals occur separately, with a temporal lag between them, when expressing an utterance.
Multimodal Hypertiming refers to the fact that both sequential and simultaneous integrators will accentuate their habitual multimodal integration pattern further during system error handling, or when completing increasingly difficult tasks. This entrenchment results in a form of hyper-clear communication.
Impulsive Individuals represent one end of the spectrum on individual differences in attentional self-regulation. Their shorter attention span and weaker impulse control make them more susceptible to distraction by many computer interfaces, especially mobile ones.
Reflective Individuals have the ability to self-regulate their attention, including a longer attention span and the ability to resist impulses and distractions to the focus of their attention. These skills support better learning, and make them more robust to interface distractions.
Universal Access Interfaces make it easier for disabled, elderly, and otherwise diverse individuals to use an interface by providing them with alternatives for input and output on a multimodal interface. Such interfaces often include user-centered adaptation and personalization of information delivery (e.g., volume or rate of speech output), and other system features designed to support interaction.

> ***Performance Gap*** refers to the habitual difference between low- vs. high-perfoming groups in achievement level, which can be exacerbated or minimized by computer interface design. An interface characterized by high cognitive load can expand the performance gap, while a low-load one can have the opposite effect of minimizing it. Interface design, especially for educational technologies, aims to improve average performance for all users, and also to "do no harm" in adversely affecting low performers. Whenever possible, it aims to minimize the performance gap between groups.

One implication of the above findings is that change in the degree of users' multimodal hy-pertiming could provide a sensitive index of cognitive load during real-time system use. Another implication is that adaptive rather than fixed temporal thresholds potentially could support a more robust and personalized approach to multimodal fusion (see Chapter 7). Ideally, an adaptive multimodal system would detect, automatically learn, and adapt to a particular user's dominant multimodal integration pattern. This could result in substantial improvement in system processing speed, accuracy of interpretation, and synchronous interchange. Estimates indicate that processing delays during multimodal fusion could be reduced by 50% simply by adopting user-defined thresholds (Oviatt et al., 2005; Gupta and Anastaskos, 2004; Huang and Oviatt, 2006).

Unfortunately, multimodal integration patterns have not been studied as extensively or systematically for all possible input modes. Apart from speech and pen integration patterns, linguistics research on interpersonal communication reveals that manual gesturing and signed language both typically precede speech during joint constructions (Kendon, 1980; Naughton, 1996). Even during speech and lip movements, close but not perfect temporal synchrony is typical, with lip movements occurring a fraction of a second before the corresponding auditory signal (Abry et al., 1996; Benoit, 2000).

Major differences have been documented among cultural/linguistic groups in the information carried within modalities and in modality integration patterns (Fuster-Duran, 1996). For example, the degree to which gesturing precedes speech in word-level integration patterns is greater in topic-prominent languages like Chinese than subject-prominent ones like English (McNeill, 1992). In other research, lip movements during audio-visual speech are less active and informative among Japanese speakers, compared with Americans (Sekiyama and Tohkura, 1991). These findings have implications for the degree to which speech can be disambiguated by processing lip movements in noisy environments for some groups. Gender, age, and other individual differences likewise are common in how modalities are used, as well as in multimodal integration patterns (Argyle, 1972).

All of the above results motivate further development of data-driven adaptive multimodal interface design. In the future, multimodal machine learning approaches could provide a particularly promising way to learn and adapt to unique temporal integration patterns found between different modalities and in different user groups. The application of new techniques of this kind will be required to generalize and speed up multimodal system development in the future.

4.3.4   COMPLEMENTARITY VERSUS REDUNDANCY IN MULTIMODAL INTEGRATION

The dominant theme in users' organization of multimodal input is complementarity of content, rather than redundancy. During both interpersonal and human-computer communication, numerous examples of multimodal complementarities have been described in past research (McGurk and MacDonald, 1976; Oviatt and Olsen, 1994; Wickens et al., 1983). For example, in the literature on multimodal speech and lip movements, feature-level complementarities have been identified between visemes and phonemes for vowel articulation. Vowel rounding is better conveyed visually, and vowel height and backness is better revealed auditorally (Massaro and Stork, 1998; Robert-Ribes, et al., 1998). During interpersonal communication, linguists have documented that speech and manual gesturing also involve complementary rather than duplicate information between modes (McNeill, 1992).

In addition, users' multimodal speech and pen input to a computer consistently contribute complementary semantic information. Whereas the subject, verb, and object of a sentence typically are spoken, detailed locative information is written (Oviatt et al., 1997). These two modalities are viewed as an opportune combination largely because of their intrinsically complementary strengths and weaknesses. Precise spatial information can be uniquely conveyed using pen input. In contrast, the descriptive capabilities of speech are better suited for specifying temporally oriented or out-of-view information. Even during multimodal correction of system errors, when users are highly motivated to clarify and reinforce information, less than 1% of the time do speech and pen input express redundant information (Oviatt, 2012).

In summary, empirical studies have highlighted the importance of complementarity as a major organizational theme during multimodal communication. Recent research has documented that the ratio of complementary to redundant multimodal input increases as users' cognitive load rises (Ruiz et al., 2010). One explicit goal of multimodal interface design is to integrate complementary modalities in a manner that yields a synergistic blend, such that each mode contributes its major strengths while overcoming weaknesses in the other mode (Cohen, et al., 1989). This approach to system design has promoted the philosophy of using modalities and component technologies for their natural advantages, which also supports optimal mutual disambiguation of joint signal input. By achieving a synergistic blend, the resulting multimodal system can function more robustly than either a unimodal recognition technology or a multimodal system that lacks complementarities between modes. For a fuller description of this topic, see Chapter 8.

CHAPTER 5

Theoretical Foundations of Multimodal Interfaces

This chapter discusses the theoretical foundations of multimodal interaction and interface design. Six different theories, including Gestalt theory, Affordance theory, Communication Accommodation theory, Working Memory theory, Cognitive Load theory, and Activity theory, all provide explanatory insights into central aspects of multisensory perception and multimodal communication. They provide context for understanding why multimodal interfaces have cognitive benefits for users.

5.1   GESTALT THEORY: GREATER MULTIMODAL COHERENCE, STABILITY, AND ROBUSTNESS

Gestalt theory presents a holistic systems-level view of perception, which emphasizes self-organization of perceptual experience into meaningful wholes, rather than analyzing discrete elements as isolates. It asserts that the whole is greater than the sum of its parts. When elements are combined, emergent properties arise that transform a percept qualitatively. Unexpected perceptual phenomena have been demonstrated widely in multisensory processing, as described in Section 4.2. In these cases, integrated percepts typically do not involve equal weighting of individual stimuli or simple additive functions (Calvert et al., 2004). Reports abound of perceptual "illusions," once thought to represent exceptions to unimodal perceptual laws. A classic example is the case of Wertheimer's demonstration in 1912 that two lines flashed successively at optimal intervals appear to move together, an illusion related to human perception of motion pictures (Koffka, 1935). Although Gestalt theory's main contributions involve perception of visual-spatial phenomena, its laws also have been applied to the perception of acoustic, haptic, and other sensory input (Bregman, 1990), and to the production of multimodal communication (Oviatt et al., 2003).

Gestalt theory describes different laws for perceptual grouping of information into a coherent whole (Koffka, 1935; Kohler, 1929). The principle of proximity states that spatial or temporal proximity causes elements to be perceived as related. During multimodal pen/voice communication, speech is an acoustic modality that is structured temporally, but pen input is a visible one that is structured both spatially and temporally. In this case, Gestalt theory predicts that the common temporal dimension provides organizational cues for binding them into a whole multimodal unit. That is, the co-timing of these modalities provides the main information conveying proximity and relatedness (Oviatt et al., 2003).

The principle of symmetry states that people have a tendency to perceive symmetrical elements as part of the same whole. During pen/voice multimodal communication, perceived symmetry depends on closer temporal correspondence between signal pieces, especially their start and end. A more symmetrical multimodal integration pattern involves increased co-timing of the onsets and offsets of the two component signals in a multimodal construct (Oviatt et al., 2003).

A third Gestalt principle that is relevant to multimodal integration patterns is the principle of area. It states that people tend to group elements to form the smallest visible figure or briefest temporal interval. This Gestalt principle predicts that most people will deliver speech and pen input simultaneously, or in a completely overlapped way during multimodal communication, rather than distributing them sequentially with one preceding the other. Research on over 100 users from children through seniors has confirmed that 70% of people are simultaneous signal integrators, whereas 30% are sequential ones (Oviatt et al., 2003). Other Gestalt principles of perceptual organization include the principle of closure, similarity, continuity, and common fate. In addition, Gestalt theory maintains that more than one principle can operate at the same time.

With respect to processing, Gestalt theory claims that the elements of a percept are first grouped rapidly according to its main principles. This economizes mental resources, and permits focal attention to be allocated elsewhere. In this respect, Gestalt principles maintain that we organize experience in a way that is rapid, economical, symmetrical, continuous, and orderly. In addition, the Gestalt principle of psychophysical isomorphism states that there is a correlation between brain activity at the neuronal level and conscious perception as outlined in Gestalt laws.

An important meta-principle underlying all Gestalt tendencies is the creation of a balanced and stable perceptual form that can maintain its *equilibrium*, just as the interplay of internal and external physical forces shape an oil drop (Koffka, 1935; Kohler, 1929). Gestalt theory states that any factors that threaten a person's ability to achieve a goal create a state of tension, or *disequilibrium*. Under these circumstances, it predicts that people will fortify basic organizational phenomena associated with a percept to restore balance (Koffka, 1935; Kohler, 1929). See Table 5.1 for italicized terms.

As an example, if a person interacts with a multimodal computer system and it makes a recognition error so she is not understood, then this creates a state of disequilibrium. When this occurs, research has demonstrated that a user will fortify or accentuate her usual pattern of multimodal signal co-timing (i.e., either simultaneous or sequential) by approximately 50%, a phenomenon known as multimodal hyper-timing (Oviatt et al., 2003). This results in a more coherent multimodal percept, which contributes to hyper-clear communication, which increases the speed and accuracy of perceptual processing by a listener.

In summary, the Gestalt principles outlined above have provided a valuable framework for understanding how people organize their perception of both unimodal and multimodal information. These principles also have been used to establish new requirements for multimodal interface design (Oviatt et al., 2003), as well as computational analysis of pen and image content (Saund et al., 2003).

In addition to making seminal contributions on perception, including multisensory perception, Gestalt theory has had a major impact on understanding thinking and problem solving. It introduced the view that productive thinking involves problem solving with insight, or the rapid and subconscious apprehension of solutions primed by prior perceptual experience. Wertheimer believed that our subconscious minds are active in gradually organizing information before it becomes the focus of conscious attention and insight occurs (Wertheimer, 1945). Insight is a foundational concept for understanding the process of creative thinking and innovative problem solving. Basic research is critically needed at both the brain and behavioral levels on the process of insight, including the self-organization of perceived information and the conditions that support it. Affordance theory, a derivative of Gestalt views, is outlined in the next section.

5.2   AFFORDANCE THEORY: MULTIMODAL INTERFACES GUIDE HUMAN COMMUNICATION AND ACTIVITY

Affordance Theory states that people have perceptually-based expectations about objects, including computer interfaces, that involve different constraints on how one can act on them to achieve goals successfully. These *affordances* of objects establish behavioral attunements that transparently but powerfully prime the likelihood that people will act on them in specific ways (Gibson, 1977, 1979). In this sense, perception of objects and their environmental context precedes and guides actions, which must be available within an organism's repertoire. For example, a cat door may afford passage for a cat or small mammal, but not a person (Gaver, 1991; Norman, 1988). Affordance theory originated in perceptual and ecological psychology, and is considered a systems-theoretic view closely related to Gestalt theory. The concept of environmental affordances that attune and constrain people to act on objects in certain ways also is central to Situation Theory accounts of behavior (Greeno, 1994). See Table 5.1 for terms.

As described in Chapter 4, object perception is multisensory. That is, people are influenced by an array of multimodal object affordances (e.g., auditory, tactile), not just their visual properties (Gaver, 1991). For example, the acoustic qualities of an animated computer persona's voice can influence a user's engagement and participation in a dialogue with it. In one study, when an animated persona sounded like a master teacher, including speaking with high amplitude and wide pitch excursions, children engaged in higher rates of question asking about marine science (Oviatt et al., 2004b). Animated computer characters typically are audio-visual instantiations, so their affordances are multimodal rather than either visual or auditory alone. This means they can provide more powerful cues for guiding human responding. One important impact of interfaces that present information multimodally is that they potentially can facilitate transfer of learning to a wider range of contexts, including ones in which the unimodal elements later may be presented individually. In this regard, exposure to multimodal patterns can fortify learning.

The above example also illustrates that Affordance Theory has been generalized from physical objects to social agents, including computational ones. In addition, it has been generalized from the impact of objects on people's physical activity patterns to their communicative actions (Greeno, 1994; Oviatt et al., 2012). This includes human communication patterns involving all modalities, not just spoken language (Oviatt et al., 2012). For example, as described in Sections 3.7 and 11.1.1. Affordance theory predicts that people's perception of a pen interface as a digital tool will elicit more total communication and more nonlinguistic content, compared with a non-digital pen.

Recent interpretations of Affordance theory, especially as applied to computer interface design, specify that it is human perception of interface affordances that elicits specific types of activity, not just the presence of an object's physical multisensory attributes. Affordances can be described at different levels, including biological, physical, perceptual, and symbolic/cognitive (Zhang and Patel, 2006). From a Distributed Cognition theoretic viewpoint, affordances are distributed representations that are the by-product of external representations of an object (e.g., streetlight color) and internal mental representations that a person maintains about their action potential (e.g., knowledge in some cultures that "red" means stop), which determines the person's subsequent physical activity. This example of an internal representation involves a cognitive affordance, which originates in cultural conventions mediated by symbolic language (i.e., "red") that are specific to a given person and their cultural/linguistic group.

In an important sense, Affordance theory is a complement to Activity theory (see Section 5.6), because it specifies the type of activity that people are most likely to engage in when using different physical tools. It has been widely applied to human interface design, especially the design of input devices (Gaver, 1991; Norman, 1988). This application of Affordance theory emphasizes that interfaces should be designed to facilitate easy discoverability of the actions they are intended to support. For complex computer tasks, an interface may guide a user's attention through a series of affordances so user actions can be successfully executed (Gaver, 1991).

From an educational viewpoint, it is important to note that the behavioral attunements that arise from object affordances depend on perceived action possibilities that are distinct from specific learned patterns. They are potentially capable of stimulating human activity in a way that facilitates learning in contexts never encountered before. As such, if interface affordances are well matched with a task domain, they can increase human activity patterns that facilitate exploratory learning. They also can stimulate transfer of procedural skills and related domain knowledge across different tasks and environmental contexts.

Table 5.1: Terminology for theoretical foundations of multimodal interfaces
Equilibrium refers to the original Gestalt meta-principle that people are driven to create a balanced, stable, and meaningful whole perceptual form. When this goal is not achieved or is disrupted, a state of tension or disequilibrium arises.
Disequilibrium refers to the fact that people will attempt to fortify basic organizational principles described in Gestalt laws to restore a coherent whole percept. The dual concepts of equilibrium and disequilibrium were later used in Piagetian theory to characterize the process of cognitive development.
Affordances are perceptually based expectations about actions that can be performed on objects in the world, which derive from people's beliefs about their properties. Affordances invite and constrain people to interact with objects, including computer interfaces, in specific ways. They establish behavioral attunements that transparently prime people's use of objects, as well as further exploratory learning. Affordances can be analyzed at the biological, physical, perceptual, and symbolic/cognitive level, and they are influenced by cultural conventions.
Semiotic Mediation refers to the Activity theory concept that external artifacts or tools can directly stimulate, guide, and refine human cognition and task performance. These tools can be physical objects, linguistic symbols, or human agents. For example, when people engage in self talk, which they do across the lifespan as tasks become harder, they externalize language in a way that supports their performance.
Convergent Communication refers to the mutual accommodation of communication patterns during interpersonal exchange, which includes adapting signal characteristics, grammar, lexical content, gesturing, body posture, and other behaviors. These adaptations occur in both humans and animals, and they are grounded in the multimodal echo and mirror neuron systems. These interpersonal adaptations enhance the predictability, intelligibility, learnability, and other aspects of communication.
Extraneous Cognitive Load refers to the level of working memory load that a person experiences due to the properties of materials they are using, including computer interface features, which is independent of the inherent difficulty of a task. Extraneous cognitive load can undermine a user's primary task performance.
Intrinsic Cognitive Load refers to the inherent difficulty level and related working memory load associated with a user's primary task, such as driving a car.

Germane Cognitive Load refers to the level of users' effort and activity compatible with mastering a new skill or content, which may be increased or decreased by the properties of educational materials or interfaces. For example, in some cases automation can undermine the germane cognitive load required for a person to master or maintain mastery of an important task, which is counterproductive. However, in other cases carefully targeted automation can assume a task that people are unable to do or have no need to master (e.g., visual detection in darkness, counting massive numbers).

5.3   COMMUNICATION ACCOMMODATION THEORY: MULTIMODAL DIALOGUE CONVERGENCE IMPROVES INTELLIGIBILITY

Communication Accommodation theory recognizes that human dialogue is socially situated and involves extensive co-adaptation of communication patterns between interlocutors. Interpersonal conversation is a dynamic adaptive exchange in which speakers' lexical, syntactic, and speech signal features all are tailored in a moment-by-moment manner to their conversational partner. In most cases, children and adults adapt all aspects of their communicative behavior to converge with those of their partner, including speech amplitude, pitch, rate of articulation, pause structure, response latency, phonological features, gesturing, drawing, body posture, and other aspects (Burgoon et al., 1995; Fay et al., 2010; Giles et al., 1987; Welkowitz et al., 1976). The impact of these communicative adaptations is to enhance the intelligibility, predictability, and efficiency of interpersonal communication (Burgoon et al., 1995; Giles et al., 1987; Welkowitz et al., 1976). For example, if one speaker uses a particular lexical term, then their partner has a higher likelihood of adopting it as well. This mutual shaping of lexical choice facilitates language learning, and also the comprehension of newly introduced ideas between people.

Although communication accommodation originally was documented during interpersonal spoken dialogue, these adaptions also occur during human-computer interaction (Oviatt et al., 2004b; Zoltan-Ford, 1991). In addition, they occur across different modalities (e.g., handwriting, manual signing), not just speech. When drawing, interlocutors typically shift from initially sketching a careful likeness of an object to converging with their partner's simpler drawing (Fay et al., 2010). A similar convergence of signed gestures has been documented between deaf communicators. Within a community of previously isolated deaf Nicaraguans who were brought together in a school for the deaf, a novel sign language became established rapidly and spontaneously. This new sign language and its lexicon most likely emerged through convergence of the signed gestures, which then became widely produced among community members as they formed a new language (Kegl et al., 1999; Goldin-Meadow, 2003).

At the level of neurological processing, *convergent communication* patterns are controlled by the mirror and echo neuron systems described in Section 4.2. Mirror and echo neurons provide the multimodal neurological substrate for action understanding, both at the level of physical and communicative actions. Observation of an action in another person primes an individual to prepare for action, and also to comprehend the observed action. For example, when participating in a dialogue during a cooking class, one student may observe another's facial expressions and pointing gesture when she says, "I cut my finger." In this context, the listener is primed multimodally to act, comprehend, and maybe even reply verbally. The listener experiences neurological priming, or activation of their own brain region and musculature associated with fingers. This prepares the listener to act, possibly by also retracting their fingers from the cutting board. This same neurological priming enables the listener to comprehend the speaker's physical experience and emotional state, such that she might respond, "Do you need a bandaid?" This basic perception-action loop provides the evolutionary basis for imitation learning, language learning, and mutual comprehension of ideas. See Table 5.1 for italicized term.

This convergence of multimodal communication patterns facilitates the mutual intelligibility of ideas during both interpersonal and human-computer exchanges. During human-computer multimodal dialogue, the nature of system output can effectively constrain users to produce input that is within the system's linguistic coverage. For example, this can include transparently guiding users to speak within a certain volume range, or to use specific lexical terms that facilitate successful system processing.

5.4   WORKING MEMORY THEORY: DISTRIBUTED MULTIMODAL PROCESSING IMPROVES MEMORY

Working memory is the ability to store information temporarily in mind, usually for a matter of seconds without external aids, before it is consolidated into long-term memory. Working memory span is a limited capacity system that is critical for cognitive functions, including planning, problem solving, inferential reasoning, language comprehension, and written composition. It focuses on goal-oriented task processing, and is susceptible to distraction, especially from simultaneous processes and closely related information. The term working memory was introduced 50 years ago by Miller and colleagues (Miller et al., 1960), although the most salient theory was proposed by Baddeley and colleagues (Baddeley and Hitch, 1974).

Working memory is a theoretical concept that is actively being researched in both cognitive psychology and neuroscience. Memory theory is well aligned with Activity Theory in emphasizing the dynamic processes that construct and actively suppress memories, which are a by-product of neural activation and inhibition processes. For example, active forgetting is now understood to be an inhibitory process at the neural level that is under conscious control (Anderson and Green, 2001).

The working memory concepts presented in this section represent limited-resource theoretic views that are related to Sweller's Cognitive Load theory and Wicken's Multiple Resource theory, which are described briefly later in this section.

According Baddeley's theory, working memory consists of multiple semi-independent processors associated with different modalities (Baddeley, 1986, 2003). A visual-spatial "sketch pad" processes visual materials such as pictures and diagrams, whereas a separate "phonological loop" stores auditory-verbal information in a different area of the brain. These lower-level modality-specific processing systems are viewed as functioning largely independently. They are responsible for constructing and maintaining information in mind through rehearsal activities. The semi-independence of modality-specific processing enables people to use multiple modalities during a task in a way that circumvents short-term memory limitations—effectively expanding the size of working memory. This "expansion" of working memory reserves is especially important as tasks become more difficult. In addition, Baddeley describes a higher-level "central executive" component that plans actions, directs attention to relevant information while suppressing irrelevant ones, manages integration of information from the lower-level modality stores, coordinates processing when two tasks are performed at a time, initiates retrieval of long-term memories, and manages overall decision-making processes (Baddeley, 1986, 2003).

The limited capacity nature of working memory is a critical feature of the theory. Miller originally described the span of working memory as limited to approximately seven elements or "chunks," which could involve different types of content such as digits or words (Miller, 1956). Expansion of this limit is achievable not only through multimodal processing, but also through the development of expertise. Expertise enables a person to perceive isolated units of information as organized wholes. For example, a chess master can rapidly perceive a series of individual moves as one strategy play. In this case, specific units of information have been grouped through repeated activity procedures, which results in learning to apprehend them as a meaningful whole. When a person becomes a domain expert, they do not need to retain and retrieve as many units of information from working memory when completing a task, which frees up memory reserves for focusing on more advanced tasks.

Another central concept of working memory is that units of information must be continually rehearsed, or else they become unavailable for consolidation into long-term memory. Loss of information from working memory can be influenced by cognitive load, which can be due to task difficulty, dual tasking, interface complexity, and similar factors. It also can occur when the content of distractors interfere with to-be-remembered information (Waugh and Norman, 1965). When dual tasking, it is easier to maintain digits in mind while working on a spatial task than another numeric one (Maehara and Saito, 2007). Likewise, it is easier to simultaneously process information presented auditorally and visually than it is two auditory tasks, which confirms the semi-independence of working memory components described in Baddeley's model.

Multiple Resource theory presents related concepts (Wickens et al., 1983; Wickens, 2002). It states that there can be competition between modalities during tasks, such that attention and processing required during input and output will result in better human performance if information is distributed across complementary modalities. For example, simultaneous verbal input is more compatible with visual than auditory output. This theory states that cross-modal time-sharing is effectively better than intra-modal time-sharing. The implication of both Working Memory and Multiple Resource theories is that multimodal interface design that permits distributing processing across different modality-specific brain regions can minimize cognitive load and improve performance.

The neural basis of memory function has advanced rapidly during the past few decades (D'Esposito, 2008). Among other things, it has confirmed the presence of modality-specific brain regions. Neurological evidence indicates that working memory is lateralized, with the right prefrontal cortex more engaged in spatial working memory, and the left more active during verbal working memory tasks (Owen et al., 2005; Daffner and Searl, 2008).

5.5   COGNITIVE LOAD THEORY: MULTIMODAL PROCESSING MINIMIZES LOAD

Cognitive Load theory, which was introduced by John Sweller and colleagues, applies working memory concepts to instructional theory (Sweller, 1988). It maintains that during the learning process, students can acquire new schemas and automate them more easily if instructional methods or computer interfaces minimize demands on attention and working memory, thereby reducing *extraneous cognitive load* (Baddeley, 1986; Mousavi et al., 1995; Oviatt, 2006; Paas et al., 2003; van Merrienboer and Sweller, 2005). Cognitive load researchers assess the extraneous complexity associated with instructional methods and tools separately from the intrinsic complexity of a student's main learning task, which causes *intrinsic cognitive load*. Assessments compare performance indices of cognitive load as students use different learning materials or interfaces. Educational researchers then focus on designing instructional materials and computer tools that decrease students' extraneous cognitive load, in order to keep it below the threshold that would sacrifice performance. Table 5.1 defines italicized terms.

In parallel, a second major objective has been the design of instructional materials and tools that increase students' *germane cognitive load*, or effort compatible with learning. This concept is central to the constructivist view of learning, which aims to increase students' level of physical and communicative activity so they can consolidate schemas. Multimodal interfaces, conversational interfaces, games and embodied simulations, and similar strategies all can be effective at supporting students' task engagement and performance during learning activities. The concept of stimulating germane load is contrary to the view that digital tools should be designed to "off-load" effort and automate tasks so they are experienced as easier.

Numerous learning studies have shown that a multimodal presentation format, for example one that includes diagrams and audiotapes, supports students' ability to solve geometry problems more successfully than unimodal visual-only presentation (Mousavi et al., 1995). When using the multimodal format, there also are larger performance advantages on more difficult tasks, compared with simpler ones (Tindall-Ford et al., 1997). These advantages of a multimodal presentation format for students' performance have been replicated for different domains, dependent measures, and materials, including computer-based multimedia animations (Mayer and Moreno, 1998; Tindall-Ford et al., 1997). These results are consistent with the literature on multimodal processing, and in particular with working memory studies showing that the effective size of working memory expands when information is processed multimodally.

One goal of Cognitive Load theory has been to provide a framework that assists in developing instructional materials and interfaces that are appropriately tailored for diverse students (Oviatt et al., 2006; Oviatt and Cohen, 2010a). Low-performing students typically experience higher load and performance deterioration when completing easier tasks and using less complex computer interfaces, compared with high performers. As discussed in Section 3.6, multimodal interface design of instructional technology permits students to self-manage their working memory in a way that reduces cognitive load.

5.6 ACTIVITY THEORY: INTENSITY OF MULTIMODAL COMMUNICATION STIMULATES THOUGHT

Activity Theory is a meta-theory with roots in Russian cultural-historical psychology, which has many variations that have developed over the years. It claims that consciousness and activity are dynamically interrelated. One major theme is that physical and communicative activity play a major role in mediating, guiding, and refining mental activities, which is evident in people's thinking and problem-solving performance (Luria, 1961; Vygotsky, 1962, 1978, and 1987). In Vygotsky's view, the most powerful tools for *semiotic meditation* are symbolic representational ones such as language (see Table 5.1).

Vygotsky was especially interested in speech, which he believed serves the dual purposes of (1) social communication and (2) self-regulation during physical and mental activities. He described self-regulatory language, also known as self talk or private speech, as a think-aloud process in which individuals verbalize poorly understood aspects of difficult tasks to assist in guiding their own thought (Berk, 1994; Duncan and Cheyne, 2002; Luria, 1961). During human-computer interaction, it is also the case that the highest rates of self talk occur during more difficult tasks (Xiao et al., 2003). For example, when using a multimodal interface during map tasks, people typically have difficulty with relative directional information. As a result, they will subvocalize, "East, no, west of…" when thinking about where to place a landmark on the map. As they complete map tasks increasing in difficulty, self talk progressively increases and serves to improve their performance (Xiao et al., 2003).

Since Vygotsky's original work on the role of speech in self-regulation, further empirical research has revealed that activity in all communication modalities mediates thought, and thereby plays a critical self-regulatory role in improving performance (Luria, 1961; Vygotsky, 1962, 1987). As tasks become more difficult, speech, gesture, and writing all increase in frequency, and serve to reduce cognitive load and improve performance (Comblain, 1994; Goldin-Meadow et al., 2001; Oviatt et al., 2007; Xiao et al., 2003). For example, research has shown that manual gesturing reduces cognitive load and improves memory during math tasks, with greater benefit on more difficult tasks (Goldin-Meadow et al., 2001). In the written modality, students substantially increase diagramming as geometry problems became harder, and diagramming improves the correctness of solutions by 30–40% (Oviatt et al., 2006, 2007). In addition, written marking on problem visuals is associated with substantially higher solution scores. This performance improvement occurs more frequently on harder tasks and in low-performing students (Oviatt and Cohen, 2010a). In summary, research across modalities is compatible with Vygotsky's basic theory that communicative activity mediates thought and serves to guide improved performance (Luria, 1961; Vygotsky, 1962).

Activity theory is well supported by neuroscience findings on activity- and experience-dependent neural plasticity. See Table 4.1 for term. Activity-dependent plasticity adapts an individual's brain according to the frequency of an activity. Activities have a profound impact on human brain structure and processing, including changes in the number and strength of synapses, dendritic branching, myelination, the presence of neurotransmitters, and changes in cell responsivity, which are associated with memory and learning (Markham and Greenough, 2004; Sale et al., 2009). For example, within hours 10–20% of dendritic spines can spontaneously appear or disappear on pyramidal cells of the cerebral cortex (Xu et al., 2009). These adaptations reinforce particular neural pathways as a function of new experiences, which mediate long-term memory and learning. The extent of this spine remodeling has been documented to correlate with the degree of successful learning (Yang et al., 2009).

The speed and durability of neural plasticity also has been documented in students, for whom one study showed that studying resulted in significant growth of the posterior and lateral parietal cortex within a few months (Draganski et al., 2006). When learning new letters, recent neuroscience data indicates that self-generated actions by young children recruit greater neural activation than more passive observational learning. For example, writing a letter with a pen results in greater neural activation than viewing, naming, or typing it, and active writing also is associated with more accurate letter recognition (James and Engelhardt, 2012; James and Swain, 2010; Kersey and James, 2013; Longcamp et al., 2008).

The major themes uncovered by neuroscience include the following. (1) Neural adaptations are most responsive to direct physical activity, rather than passive viewing or vicarious experience (Ferchmin and Bennett, 1975). The implication of this finding for computer interfaces is that the design of input tools is particularly consequential for eliciting user actions that stimulate neurogenesis and thought, compared with system output. (2) All activity is not created equal in the sense that exposure to novel and complex activities stimulates synaptogenesis, whereas familiar and simple activities do not have the same impact (Black et al., 1990; Kleim et al., 1997). One implication of this theme is that multimodal interfaces that excel at supporting users during difficult tasks will be more effective at stimulating synaptogenesis than alternative interfaces that cannot. (3) Multimodal communicative activity represents more total activity across a range of modalities, more intense bursts of neural activity, more widely distributed activity across the brain's neurological substrates, and longer distance connections. Since multimodal interfaces elicit more extensive neural activity along many dimensions, compared with other interfaces they will have a greater impact on stimulating thought, improving memory, elaborating learning, and improving overall performance.

CHAPTER 6

Human-Centered Design of Multimodal Interfaces

This chapter introduces the data-intensive methodologies that are used to envision, prototype, and evaluate new multimodal interfaces. The design of human-centered multimodal interfaces has been directly enabled by two main things: (1) the cognitive science literature on multisensory processes and multimodal interaction, which has provided a foundation for user modeling; and (2) high-fidelity semi-automatic simulation methods, which have played an especially important role in prototyping entirely new types of multimodal system (Dahlbäck et al., 1992; Oviatt et al., 1992; Salber and Coutaz, 1993). In the next section, we focus on prototyping and iterative design tools for creating new multimodal interfaces, as distinct from tools for visualizing multimedia output or for making more minor system modifications. The methods outlined are optimal for developing multimodal interfaces for new devices and applications, including evaluating the trade-offs associated with different prototypes so that final design choices are well informed. Chapter 9 presents further information on commercial toolkits for developing and implementing multimodal systems.

6.1 METHODS FOR PROTOTYPING AND EVALUATING MULTIMODAL INTERFACES

When a new multimodal system is in the planning stages, *low-fidelity prototyping* based on design sketches, walk-throughs of scenarios, and similar techniques initially are used to visualize the new system and plan the sequential flow of human-computer interaction (Beaudouin-Lafon and Mackay, 2012; Rosson and Carroll, 2012). In addition, *contextual analysis* methods, like situated user interviewing and task analysis, typically are used to conduct a detailed user needs and requirements analysis (Holtzblatt, 2012). However, early prototyping methods like user self report and focus group interviews, without any exposure to the technology, have limited value in designing new multimodal interfaces. One reason is because users often have never experienced the type of multimodal interface being developed, so their stated preferences are uninformed and rarely match how they will interact with it after implementation. These prototyping methods also cannot provide information on users' specific behavior patterns, multimodal vocabulary, errors, or other critical information that multimodal system designers need to know. In addition, most traditional software tools that support interface design are intended for visualizing screen layouts and system feedback, but not for designing multimodal user input and interaction. See Table 6.1 for terms.

After low-fidelity prototyping, design plans typically are rapidly transitioned to a higher-fidelity simulation of the multimodal interface or system, which is used for proactive data collection with intended users. *High-fidelity semi-automatic simulations* have been the preferred method for designing and evaluating new multimodal systems, largely because of the complexity of the user interface design space. It is not possible for engineers to anticipate, for example, how users will interact with a given collection of modalities, what multimodal language patterns will emerge that require processing, and so forth. As a result, extensive data collection with relatively high-fidelity simulation tools, a form of Wizard-of-Oz method, preferably is completed before one or more fully functional prototypes of the system ever is built (Dahlbäck et al., 1992; Oviatt et al., 1992; Salber and Coutasz, 1993). See Table 6.1 for terms.

During high-fidelity simulation testing, Figure 6.1 illustrates that a user interacts with what he believes is a fully functional multimodal system. However, the interface is actually a simulated front-end that is designed to appear and respond like a fully functional system. During the interaction, a programmer assistant at a remote location provides simulated system responses. As the user interacts with the front-end interface, the programmer tracks his multimodal input and provides system responses as quickly and accurately as possible. To support this role, the programmer makes use of automated simulation software that is designed to support interactive speed and realism with the targeted system. For example, with these automated tools, the programmer can make a single selection on a workstation field to rapidly send simulated system responses to the user during a data collection session.

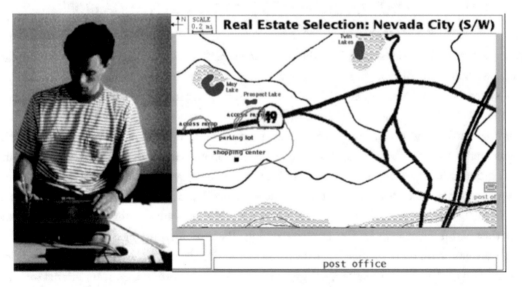

Figure 6.1: User interacting multimodally with speech and pen input while searching for homes on a real estate map during simulation data collection. From Oviatt (1996). Copyright ACM. Used with permission.

High-fidelity simulations have been the preferred method for prototyping multimodal systems for numerous reasons. Simulations are relatively easy and inexpensive to adapt, compared with building and iterating a whole system. They also permit researchers to alter a planned system's characteristics in major ways (e.g., input and output modes available), and to study the impact of different interface features in a systematic and scientific way (e.g., type and rate of system errors). In comparison, a particular system with its fixed characteristics is a less flexible and suitable research tool, and assessment of any specific system only provides a case study. Using simulation methods, interface designers can rapidly collect data and adapt the planned system's features to gain a broader and more principled perspective on the potential benefits of entirely new multimodal systems. Simulation research assists with evaluating the main performance tradeoffs associated with a particular system design, and with making decisions about which of the alternative designs performs best.

Some high-fidelity simulation tools have been designed to support prototyping of new multimodal systems that support collaborative group interactions (Arthur et al., 2006; Schiel and Turk, 2006). Others have supported processing of signal, semantic, and activity-level dimensions of users' input (Cohen et al., 2008; Oviatt et al., 2008). In some cases, prototyping a collaborative multimodal interface has required a dual-wizard simulation environment, as illustrated in Figure 6.2. The illustrated simulation collected speech, images, and digital pen data from groups of students during math problem-solving sessions (Figure 6.2, left). Two wizards were required in this simulation, as shown in Figure 6.2 (right), to process user data involving (1) linguistic content of requests and (2) signal characteristics of speech and pen input (i.e., amplitude, pressure). Specialized simulation software and wizard training both were needed to support fast and error-free teamwork between the two wizards (Cohen et al., 2008).

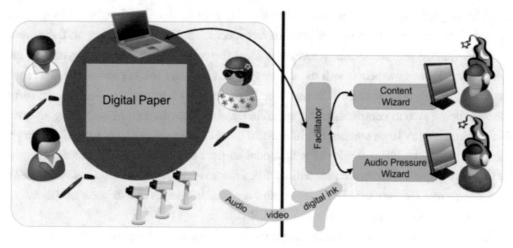

Figure 6.2: Dual-wizard simulation environment for prototyping collaborative multimodal interfaces capable of real-time adaptive processing based on users' signal features and language content. From Cohen et al. (2008). Copyright© 2008 ACM. Used with permission.

To support the further development and commercialization of multimodal interfaces and systems, additional infrastructure would be beneficial, including: (1) simulation tools for rapidly building and reconfiguring collaborative multimodal interfaces, (2) multimodal data analytics for accelerating iterative system development, and (3) tools to support integrating newer input modes into multimodal systems (e.g., gaze tracking, pen input), since they typically lack adequate infrastructure. Since most multimodal systems focus on field and mobile usage contexts, including in-vehicle and cell phone design, prototyping tools also are needed that (4) can simulate realistic types of multi-tasking that are encountered in mobile environments. In addition, (5) high-quality, large multimodal databases are needed. In some cases, innovative techniques like *crowdsourcing* could be a particularly valuable approach for collecting unique global multimodal data. For example, crowdsourcing has been used to collect data on multimodal vocabulary and language use by community members of minority languages, such as Lohorung in Nepal (Allwood et al., 2011). See Table 6.1 for term.

Following simulation-based design of new multimodal prototypes, a fully functional system prototype typically is built of the most successful concept. The specific implementation of multimodal signal processing, language processing, system architecture, and software processing is determined by the simulation's empirical findings on (1) what modalities and system functionality users actually engaged, (2) users' multimodal language and vocabulary, (3) users' interaction and error patterns, (4) the type of applications best supported by the multimodal implementation, and other major results. Once these decisions have been made about how to proceed in developing the complete system, a full system prototype is built to test the implementation—including functioning of each component, the overall system, and testing with users in realistic usage conditions. If a device and its multimodal interface is expected to be widely multi-functional, as in the case of smart phones, then further evaluation is conducted to test specific applications running on the system.

High-fidelity simulation infrastructure is ideal for collecting and evaluating a wide range of information about how people will use a new system, and what the key system design requirements are. However, it also can be valuable to make use of any closely related multimodal corpora for bootstrapping system components, for example training recognizers and evaluating alternative fusion architectures. A large number of multimodal corpora now are available from different projects around the world. For examples of multimodal corpora and a discussion of issues involved in collecting and preparing them, see proceedings from the series of *International Conferences on Language Resources and Evaluation* (LREC, 2014) and the affiliated series of *International Workshops on Multimodal Corpora, Tools and Resources* (MCTR, 2014).

Both empirical and machine learning analyses of multimodal corpora, whether of an existing corpus or one collected by a simulation, require tools for data annotation and exploration. A variety of tools are available that display time-coded modalities (e.g., multiple video, ink, and speech streams) in a precisely synchronized fashion. Examples include ANVIL (Kipp, 2014),

Chronoviz (Fouse, 2013), MACVisSTA (Quek et al., 2002), and Nomos (Niekrasz and Gruenstein, 2006). These systems assist annotators with exploring, labeling, and evaluating different aspects of time-synchronized data. Nomos also enables using logical statements and queries to enforce cross-annotation constraints and to retrieve matching data. Many of these systems can incorporate specialized data analysis tools for analyzing individual modalities, such as Praat for speech (Boersma and Weenink, 2015). For a comparison of multimodal annotation and analysis tools, see Rohlfing et al. (2006).

In addition to the above corpus-related issues, Section 9.9 describes commercial toolkits for developing fully functional multimodal systems, including Microsoft's Kinect (Microsoft, 2015c), Intel's RealSense (Intel, 2015), and Openstream's CueME (Openstream, 2015). Section 9.9 also presents information on international multimodal system development standards.

It cannot be emphasized enough what a critical role empirical prototyping methods and tools play in supporting the design of new multimodal mobile systems. This is especially true in rapidly changing and competitive areas like smart phone and in-vehicle interface design, where redesign is continuous to develop new products that are futuristic and attractive commercially. There is always pressure to add new input modalities—for example, gaze tracking to turn on the phone or select application icons. However, to develop sustainable products in line with durable long-term technology trends, we need to know more than simply whether a new modality is viable from an engineering viewpoint. Advance simulation testing can reveal whether users ever engage it, for what functionality, what specific behavioral patterns will need to be recognized by the system, what errors can be expected, users' attitudes toward the new capability, and similar issues. After initial user-centered prototyping, iterative testing of the new system then would assess issues such as how well the gaze-tracking implementation performed, what processing capacity and battery life were required, how fusion of gaze with other modes improved system reliability, and so forth.

The above issues are common concerns in the design of new smart phones, which currently are always striving to add new sensors, input modes, visual processing capabilities (e.g., motion tracking, depth sensing), dialogue processing capabilities, predictive processing of users' activities and needs, and a host of other non-trivial innovations. Each change that is made has an impact on other functional components, requiring re-evaluation of the overall system's functioning and usability during iterative test cycles. This is certainly true when redesigning a multimodal interface, which by its nature involves multiple distributed components that interact extensively with other system capabilities.

In spite of the extensive advantages of simulation tools, many corporate environments actually lack adequate tools for designing and evaluating alternative multimodal prototypes in order to determine which functions best. Instead, they often build and test components and a whole system, and then place it on the open market to obtain user feedback. This approach can work when an existing system has been changed in minor incremental ways, but it risks the vendor's reputation and market share when a product is poorly designed or premature. In addition, building a fully functional system can be extraordinarily expensive in software development costs, and adopting this approach as part of a trial-and-error commercialization policy can escalate costs without ensuring that any product ever will be successful. Finally, this approach to product development risks undermining marketplace adoption of potentially valuable new types of technology simply due to customers' negative first impressions.

Table 6.1: Terminology for design methods
Human-Centered Design is based on knowledge and modeling of users' natural communication and behavior patterns, as opposed to technology-centric design. It aims to develop more transparent interfaces that minimize cognitive load and errors, while supporting human cognition and performance.
High-Fidelity Semi-Automatic Simulations are a relatively sophisticated methodology for designing technology that is still in the planning stages, before a fully functional system ever is built. They support extensive data collection, assessment, and iterative design of newly conceived interface prototypes and their detailed requirements (e.g., speech vocabulary). They are a type of Wizard-of-Oz method.
Low-Fidelity Prototyping involves relatively rapid low-cost methods to initially visualize the new system and plan the sequential flow of human-computer interaction, including design sketches, walk-throughs of scenarios that represent intended use, and similar techniques.
Contextual Analysis refers to a combination of methods used to establish the main needs and constraints for developing a computer interface, including task analysis, interviewing and observing user behavior in the location where the system will be used, and similar methods.
Crowdsourcing refers to distributed web-based performance of a task. It has been used to collect multimodal data (e.g., audio, visual, text), for example, on multimodal vocabulary and language use by community members of minority endangered global languages. In such cases, simple tools sometimes are developed so community members with minimal or no computer skills can create multimodal dictionaries and document situated language use. One trusted community expert is nominated to be the administrator who checks the data. These rich multimodal data then serve the dual purpose of documenting the language, and providing information for language revitalization efforts.
User Juries refer to hands-on evaluation of new technologies by active-duty personnel returning from deployments, who report their assessment of technology benefits and limitations to the government. They are distinct from "focus groups" conducted by marketing teams, which attempt to solicit user preferences and opinions without any exposure to the targeted technology (see Section 9.2).

Community-Based Participatory Design engages end-users of a computer interface in the system design process, with research conducted at the intended field site. It aims to engage communities more deeply in designing new systems for and by themselves, so linguistic, cultural, functional, ethical, and other core dimensions of community needs and values are adequately captured in the design outcome.

6.2 HUMAN-CENTERED PHILOSOPHY AND STRATEGIES FOR MULTIMODAL INTERFACE DESIGN

Historically, the development of computer systems has been a technology-driven phenomenon, with technologists believing that "users can adapt" to whatever they build. They typically have relied on instruction, training, and practice with an interface to encourage users to interact in a manner that matches a system's processing capabilities. *Human-centered design* advocates that a more promising and enduring approach is to model users' natural behavior, including any constraints on their ability to attend, learn, and perform, so that interfaces can be designed that are more intuitive, easier to learn, and freer of performance errors. In the case of multimodal interfaces, this requires modeling modality-specific features of natural communication patterns, upon which the system must be built. People have many highly automatic behaviors, such as speech prosody and timing, which are organized in modality-specific brain centers and not under full conscious control. Given these challenges, one human-centered strategy is to proactively model and design for such behaviors. In short, a human-centered design approach can leverage a more usable and robust system by modeling users' pre-existing behavior and language patterns, rather than attempting to retrain strongly entrenched behaviors. See Table 6.1 for term.

Human-centered design of multimodal interfaces acknowledges that people are experienced at communicating multimodally and know when to use a particular mode to communicate accurately. They will use the input mode they judge to be least error prone for conveying specific lexical content, including switching modes if an error is encountered. They also will shift to communicating multimodally as tasks become harder, which improves performance. As discussed in Sections 3.6 and 8.1, their language often is briefer and simpler when communicating multimodally, which improves system processing. As also discussed previously, multimodal interfaces can substantially minimize users' cognitive load and improve performance by distributing processing across different brain areas to conserve working memory.

The following summarize basic human-centered design principles that improve performance when using a multimodal interface:

- support users' natural multimodal communication and activity patterns in different contexts, rather than attempting to retrain them;

- identify and model any major sources of variability in natural human input that a multimodal system must process, especially difficult-to-process ones (e.g., speech disfluencies);

- devise interface techniques that can effectively but transparently reduce these difficult sources of variability, thereby enabling more robust multimodal system processing (Oviatt, 1996, 2006);

- give users the flexibility to exercise their own intuitions about when to use one mode, the other, or both—which supports minimizing their cognitive load, and also improves system robustness;

- support user input for all types of representation (e.g., linguistic, diagrammatic, symbolic, numeric) that will be needed to perform a task, which directly facilitates cognition;

- minimize cognitive load associated with non-intuitive and complex interfaces, which distract attention and undermine users' ability to engage in high-level planning, integrative thinking, and correct problem solving; and

- minimize cognitive load associated with users' utterance planning.

6.3   COMMUNITY-BASED PARTICIPATORY DESIGN OF GLOBAL MULTIMODAL INTERFACES

As the development of new multimodal systems (e.g., smart phones) is expanded for diverse cultural/linguistic groups on a global scale, a major requirement will be *community-based participatory design* by the intended users. Global expansion of technology depends on more sophisticated cross-cultural and linguistic teamwork skills than other system design projects. It also requires international design partnerships, and more extensive logistical arrangements. See Table 6.1 for italicized term.

This type of design process requires understanding not just the multidisciplinary issues involved in designing technology with different component modalities, but also the human-centered issues involved in supporting successful multilingual communication and cultural adoption. For technology to be adopted rather than abandoned, different stakeholders need to be involved in designing and vetting the new technology and its applications. This means that when new multimodal interface designs are prototyped, researchers representing the planned native language group need to be included on the design team. Their role should include all aspects of design, from ideating new interface features, to walk-throughs of interface use from the perspective of an intended user, to critical analysis of functionality and features, and full system assessment to improve technology design.

While some work of this type can be conducted in laboratory settings, part of the iterative design process will require testing new technologies with native communicators in their country. Community-based participatory design (CBPD) includes local native language speakers on the design team, who recruit and work with other local users during testing, interpret the data based on local knowledge (e.g., linguistic meaning, ethics, values), and contribute to iterating technology redesign appropriately (Friedman et al., 2006; Jahnke, 2008; Minkler and Wallerstein, 2008; Muller, 2007; Nielsen and Gould, 2007). In this regard, the new technology is designed by and for the target community, which is at the heart of human-centered design. This ensures that its functionality and critical features are acceptable, and that usability is optimized. It also ensures that the design process is cooperative and productive. Ideally, this process includes extended periods of longitudinal testing.

This type of design process involves advanced methodological skills. The time frame for accomplishing it is longer, because the design team must cultivate the community's trust before team building and information exchange can occur. For example, many indigenous cultures are wary of the potentially adverse culture-transforming effects of existing computers, which can differ profoundly from their own community values and practices (Bowers et al., 2000; Marker, 2006). The Internet may be perceived as introducing expensive products and foreign or disrespectful values, which many cultures don't want their children to learn. In this case, the basic assumption that everyone wants access to the Internet may be untenable. In other cases, the host community may hold beliefs that cause the design process to change radically, or even to halt. For example, some indigenous groups believe their language is sacred, and will not share information about it with "outsiders" when efforts aim to design new communication technologies. In more routine cases, CBPD simply ensures that a member of the design team from the host community helps to navigate local politics, and expedites planned teamwork without major obstacles and delays. In summary, successful CBPD research and technology design requires developing trust and reciprocity with the host community, and patience on the part of researchers who typically expect rapid results. It also requires developing a sustained long-term relationship that engages community members as partners, and that may extend beyond technology design to collaborating on other community projects.

Technology design professionals who do global work need specialized training in advanced human interface design, as well as exposure to cross-cultural fieldwork practicum experiences. The longer-term goals of CBPD include that end users will become trained and able to develop their own technology. This requires continuous involvement in the design process and gradually building technical knowledge. End-user design of technology ensures that one cultural group will not be subjected to predatory practices by another "outside" group, who otherwise could develop and use the technology for their own financial or political gain.

The following chapters turn to specific design and implementation issues that are central to developing multimodal interfaces and systems. Chapter 7 introduces basic concepts required for multimodal signal processing, architectures, and approaches to fusion. Chapter 8 continues with a summary of multimodal language processing and semantic integration, including techniques required for developing more advanced fusion-based systems (i.e., level 6 systems, as shown in Figure 1.1).

CHAPTER 7

Multimodal Signal Processing, Fusion, and Architectures

The next two chapters discuss the fusion of information from multiple modalities, beginning at the level of sensors and then at the level of semantics. Sensor fusion has been a long-standing topic of signal processing research within engineering, often for tracking objects from aircraft and satellites. For example, advanced aircraft automatically fuse multiple types of radar and infrared imaging to provide the pilot with a rapidly changing scene of objects in air and on the ground (Lockheed Martin, 2015). During the past decade, as smart phones, cars, and computers have become increasingly instrumented with cameras, microphones, GPS, accelerometers, biometric and other sensors, fusion techniques have begun to be applied to combining signal information for computer interface design. The terms *multimodal fusion* (*fusion-based multimodal interfaces*) and *multimodal-multisensor fusion or interfaces* now refer to joint processing of human communication modalities, sometimes combined with other sensor information, during human-computer multimodal interaction. See Table 1.1 for terms.

   With respect to multimodal fusion for computer interface design, Chapter 2 summarized the history of multimodal system development over the past 30 years. The wide variety of multimodal systems, including ones that jointly processed speech with gesturing and speech with sketching/writing, were based on different fusion techniques derived from computer science, artificial intelligence, and linguistics. Both the engineering and computational literatures use the term "multimodal fusion," and they are beginning to share techniques from statistical machine learning. However, their fusion aims and techniques are sufficiently different that we will separate our discussion of them. In Chapter 7, we examine the process of fusing information from multiple signals collected by different sensor devices (e.g., cameras, microphones) at different processing levels. The typical goal of such multimodal fusion is classification or recognition, which will be discussed synonymously in this chapter. That is, given a finite but potentially large number of labeled classes that can be associated with combined multimodal signal input, the purpose of multimodal fusion is to identify the most likely class or classes that characterize the signals. Atrey et al. (2010), Kittler et al. (1998), and Tulyakov et al. (2006) provided excellent detailed reviews of the multimodal fusion and classifier combination literatures from a signal processing perspective. We refer readers to these summaries as general background.

   One of the main techniques discussed in the signal processing literature is called *decision fusion*, which refers generically to reaching a final classification—or the best label that classifies the various signals by combining the classification decisions of individual classifiers. In Chapter 8, we use the term *semantic multimodal integration* to refer to fusion of semantic or representational information based on processing of human communication modalities (see Table 7.1). This might include speech and non-speech audio, handwriting that results in an x,y coordinate stream of digital ink, visual information about facial expressions, gestures and body movements, eye movements, physiological signals (e.g., heart rate, galvanic skin response, brain signals), and other sensor information (e.g., GPS). Semantic multimodal integration can be considered a type of decision fusion that attempts to generate a joint meaning interpretation, rather than just assigning a simple class label.

7.1   DIMENSIONS OF MODALITY FUSION

In both Chapters 7 and 8, we discuss the problem of modality fusion in terms of five dimensions:

- Why fuse—what benefits are available?

- What to fuse—what types of input are involved?

- When and how to fuse—When should processing fuse input from multiple modalities, rather than interpreting the signals individually? And how should signals be processed and fused?

- What fusion architectures are available for coordinating fusion?

- How robust is the implementation of multimodal fusion, as measured by evaluation metrics?

7.1.1   WHY FUSE?

Chapter 3 summarizes numerous documented benefits of designing an interface multimodally, compared with keyboard-and-mouse or unimodal interfaces. These include many substantial usability advantages, such as accommodation of individual differences, reduction of cognitive load, and support for more flexible and expressively powerful communication. A major theme throughout both the biological and engineering literatures has been that signal fusion can produce a major reduction of uncertainty, yielding highly robust systems. As described in Chapter 4, the human brain achieves its remarkable cognitive abilities through multi-sensory fusion, which is supported by multimodal neurons, multi-sensory convergence regions, and similar neurological substrates. These features reveal that the brain's architecture is fundamentally designed to support fusion of incoming signals. Multisensory fusion produces *super-additivity*, or responses larger than the sum of component input modes, which increases perceptual speed, reliability, and stability (see Section 4.2, Figure 4.1, and related term in Table 4.1). In addition, it can support qualitatively unique capabilities based on the blended input. Likewise, parallel engineering work on signal fusion has demonstrated improved system reliability, with the largest improvements occurring when an input signal is noisy (e.g., accented speech, high environmental noise).

Many recognition and classification problems that form the core of interactive systems can benefit from combining multiple input signals. Examples of the purpose of fusion include:

- engaging a system, or a recognizer;

- identifying a user from a database;

- identifying and retrieving content from a database;

- interpreting users' meaning, whether verbal or nonverbal;

- identifying a users' permanent or temporary state (personality, domain expertise, emotion, truthfulness, wellness); and

- identifying individual or group activity patterns, or a preferred sequence of actions for a robot to take in a given context.

We discuss specific multimodal systems that pursue these various aims in Chapters 9 and 10, including both commercial and research-level ones.

7.1.2   WHAT TO FUSE?

Many different types of data have been fused in multimodal systems and applications, including:

- continuous signals, which have been pre-processed, sampled, and segmented temporally and/or spatially at different levels of granularity;

- feature vectors that abstract and transform various signal parameters in a given window of space-time;

- discrete events, such as events transpiring in a game;

- words in text;

- class labels (e.g., image tags, words, phoneme labels, viseme labels, gesture labels, emotion labels); and

- structured meaning representations.

We give examples of many of these data types in this chapter.

In progressing from signals to semantics, signals are sampled, transformed, and provided to classifiers that determine their most likely labeling. For example, this may involve distinguishing emotional states, or a sequence of words associated with sounds and lip movements. During multimodal signal processing, the same set of classifications typically is used to categorize the different signals, such as common emotional state labels derived from voice quality and facial expressions (Busso et al., 2004). If the classifications used for different input signals are distinct, such as spoken words and manual gestures, then the fusion process may produce a more fully specified overall classification that incorporates information from each individual modality.

Subsequent processes then may incorporate the classification decisions. The discrete words may be analyzed by a natural language engine, or combined with input from another modality (e.g., location of eye gaze, emotion labels, or type of gesture). This may generate a more abstract type of data, such as a meaning representation. As a result, a *multi-level architecture* is the most common approach for multimodal signal processing and interpretation. However, there are numerous examples of systems that combine data types at different levels of abstraction. See Table 7.1 for term.

7.1.3   WHEN AND HOW TO FUSE?

This section outlines how input signals are sampled, aligned, segmented, and what determines when signals are interpreted jointly rather than individually.

Pre-processing, Sampling, and Alignment. Multimodal interfaces need to capture human input that arrives from different modalities, which may be processed at different rates. Signal processing algorithms sample continuous signals, and bin them into a "frame" for further processing. For instance, speech sampling may occur 48,000 times per second (Hertz, or Hz), but corresponding video frame sampling may occur at 30 Hz. One video frame then would include 1600 auditory samples. Other types of pre-processing include normalization of skew, slant, and baseline positioning during handwriting recognition (Bertolami and Bunke, 2006).

Since multimodal architectures are time-sensitive, the beginning and end of any incoming signal fragments (e.g., articulation bursts) also are time stamped prior to fusion with other incoming signals. This is standard pre-processing prior to any modality-specific recognition. Then a multimodal fusion algorithm will automatically time-align the incoming signals. During audio-visual speech recognition, signal information for corresponding visemes and phonemes is closely coupled, or time aligned, although visual movement occurs slightly in advance of the articulated phoneme. In contrast, other types of multimodal signal fusion (e.g., joint speaking and sketching) involve more loosely coupled or time-aligned signals, with written input often occurring several seconds before speech. Some multimodal fusion algorithms also will automatically co-process incoming signals based on their spatial features and relation. For example, when processing handwriting, different feature types (e.g., pixel-based, geometric) may be implicitly synchronized based on the input image (Bertolami and Bunke, 2006).

Segmentation and Coarticulation. The next major problem is to segment the signal for regions of interest. Thus, the system might try to separate speech from non-speech audio, such as road noise or laughter, or to segment out faces and hands from complex video imagery. A system typically needs to separate, identify, and localize multiple signal sources of interest, such as the speech and/or movement patterns of different specific people. In the visual domain, *space-time interest points* (i.e., STIPs) are regions of an image sequence that vary significantly in both time and space (Laptev, 2005). They are used to focus face and body recognition algorithms for analysis of human motion and gesture (Song et al., 2013). For term, see Table 7.1.

The segmentation of gestures during continuous movement, phonemes in continuous speech, and cursive handwriting in a digital ink stream, are difficult problems partly because of coarticulation effects. These are caused by adaptation in a movement pattern, for example movement of the lips and tongue in the production of a sound, when it is produced within a stream of other movements rather than in isolation. For example, the sound of a phoneme will vary depending on whether it is in initial, medial, or final position in a word. Similar context effects occur during gesturing, due to transitions from one position (e.g., resting) or movement pattern (e.g., earlier gesture) to another.

Feature Selection. Among the most important decisions that influence recognition quality is the set of signal features used. Researchers in every subfield of pattern recognition have manually studied a particular set of features. For example, handwriting recognition algorithms often use pixel and geometric features, and computer vision algorithms may identify images for edges and corners, density of black pixels, and so forth. Speech recognition has typically used features that include, among many others, 12 Mel Frequency Cepstral Coefficients per 10-ms acoustic frame (Davis and Mermelstein, 1980). The reader is referred to introductory textbooks on recognition and classification technologies for details on the many different feature sets.

However, a radical shift has occurred recently in using deep neural networks that can select their own features. This approach has shown significantly better performance than state-of-the-art systems based on manually engineered features sets. For speech, a deep learning network can derive its own features from raw unfiltered speech signal spectrograms (Dahl et al., 2012; Sainath et al., 2015). For computer vision, it can derive image features directly from pixel representations (Krizhevsky et al., 2012). In addition, a deep learning approach has recently shown promise in automatically learning multimodal features for audio-visual speech recognition (Ngiam et al., 2011), including reproducing human multisensory blending observed in the *McGurk effect* (see Section 4.2, and Table 4.1 for term).

Decision to Process Signals Jointly vs. Separately. Once signals are sampled, aligned and segmented, the system needs to determine if they should be interpreted together. As discussed in Chapter 1, speech typically is an active and intentional input mode that users direct to a person or computer, whereas other information sources (e.g., facial expressions, eye movements) may be passively tracked without a user's intending to communicate to the system. Multimodal fusion can incorporate both active and passive types of input mode, and their joint processing may support qualitatively different and improved interpretations beyond accurately assigning a common set of labels. For example, processing of facial expressions, eye movements, or voice quality may reveal whether the user's literal spoken utterance is truthful or not. That is, the multimodal system may provide extra information about how to interpret the classification.

As introduced earlier, input signals vary in how closely coupled (e.g., speech and lip movements) vs. loosely coupled (e.g., speech and gestures) they are along a temporal dimension. In the case of more loosely coupled input like spoken utterances and gestures, they also can occur by themselves. For example, a body motion may be culturally meaningful as a stand-alone *emblematic gesture* (McNeill, 1992), such as a traffic policeman displaying an outward facing palm to a driver. However, the same body motion can change in meaning if accompanied by speech, such as "Hello." Indeed, researchers have argued that certain types of gestures, *iconic gestures*, cannot be interpreted without reference to co-occurring speech (Kopp et al., 2007). For terms, see Table 8.3. In some cases, these two signals could even be produced by different people during a conversation. For example, one person might ask, "How big was the fish?" while their conversation partner responds with a two-handed gesture indicating its length. As another example, a person's head nods, indicating confirmation of understanding must be interpreted in relation to preceding speech from a partner. However, not all gestures or body movements that overlap with speech should be treated as meaningful and jointly interpreted with it. A separate gesture, such as a hand wave, may be intended for a distant person entering the room. Movements also may involve involuntary fidgeting or tics. Even when speech and gestures are intended to jointly convey meaning, they do not necessarily overlap in time (see Section 4.3.2; McNeill, 1992; Oviatt, 1997). The upshot is that it is often nontrivial for a multimodal system to determine when to fuse two signals, and when to process them individually.

As discussed in Section 4.3.1, the likelihood that a user will issue unimodal vs. multimodal input to a computer varies depending on the task. Sections 4.3.2 and 4.3.3 also clarify that individual users have an identifiable pattern of synchronizing input modes, with some users habitually simultaneous integrators while others are sequential integrators. Users' signature pattern is resistant to change during training. In fact, they will actually entrench further in their habitual pattern when tasks become difficult or system errors increase. The pattern of synchronizing signals also depends on the specific input modes in question.

In the past, the most common approach has taken into account the type of input modalities. It then has used empirical data from a group of users interacting with the system to determine: (1) whether one input mode typically precedes the other and (2) what the longest average lag is between modes. After discarding outliers, a system threshold is set for when to fuse signals. For example, if writing typically precedes speech with no more than a 4 second lag, then when the system receives input in that order it may adopt a threshold of 4 seconds to ensure that 98–100% of all multimodal input is correctly co-processed. Alternatively, the decision may be made to adopt a 2–3-s lag threshold if speed of processing is high priority, in which case the tradeoff is that a lower percentage of multimodal input will be correctly co-processed initially. In both cases, processing is unimodal whenever (1) speech precedes gesture or (2) the temporal threshold is exceeded. Given continuous signal input from both modes, if the system encounters a sequence of user input that is **Speech₁ Drawing Speech₂**, it will analyze it as unimodal **Speech₁**, followed by multimodal **Drawing+Speech₂**, assuming the threshold is met.

Given available data, the best current approach to deciding whether two signals should be co-processed is a large corpus data-driven one based on machine learning, which incorporates relevant contextual information about the input modes, user's task, and individual user integration pattern. It ideally would develop a user-centered threshold for co-processing of two signals (Huang et al., 2006). The multimodal system then would adaptively process multimodal input based on user-centered and contextual information to optimize performance. Given this approach, system processing could be sped up by not waiting at all whenever (1) the user is a simultaneous integrator (the majority or 70% of users) or (2) the user is a sequential integrator, and the upper bound of their personal user-centered threshold has been exceeded. Ultimately, this approach would result in system processing being sped up substantially in almost all cases. Note that this approach depends entirely on the availability of relevant data, which in the past has not been readily available.

Finally, a completely different approach is to process signals in parallel as both unimodal and multimodal. Then, based on the alternative semantic interpretations, the system would determine which resulting meaning makes the most sense in the given situation and conversational context.

7.2   FUSION ARCHITECTURES

In this section, we discuss different approaches to classification and their organization within an overall system architecture. There are numerous types of classifiers, including K-nearest neighbor, decision trees, neural networks, support vector machines, and others. Classifiers separate vectors of data into clusters that can be assigned class labels. Learning algorithms for such classifiers are "supervised," in that they are given a set of labeled vectors for training. Once trained, the algorithms are given a new set of unlabeled vectors and attempt to find the best class labels for them. Typically, classifiers such as those above are applied to static data. For sequential data, *hidden Markov models* (HMM; Rabiner, 1990), dynamic Bayesian networks (Garg et al., 2003), time-delay neural networks (Vo and Waibel, 1993), and others are often used. For background on the more frequently used classifier/recognizer architectures, and the meaning of related terms, there are several excellent textbooks and review articles on machine learning and recognition (Alpaydin, 2010; Jurafsky and Martin, 2009; Manning and Schütze, 2003; Rabiner and Juang, 1993; Salakhutdinov, 2014).

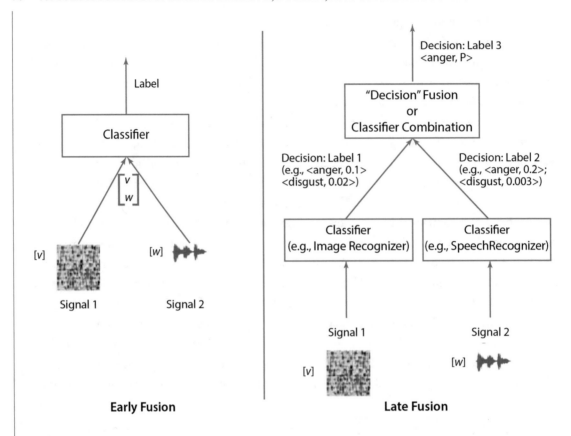

Figure 7.1: Early fusion (left): Feature vectors v and w, for example from image and auditory signals respectively, are concatenated for a given time frame and provided to a joint classifier, which assigns a category label. Late fusion (right): Vectors v and w are classified separately, typically as lists of labels, each with a score or probability. Those classifications, which use the same set of labels, are then combined to form a decision about the best label. Here the labels are emotion categories that are based on Ekman and Friesen (1978).

One possibility is to classify multiple synchronized signal or feature vectors with the same classifier, a process called *early fusion*. Figure 7.1 (left) illustrates an early fusion architecture in which vector v is combined with vector w to form the joint vector $[v\ w]$, which is processed by a classifier. If v is a representation of an image and w represents synchronized speech, an early fusion system could be used to perform audio-visual speech recognition. For other applications, such as multimodal biometrics, the concatenated vectors might be two different ways to image a finger (Ross and Jain, 2004), or pixel-based and geometric vectors derived from images of handwriting (Bertolami and Bunke, 2006). However, since feature vectors can be high-dimensional, one disadvantage of early fusion is that concatenation can lead to long processing times. Since the vectors for individual modalities have been merged, another disadvantage is that the resulting classification cannot model the reliability of each modality under different conditions—such as the effects of high noise on speech recognition, changes in lighting on visual recognition, and other characteristic types of channel degradation for individual signals (Kolossa et al., 2009; Papandreou et al., 2009; Potamianos et al., 2015). See Table 7.1 for term.

An alternative to early fusion is that signals can be classified independently. Then classifications or decisions can be combined to arrive at a joint classification. This is called *late fusion or decision fusion* (see Figure 7.1, right, and Table 7.1 for term). There are many advantages to considering a late fusion approach, including:

- tailorability: a given type of signal may best be analyzed with a particular type of classifier;

- synchrony: modalities that are not time-synchronous, such as speech and gesture, frequently benefit from independent recognition;

- efficiency: often it is computationally advantageous to process each type of signal with a separate classifier so input vector size is reduced, which prevents exponential growth in classifier computation time;

- accuracy: late fusion generally outperforms early fusion, although this is not always the case and can depend on the modality combination; and

- simplicity of system development: a late fusion approach enables researchers to use commercial recognizers that provide only a "black box," with no access to the internal state or data of the recognizer/classifier. This permits a larger choice of recognizers, and also the ability to swap in an improved recognizer with the same applications programming interface.

Late/decision fusion combines the output of two classifiers, and can be accomplished in a number of different ways. If the recognizers only provide a ranking of their outputs, and those outputs have the same labels, then a *majority-voting scheme* can be used (Song et al., 2013). Alternatively, one can provide a *Borda count* that provides a numerical rank to each label assigned by each classifier. The sum of the ranks for each label across classifiers then is maximized (Tulyakov et al., 2006). See Table 7.1 for terms. In some cases, such as for commercial recognizers that provide no access to their internal algorithms, these simple combination functions may be the only alternative possible.

In other cases, the individual modality classifiers might generate a list of class labels, each with a numerical score that may be expressed as a *confidence value* or probability. The question then becomes how to combine the numerical results from these classifiers. A typical way to combine classifier scores that are likelihoods is to sum their weighted log-likelihoods, as long as the modalities are conditionally independent. This often is accepted as a simplifying assumption for late fusion. Many algorithms can be used to train the weights, such as neural networks. If the scores are not likelihoods, they are often normalized to the interval [0,1] by a *softmax function*. See Table 7.1 for term. Kittler et al. (1998) examined multiple classifier combination functions, including sum, product, average, minimum, and maximum, and found that a simple sum rule outperforms the other combination functions because it is less perturbed by errors in the original data or classification results.

In some cases, early fusion of synchronized feature streams, such as using pixel-based and geometry-based recognizers for handwriting, has performed better than late fusion. This may occur partly because one of the classifiers performs poorly by itself. For example, Bertolami and Bunke (2006) found that a classifier that used both pixel and geometric features concatenated into a single vector outperformed a late-fusion architecture. In this case, the late fusion architecture used a pixel-based handwriting classifier with an relatively high error rate. Other research has argued that highly correlated modes should in principle be handled better using early fusion. However, a major limiting factor is computational complexity that can result from the high dimension of combined input features, which often results in a performance disadvantage.

A number of variants to these two basic architectures have been developed. For instance, an *intermediate fusion* architecture, such as the coupled hidden Markov model (Brand et al., 1997), sends synchronized streams of vectors to modality-specific recognizers, whose internal states are synchronized at specific times or events (see Figure 7.2, left; see Table 7.1 for term). An example is an audio-visual speech recognition architecture in which the hidden states for audio and visual HMMs may be asynchronous within a phoneme, but synchronized at phoneme boundaries (Potamianos et al., 2015).

As discussed earlier, human signals may be continuously available to process (e.g., emotional expressions, body posture), or they may be discrete and/or occur intermittently (e.g., pointing, writing). Although it is not yet common practice, continuous and discrete signals may also be combined in *hybrid fusion architectures* (see Figure 7.2, right; see Table 7.1 for term). In this case, a classifier receives a raw signal from one modality, and a discrete event or decision from another. An example of such a hybrid architecture involves fusing events in a game with players' continuous skin conductance in order to predict their emotional states during play (Martinez and Yannakakis, 2014). A second example is incorporation of a recognized gesture label into a statistical language model during speech recognition (Johnston and Bangalore, 2000).

As mentioned earlier, a multimodal interface may involve fusion of classifiers at multiple levels of abstraction. The same type of recognizer/classifier could be used at the different levels.[6] For example, a three-level layered Hidden Markov Model was used to combine audio, video, keyboard, and other signals at multiple levels of temporal resolution in order to recognize office activities (Oliver et al., 2004). Other researchers have used different types of classifiers at each level. For example, a deep learning neural net might be the classifier of choice for automatically learning and classifying acoustic features. It then could provide those results to an HMM for recognizing utterances. Similarly, a three-level member-team-committee architecture was used to combine speech, which had been recognized by an HMM and parsed into a meaning representation, with pen gestures that were recognized by a neural network (Wu et al., 2002).

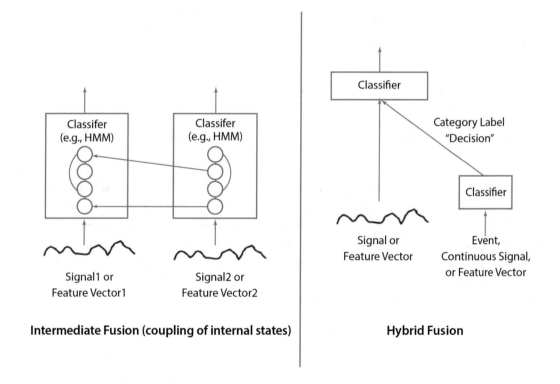

Figure 7.2: Intermediate and hybrid fusion.

---

[6] The "level" of the recognition system refers to the functional distance from the raw signal. The lowest levels of the system examine the raw signal. Middle levels receive the outputs of the lower level ones, and combine those results to provide data to higher levels. Any levels in the middle of the hierarchy are "hidden" in that their structure is not observable.

More recently, a late-fusion, multi-level *deep learning neural network architecture* has also been used to perform multimodal retrieval of labeled images (see Figure 7.3; Srivastava and Salkhutdinov, 2012). See Table 7.1 for term. Ngiam et al. (2011) have shown that a deep neural network can learn a shared feature representation from raw audio and video data. It can use that representation to recognize speech, given audio training alone, video alone (i.e., "lip reading"), or both types of input. Moreover, the deep neural network's recognition of noisy speech, which is based on learned multimodal features combined with audio-only features, results in superior reliability to using audio features alone.

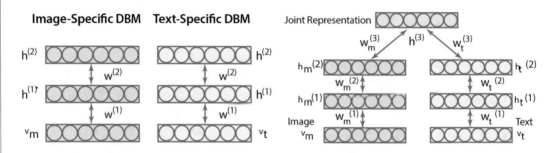

Figure 7.3: Multimodal deep learning with neural networks using a *Deep Boltzmann Machine* (DBM) for multimodal image retrieval. Vectors v_t and v_m are text and image vectors, and $w^{(1)}$ are weights at level i of the network. Hidden layers are $h^{(1)}_t$ for image (m) and text (t). The image-specific and text-specific two hidden-layer DBMs use different statistical models of their input features. In the multimodal DBM, they feed their results to a joint layer that is trained to classify images from the two types of output. Based on Srivastava and Salkhutdinov (2012). Copyright© 2012 Neural Information Processing Systems Foundation (NIPS). Used with permission. For term, see Table 7.1.

7.3   MULTIMODAL EMOTION RECOGNITION EXAMPLE

Consider the recognition of human emotion (Scherer, 2000) or affect from audio-visual video images of a person's face and hands. Fusion algorithms can treat signals from the face and from the body together (early fusion) or separately (late fusion). Likewise, audio signals could be combined with visual ones via early or late fusion. In this section, we present an example of emotion classification from a recent conference (Song et al., 2013) that illustrates the concepts we have discussed feature selection, classification, and both late and early fusion to produce state of the art results (see Figure 7.4). The data analyzed is from the Audio-Visual Emotion Challenge dataset, or AVEC (Schuller et al., 2012). Using this approach, video images were scanned for space-time interest points (STIPs; Laptev, 2005) of a subject's face and body. Both static image features (i.e., Histograms of Oriented Gradients, HOG; Dalal and Triggs, 2005), and motion features (i.e., Histograms of Optical Flow, HOF; Dalal et al., 2006) were extracted. The features were clustered into bins, or codes in a *sparse codebook*, which formed a table. The maximum values of these vector codes were expressed over time as histograms of combinations, or max-*poolings* of features. Then, a support vector machine classifier was trained to map a sequence of such max-pooled feature codes, combining both face and body features, into emotional dimension classifications that were expressed during that video segment. For terms, see Table 7.1.

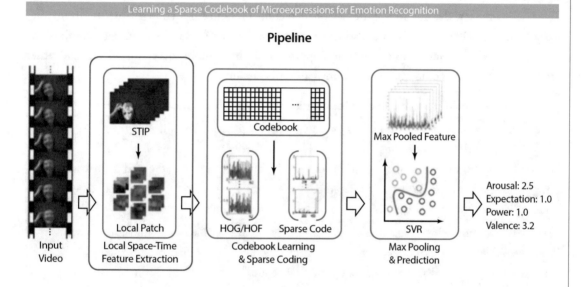

Figure 7.4: *Pipeline architecture* for emotion recognition. Based on Song et al. (2013). Copyright© 2013 ACM. Used with permission. See Table 7.1 for term.

This Song et al. (2013) system, and others in the AVEC competition, also analyzed the subject's co-occurring audio, which was represented by more than 1400 audio features (e.g., spectral, energy, voicing, prosody). One approach combined audio and visual features using early fusion, but the joint audio-visual recognition was degraded when speech was absent (cf. Ngiam et al., 2011). This research also reported using a late fusion approach in which audio and visual classifications of emotion were combined with a modified voting method. In this case, if no audio was present, the video was used alone (see Table 7.2). Emotion recognition using late fusion of audio with visual was marginally better than using visual information alone, but clearly better than using an early fusion strategy. Other participants in the AVEC challenge (e.g., Nicole et al., 2014) have also obtained a similar benefit for late audio-visual fusion.

However, not all classes are equally captured by one multimodal fusion method. Nicolaou et al. (2011) found that one emotional dimension (Arousal) is best analyzed by audio information, while another (Valence) is better analyzed multimodally. They argued that although in principle feature fusion should be an appropriate method when audio and visual are correlated, in practice this early fusion principle does not always yield better performance. They hypothesize that the reason for this disadvantage is the high dimensionality of the combined features, as well as inaccuracies in synchronization.

In summary, the audio-visual emotion detection literature has shown benefits from using early fusion for video analysis, and also late fusion to incorporate audio with visual classifications (Zeng et al., 2009). Generally, a late fusion approach has been more successful on this and other tasks whenever close audio-visual synchrony cannot be assumed.

Table 7.1: Terminology for multimodal information processing, fusion, and architectures

Early Fusion, or Feature-Level Fusion concatenates two time-synchronized signals or feature vectors and sends them to a single classifier. For example, two video streams taken from different angles might be fused for purposes of object identification, or an audio and a video stream might be abstracted as feature vectors and sent to the same emotion recognition classifier. Importantly, the signals or feature vectors must be time synchronized.

Intermediate Fusion involves combining or coupling the internal states of multiple classifiers, such as hidden Markov models (e.g., Coupled HMMs), each of which has been sent its own signal for processing. This can lead to a joint or "product" state of recognition, in which recognizer A is in state S_A and B is in state S_B, so the coupled or product classifier is in state $S_A S_B$. There is no requirement that the two signal or feature vector streams be precisely synchronized. An example is audio-visual speech recognition in which a phoneme may precede the corresponding viseme by up to 120ms.

Late Fusion, or Decision Fusion refers to the combination of results from separate classifiers with their own signal or feature stream. Depending on the types of output produced by the individual classifiers, the combination can be as simple as summing the ranks of those outputs, or as complex as providing a weighted probabilistic combination whose weights are trained through machine learning.

Semantic-Level Fusion, or Semantic Multimodal Integration is a method for integrating semantic information derived from two or more input modes in a multimodal architecture, which generally has been used to process modes that are more loosely coupled temporally (e.g., speech and manual gestures, speech and writing). It involves applying fusion later during signal processing.

Case Frame is a collection of semantic roles that entities play within an action. They often have names such as "agent" (A), "object" (O), "beneficiary (B)," some of which are obligatory in a sentence, and some optional. Thus, "John gave Mary a book," has John as agent, Mary as beneficiary, and book as object. The same cases are filled by the same entities in "John gave the book to Mary." Verb senses in natural language will have characteristic case frames (Fillmore and Baker, 2009).

Frame-Based Integration is a pattern matching technique for merging case frame attribute-value data structures that characterize verbs. For multimodal processing, partial attribute-value data would arrive from different modalities. Frame-based integration is a special case of typed feature structure unification, which has been more precisely analyzed.

Time-Sensitive Architectures are ones that time-stamp the beginning and end of input signals or fragments during co-processing of two or more multimodal information sources (e.g., writing and speaking). The fusion of two or more information sources depends on meeting temporal processing requirements.

Hybrid Architecture*, or *Hybrid Fusion Architecture refers generically to using different fusion techniques at the same time. For example, this can be done by having one classifier of a signal or feature vector generate a classification result (such as a gesture label), which is then input along with a separate signal or feature vector to a second classifier, such as a speech recognizer.

Multi-Level Architecture involves having classifiers that examine a signal/feature vector. They then produce a result that is input to another level of classification, which examines the distribution of results from below. A "level" of the classifier network refers to its conceptual distance from the raw signal. Any levels in the middle of the hierarchy are "hidden," in that their structure is not observable. The classifiers could be of the same type, as in neural networks and layered HMMs, or of different types, as in the Member-Team-Committee architecture.

Pipeline Architecture involves a series of processing steps in which the output of one step becomes the input to another.

Hidden Markov Model (HMM) is a statistical pattern recognition technique for modeling sequential data, such as a sequence of phonemes. The goal of an HMM is to assign a probability to its observed input sequence. The HMM model does this by assuming the observed data were generated by a system that progressed probabilistically through a sequence of unobserved or "hidden" states in a transition graph. Each state has a probability for emitting a given output (i.e., the elements of the input sequence), and for transitioning to others states. Therefore, an HMM computes the probability of the *observed data* sequence by finding the most likely *state* sequence in the model. Typically, the state graph structure will be stipulated by the researcher, and the probabilities will be learned automatically. For a more comprehensive explanation, see Chapter 6 of Jurafsky and Martin (2009). For an explanation of the relation between HMMs and more general Bayesian networks, see Ghahramani (2001).

Neural Networks are graphs of "units" that compute a nonlinear function of their inputs, propagating weighted functions of those results along edges that connect to other neural units. A neural computation starts at the input layer of units, propagating each unit's functional outputs to neighboring levels until the computation reaches the highest level that computes the recognition output. Basic neural networks learn using a supervised process to adjust their weights by minimizing errors vs. correct results.

Deep Learning Neural Networks are multi-level neural networks that have more than one hidden layer. The layers roughly correspond to levels of abstraction departing from a raw signal. For example, a layer may learn to distinguish phonemes, with a subsequent layer distinguishing syllables. Deep neural networks are trained to choose their own set of features based on the raw signal. This is accomplished with an "autoencoder" process that automatically trains weight values and selects the best performing input features simultaneously. This process works backwards from the recognition results towards the input, adjusting weights to minimize the differences between the original and reconstructed inputs. For an excellent tutorial on deep learning, see Taylor (2014).

Deep Bolzmann Machine (RBM) Neural Networks are deep neural networks consisting of stacked combinations of Restricted Bolzmann Machines. RBMs are undirected graphs of neural units that are arranged in layers such that neural units on one layer are fully connected with those on another layer. However, there are no connections among units at the same level.

N-Best List is a list of the top N hypotheses that are provided by a classifier, recognizer, or parser. They may merely be ranked 1 through N, or they may have a score that is a *confidence value* or probability.

Confidence Value is a value returned from a recognizer representing the algorithm's relative certainty that its recognition result is correct. It is not intended to be a probability value even if normalized to the interval [0,1], but rather a relative value in comparison with other alternative recognition results.

Majority Voting Scheme is a method to combine results from multiple classifiers that share the same set of labels. For instance, if classifiers provide a common set of emotion labels such as "anger," then this combination rule would provide the result that assigned by the majority of them.

Borda Count is a method for combining preferences among classifier outputs that produce the same set of labels, but rank them. Each member of the *n-best list* is given a rank score, say 1-N, with N the highest rank. A class label's score would be assigned the sum of the scores provided by each individual recognizer. The class label with the maximum score is chosen.

Sparse Codebook is method of vector quantization that finds a collection of vectors, or "code vectors," to approximately represent a much larger set of vectors in a vector space region. The collection of code vectors is a "codebook," and the goal is to find a codebook with a minimal number of non-zero vectors (e.g., see: http://www.data-compression.com/vq.shtml; retrieved 2/20/15).

Coarticulation Effects are differences in continuous movement patterns that occur due to transitioning from a preceding state and to a following one. For example, spoken articulation of a particular phoneme or vowel varies depending on its articulatory context in running speech, which is caused by biomechanical constraints on tongue and lip movements.

Space-Time Interest Points (STIPs) are regions of an image stream in which mathematical operators of interest computed in those regions show high variation over space and time.

Pooling is a method designed to reduce signal-processing complexity by combining features of a signal, for example maximum and minimum values of some image feature in a signal region. They may be performed and referred to as a "max" pooling, or an "average/mean" pooling, etc., of the feature of interest.

Softmax is a function that often is used to obtain a probability distribution. It compresses the range of an M-dimensional real-valued vector z to a new vector of the same dimension for which the M elements lie in the interval (0,1).

Table 7.2: Comparison of video only, early audio-visual fusion, and late audio-visual fusion (Song et al., 2013) for categorizing dimensions of emotion in the AVEC 2012 emotion recognition challenge. Values are Pearson correlation coefficients between system emotion classification and hand-labeled data

Fusion Method	Test Split				
	Arousal	Expectation	Power	Valence	Mean
Video Only	0.575	0.419	0.427	0.230	0.413
Early Fusion (concatenation of vectors)	0.409	0.401	0.406	0.186	0.351
Late Fusion with Voting	**0.576**	**0.429**	**0.427**	**0.235**	**0.417**

This chapter has outlined a variety of fusion techniques used for different tasks and modality combinations. Table 7.3 summarizes and illustrates the major multimodal architectural approaches, including their advantages and disadvantages.

Table 7.3. Summary of multimodal fusion architectures

Method	Examples	Type of classifier	Benefits	Drawbacks
Early fusion of signals or features	Images of the same scene with two different sensors; audio-visual speech recognition	K-nearest neighbor, support vector machine, neural network	Appropriate when modes are tightly synchronized; captures mode correlations	High-dimensional fused vectors can lead to lengthy computation; cannot weight streams to adapt processing based on situational or personal factors
Intermediate fusion	Audio-visual speech recognition	Coupled HMM Multi-stream HMM	Captures mode correlations; allows modest degree of asynchrony	Not appropriate for highly asynchronous or independent modes
Hybrid Fusion	GSR +game events; use of gesture recognition to aid speech recognition	Deep neural networks; finite state transducers	Can combine discrete + continuous information; can use classification of one mode during recognition of another	Fusion benefits classification of one mode, but not the other(s)
Late/ Decision fusion	Speech + gesture; speech + sketch; audio-visual emotion recognition; multi-biometrics involving uncorrelated sources	Neural networks; Bayesian combination; linear-weighted combinations; MTC architecture	Appropriate for uncorrelated or independent modes; Can take advantage of semantic fusion techniques; black box recognizers can be swapped; can adaptively weight different modalities depending on reliability or circumstances	Black box recognizers cannot be changed

CHAPTER 8

Multimodal Language, Semantic Processing, and Multimodal Integration

This chapter describes *semantic multimodal integration*, during which semantic or representational information based on processing human communication modalities is fused (see Table 7.1 for term). We begin by outlining the main features of multimodal language from a linguistic perspective, which differ substantially from text or spoken language.

8.1   MULTIMODAL LANGUAGE

Communication channels can be tremendously influential in shaping the language transmitted within them. From past research, there now is cumulative evidence that many linguistic features of multimodal language are qualitatively different from those of spoken or textual language (Cohen et al., 1989; Oviatt, 2012). It can differ in features as basic as greater brevity, different semantic content, reduced syntactic complexity, altered word order, reduced *disfluencies* and ambiguity, fewer referring expressions, fewer determiners, less anaphora but more *deixis*, and reduced linguistic indirectness (Oviatt and Kuhn, 1998). As discussed and illustrated in Section 3.6, multimodal language also can reduce or eliminate error-prone locative descriptions when it includes pen input or gestures. See Table 8.3 for terms.

In many respects, multimodal language is simpler linguistically than either textual or spoken language. In research on multimodal speaking and writing exchanges, people used less indirection and fewer referring and co-referring expressions than when just speaking the same information (Oviatt and Kuhn, 1998). Instead, their constructions were briefer, more direct, and noun phrase referring expressions frequently were replaced by deixis. Expression of definite and indefinite reference also was less frequent. Typical word order departed from the canonical English order of Subject-Verb-Object-Locative constituent, which is characteristic of both spoken and textual language. Instead, users' multimodal constituents shifted to a Locative-Subject-Verb-Object word order. In fact, 95% of locative constituents were in sentence-initial position during multimodal interaction, whereas the same users completing the same tasks placed 96% of locatives in sentence-final position when only speaking (Oviatt et al., 1997). By foregrounding the locative constituent during multimodal communication, the communicator can highlight the topic in a way that reduces cognitive load.

From a linguistics perspective, the act of planning complex sentences increases a person's verbal working memory. For example, composing noun-phrase referring expressions (e.g., "The tall woman in the second to last row, who wrote the book") and subsequent anaphoric tracking of pronouns (e.g., "she") is well known to generate high levels of memory load when speaking or typing. People only use a longer noun phrase when introducing a new topic. Otherwise, they conserve effort and cognitive load by using a briefer pronoun or multimodal communication (e.g., "This one," while pointing with their finger). Almor's Informational Load Hypothesis describes these adaptations in noun-phrase referring expressions as an optimizing process, in which speakers trade off the cost of exerting effort to compose a full referring expression against the cognitive load they incur (Almor, 1999). If a topic already is in the focus of a listener's attention, a pronoun often is used to reduce load.

Unlike unimodal speech or text communication, multimodal communication eliminates the need for a referring expression or anaphoric tracking, because the topic can be indicated directly by gesturing, marking with a pen, or eye gaze. As a result, multimodal communication supports a large decrease in cognitive load due to reduced sentence planning demands. In one study, users' ratio of multimodal to unimodal communication spontaneously increased from 18.6% when dialogue context already was established to 77.1% when they had to establish a new one, as was illustrated in Figure 3.3 (left). That is, as sentence generation demands increased in difficulty, there was a +315% relative increase in people's use of multimodal communication (Oviatt et al., 2004a). Just as users prefer to interact multimodally on harder tasks, they also prefer to "upshift" to multimodal interaction when planning a more complex noun phrase description.

As discussed in Section 4.1, multimodal communication provides an important intelligibility advantage, which is a by-product of human's highly evolved multisensory processing skills. Audio-visual communication of a message can be understood more accurately by a listener than a unimodal spoken one (Grant and Greenberg, 2001). In addition, the brevity of multimodal language corresponds with briefer task completion time, lower cognitive load, and reduced disfluencies and errors on a task that would require reworks (Oviatt, 1997, 2012).

One implication of the above research on multimodal language is that multimodal system design has the potential to support more robust processing than a unimodal approach. The rest of this chapter focuses on processing users' multimodal language, especially techniques for semantic integration.

8.2   SEMANTIC PROCESSING AND MULTIMODAL INTEGRATION

The previous chapter discussed multimodal signal processing, during which the system classifies joint signal input into various categories. This chapter explains later stage semantic processing, which interprets the meaning of this input. In this context, the term *semantic multimodal integration* refers to processing of semantic fragments, or the partial information from multiple individual modalities, to obtain a meaningful interpretation based on their combination. For a related survey article, see Lalanne and colleagues (2009), and for a research-level toolkit for rapidly building multimodal fusion-based applications, see Serrano and Nigay (2009).

The following illustrates semantic multimodal integration. Assume a user of a multimodal map system draws a line on a map and says "main supply route." The spoken phrase can be recognized as a sequence of words, and the drawing classified as a spatial mark specifying a series of x, y coordinates. By integrating the meanings attributed to the words and to the drawing, in a process that will be explained below, a more complete semantic representation can be obtained. In this example, the label attribute of the symbolic content is filled in with the words **main supply route**, and the drawn mark's location is filled in with the series of x, y coordinate points showing latitude and longitude. This information determines a joint *feature structure*, or attribute:value structure, which goes beyond the simpler joint signal classification discussed in the previous chapter. See Table 8.3 for term.

The earliest systems, which were discussed in Section 2.1, incorporated spoken or typed natural language with 2D or 3D pointing gestures using a mouse, light pen, or data glove. Their semantic integration was guided by a natural language parser, which looked for a gesture and its referent only if there was a deictic determiner such as "this" or "that." That is, the parser was in control of the process, and fusion was limited to deictic pointing. As discussed in Section 4.3.2, cognitive science research has shown that deictic pointing only accounts for 14–20% of manual or drawn gestures (McNeill, 1992; Oviatt et al., 1997), so focusing exclusively on them would fail to provide much functionality. Furthermore, early system processing made the assumption that a spoken deictic term would occur simultaneously with a corresponding point gesture. Once again, subsequent research showed that the required simultaneity only occurred in 25% of cases (Oviatt et al., 1997). As a result of these findings, the use of natural language parsers to control fusion was abandoned in favor of more symmetrical and flexible approaches to combining semantic meaning. Additional shortcomings of these early systems included their failure to establish a common meaning representation format, or a more powerful and well-defined method for information fusion.

For the purpose of focusing discussion, the rest of this chapter will examine a detailed example. Assume a person is giving directions to a robot, and she says "go quickly down the road around the corner" while gesturing with her hands a straight trajectory and a 60° turn (Figure 8.1). The robot receives the user's speech input via a built-in array microphone, and the user's gesture, orientation and body posture via stereo video and depth cameras. Assume the robot's speech recognition is based on one or more hypotheses for words in the utterance, and its visual perception on representations of gesture, head orientation, facial expression, gaze, and body posture. The process of semantic multimodal integration must combine possible spoken utterance meaning representations with possible interpretations of the gesture, given the context of the user's body orientation and movements.

Figure 8.1: Person giving spoken instructions while gesturing to show the robot where to go down the curved street. Robot orients to the user to listen and observe these instructions.

Figure 8.2 shows a semantic multimodal integration example with speech and vision input for this example, which could be extended to incorporate additional input as well. The visual signal has a start and end time value, and it is classified as one of several possible gestures with associated meanings (i.e., a path, vs. a hand wave), each associated with a confidence value. Likewise, the speech recognizer has classified the speech signal for the utterance, which also has a start and end time, into a set of alternative word sequences (Word, Words2...) with associated probabilities. The natural language processor maps the word sequences into meaning representation fragments, which then are combined with those from the gesture analysis. The sections that follow will explain the multimodal integration process, including meaning representations that are called *typed feature structures*. It also will explain the concept and operations involved in *feature structure unification*, which combines partial meaning from each input modality to produce a complete meaning representation. See Table 8.3 for terms.

Multimodal Grammar Rule

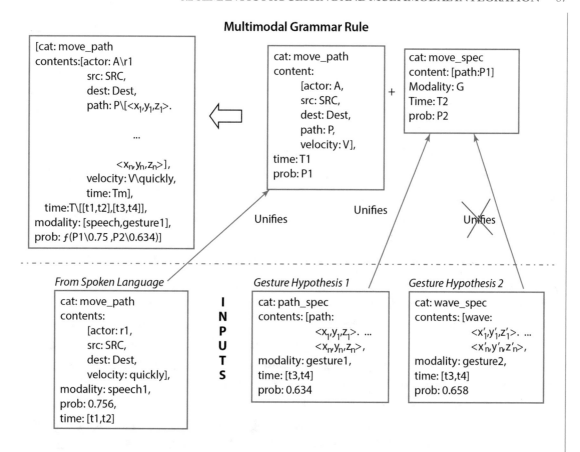

Figure 8.2: Multimodal grammar rule as applied to speech and gesture input during robot direction-giving example.

8.2.1   MEANING REPRESENTATIONS

Many different representations have been proposed to capture the meaning of a sentence. One typical example is logical representation, such as predicate logic (Genesereth and Nilsson, 1976). In such a scheme, the meanings are encoded as predicates that are applied to arguments. For example, a predicate might be "**move**" and its arguments might be the "actor" symbol (i.e., r1) denoting the robot, a "source" (**house0**) denoting an originating location, a "destination" (**house1**) denoting a geospatial coordinate or landmark, and a "path" symbol denoting a trajectory in space, such as **street2**.

```
move(r1,house0, house1,street2) .
```

In the language of predicate logic, **move** is a predicate, while **r1, house0, house1**, and **street2** are constant symbols. The relationship of the predicate to its arguments depends on their order in the above expression. Reversing the positions of **house0** and **house1** would imply a different movement. In addition to constants, predicate logic expressions can have variables, indicating that there is some value for that position in the expression, but the value is not stated. An example would be:

```
move(r1,Location, house1,street2)
```

in which **Location** is a variable by virtue of its starting with a capital letter, while the predicate **move** and constants **house1** and **street2** use lower case initial letters.[7]

Finally, such expressions above can have as arguments embedded expressions, such as the "move" term in the request to move below:

```
request( r1, move(r1, Location, house1, street2)).
```

The vocabulary of terms used here typically is drawn from an *ontology* in which types of entities are related to one another using expressions such as "isa" and "has-as-part", etc. An example would be **r1** is a kind of **robot** or **isa(r1,robot)**. Here, we speak of robot as being a superordinate or higher-level concept as compared to r1. The range of such terms can be vast, potentially as large as the vocabulary in a natural language. Authors of knowledge representations write rules and expressions that relate such concepts drawn from an ontology.

In addition, such concepts may be differentiated via an explicitly stated set of argument labels, often called roles or cases when discussed in linguistics. Examples include "actor," "source," "destination," "path," and so forth (Fillmore, 1968, 1977). A major effort has been undertaken to codify such cases, or roles, and their combinations in *case frames* in the FrameNet research project (see Table 7.1 for term; Fillmore and Baker, 2009). For such expressions, rather than use a positional notation as above, researchers have found it more convenient to be explicit about the role or case labels that arguments play in the concepts; the role/case expressions can occur in any order. So one might encode the above expression as:

```
move(actor:r1,

        [source: SOURCE,

        destination: DEST,

        path: [SOURCE,MIDDLE, DEST],

        velocity: V])
```

A move action has an actor and a list of arguments, enclosed in square brackets. Each argument is an attribute:value pair, with an attribute name and a value indicated with a variable in

---

[7] These conventions derive from the Prolog programming language. Lists are enclosed in brackets "[ ]".

capital letters. Here, the path is a list starting at **SOURCE**, ending at **DEST**, with some **MIDDLE** set of coordinates. The attributes **actor**, **source**, **destination**, **path**, **velocity**, and their values are all terms that would be drawn from the ontology. The term we will use to refer to such expressions, common in the computational linguistics literature, is *typed feature structure.* Feature structures are attribute-value structures like those above, such that "features," or attributes, are filled with values, variables, or embedded feature structures. For term, see Table 8.3. In a typed feature structure, each attribute, value, constant, and predicate is drawn from a set of types in the ontology, which are related by the "isa" predicate with subtypes. **Move** is a type that can have associated features with values, which in turn must be of a certain type. In expressions, values may be bound to the variables that begin with capital letters.

Typed feature structures have a long history in computational linguistics. They have been used for grammar rules, lexical entries, and meaning representations (Kaplan and Bresnan, 1995; Shieber, 1986). For multimodal processing, the meanings derived from input are each represented as typed feature structures. The best meaning representation of a multimodal utterance depends on a method for combining meaning from constituent utterance pieces, and also a process for obtaining high-likelihood combinations. The ideal process would be one that can represent and combine meaning fragments from a variety of different modalities. The process also requires a statistical ranking methodology to obtain the best or most likely joint interpretation. These topics are discussed in the next section.

8.2.2   MEANING COMBINATION

Continuing our example, let us assume the robot's utterance interpretation process derives a meaning representation fragment from the spoken utterance (Jurafsky and Martin, 2009). How should that fragment be combined with meaning fragments expressed in the same meaning representation language derived from other input modes? For example, how should the linguistic meaning from speech be combined with that derived from manual gesture, sketch, eye gaze, facial expressions (e.g., frown), and other diverse forms of information? Setting aside the issue that not all input may have been intended as a "meaningful" communication to the system, there are numerous techniques for combining information from multiple modalities. Below we describe a basic technique that has frequently been used, *typed feature structure unification*, along with two descriptions of algorithms that use unification as a component operation.

Typed Feature Structure Unification

The purpose of the unification of typed feature structures is to combine consistent though potentially partial information to arrive at a more specific and complete overall structure. As described earlier, feature structures (FS) contain a list of feature: value pairs, whose values can themselves be feature structures. Each FS has a type that is drawn from an ontology. A value can be a variable (specified in capital letters). Two structures, FS1 and FS2, are consistent if their types are in the "isa" relationship, and attributes in each that are the same do not contain constant values that are different. If one or more of the values are variables, they are bound together and fill in the value. If the values are both variables, they are bound together and receive the same value. A feature:value pair in one FS, provided it is not inconsistent with the other FS being matched, is included in the unified FS.

The requirement that partial interpretations from multiple modalities unify is a semantic constraint that rules out any potential interpretations that would be semantically inconsistent. This constraint can be used in a variety of different semantic multimodal integration algorithms, as long as there is a common language for meaning representation. Moreover, information is accumulated from each meaning representation into the fused one. Further details and formal definitions of typed feature structure unification are available elsewhere (Carpenter, 2005; Copestake, 2000; Kaplan and Bresnan, 1995; Shieber, 1986).

The three specific integration methods that will be discussed next are: multimodal grammars, finite state transducers, and event logic charts.

Multimodal Grammars—The QuickSet parser, described elsewhere (Johnston et al., 1997; Johnston, 1998), is a generalized *multidimensional chart parser* (Jurafsky and Martin, 2009; Kay, 1973; Wittenburg et al., 1991). It uses multimodal grammar rules to characterize the ways that input from each modality can combine to form a meaningful structure. This unification-based method of multimodal integration also is used in the Sketch-Thru-Plan multimodal planning system that will be described in Section 9.2 (Cohen et al., 2015), as well as many other systems (Holzapfel et al., 2004; Wahlster, 2006). A grammar developer would write multimodal grammar rules as typed feature structures that have a left-hand side (LHS) feature structure and a list of constituents (i.e., "daughters," or DTRs) on the right-hand side. These rules are subject to various constraints, including temporal and spatial ones. Such a grammatical rule schema is:

Grammar Rule

      lhs: L

      rhs: [DTR1 DTR2]

      constraints: [Temporal, Spatial, Other]

In Figure 8.2 (top), this multimodal grammar rule has two daughter feature structures, indicated in boxes on the right side of the arrow, which combine to form the feature structure on the left side of the arrow. (Note: The modality and time attributes will be ignored for the moment.[8]) The grammar rule says that a **request to move** along a **path** by actor **A**, starting at source

---

[8] The rule constraints stipulate that the time of speech has to overlap or follow that of the path gesture by no more than 4 s.

SRC, to destination **Dest**, along path **P**, with velocity **V**, at time **Tm** holds if there is a **move_path** action whose content is **A**, source **SRC**, destination **Dest**, path **P** and velocity **V**, along with a second constituent which is a path specification for which the content is **P**.

These right-hand side feature structures are unified against the input provided by the modality recognizers. In particular, the gesture recognizer has provided two alternative interpretations of the person's arm motion, namely as **path** or **wave** gestures. A natural language processor has taken the spoken sequence of words and determined that the speech action is a request for the robot to **move** from **SRC** to **DEST** along some **path** with a **velocity** "quickly." Because the **path** feature on the right side of the rule unifies with the **path** feature from the gesture, and because the value of the **path** feature from the **move_path** action is a variable **P**, it becomes bound to the coordinates provided by the **path** feature of the gesture. The **wave** interpretation is inconsistent with **path**, so the **wave** interpretation of the gesture does not unify with the interpretation of the language, ruling out a potential combination. The reverse of this process has also been used in generating language and gesture for virtual agents (Kopp et al., 2007).

Finally, the variables in the rule are filled in by the values provided by the modality input. Specifically, feature structure unification binds the variables in the rule's right-hand side feature structures, in particular the **path** variable **P** becomes bound to the coordinates from Gesture 1. A variable has been filled in by a value, notated by the syntax "var\val". Since **P** is shared with the left side of the rule, the coordinates are bound there too, indicated by: `'P\[<x1,y1,z1>, ...<xn,yn,zn>]')`. Also, the probability of the unified combination is a function of the probabilities of the speech and gesture hypotheses. The details of such combination functions have been the subject of much research (Kittler et al., 1998). Note that unification has ruled out the higher scoring gesture hypothesis by a process called *mutual disambiguation* described in Section 3.5 (see Table 8.3 for term). The result of this parse is to unify the attributes and values from the right hand side constituents into the left hand side, which is a representation of the meaning of the multimodal utterance. This result then can be acted upon by other system components, sent as output to the user, or queried for followup during a dialogue.

The multimodal grammar has the benefit of being declarative, enabling the grammar writer to create different rules that easily change the way multimodal constituents combine. Parsing algorithms and the basic typed feature structure unification process are well understood. The multimodal grammar also is general enough to allow more than two modes to be considered (Kaiser et al., 2003), such as speech, gesture, and vision-based object recognition. Such multimodal rules also can be used to combine information from intentional input, dialogue context, and passive sensing. However, one disadvantage is that in cases where there are many rules and constraints they could potentially become combinatorially explosive in the worst case.

Statistical Ranking—The unification-based integration of meaning representation fragments is one step in the process of combining information from different input modes, which requires that the meanings be represented with a common set of features and values. However, the recognizers that each produce a list of possible feature structure representations may also provide corresponding quantitative recognition results, which can be used to rank order the likelihood of their interpretations on an *n-best list*. For term, see Table 7.1. Once the recognizers produce their rank-ordered list of possible meaning representations, then the semantic integration process attempts to unify each interpretation on the n-best list for modality A with each interpretation on the n-best list for modality B. If a combination is not a semantically viable join, then it is ruled out as not properly unifiable. This can be accomplished by creating a table of potentially possible unifications, called an "associative map" by Wu and colleagues (1999), with a table lookup used to screen out infeasible combinations. Combinations that pass this filter and then unify successfully are retained and scored by the sum of their ranks to create a final rank-ordered multimodal list of meaning interpretations.

In our robot example, a table lookup to screen for semantically legal unifications would take place as such: The category of the top-level feature structure (FSs) from speech (e.g., **move**) would be set to index the rows of the table, and that of gesture (FSg) (e.g, **path**) to index the columns. There would be a "1" in the table if the spoken FS could in principal unify with that indexed for gesture. If so, then that combination would be saved for further comparison with other alternative joint interpretations. Recognizers/classifiers may or may not produce actual numerical scores for likelihoods,[9] rather than a simple rank ordering of interpretations, but this table lookup method can be used in either case.

If the modality recognizers provide scores that can at least be normalized into the interval [0,1], especially if they can be considered probabilities, then semantic multimodal integration can consider weighted linear combinations of the scores (Kittler et al., 1998; Wu et al., 1999, 2002). If the scores are probabilities, the usual method is to sum the weighted log probabilities derived from the individual recognizers. Numerous recognition/classification frameworks could in principle be used to learn the weights, including deep learning neural networks (Pavlakos et al., 2014; Srivastava and Salukhdinov, 2012), a member-team-committee (MTC) architecture (Wu et al., 2002), Bayes Nets (Garg et al., 2003; Oliver and Horvitz, 2005; Singhal and Brown, 1997; Muncaster and Turk, 2006), and others.

For example, MTC is a three-level architecture used for multimodal integration (Wu et al., 2002). MTC incorporates a set of individual member recognizers (e.g., multiple speech and gesture recognizers), each trained with a different set of data, features, and modeling approach. The members each produce a posterior probability estimate of the individual recognition result, given their inputs. The mid-level "team" classifiers are each trained to optimize a weighted linear combination of the posterior probability outputs of the set of members that they examine. Given the variation among the members, the distribution of member recognizer outputs provided to each team could

---

[9] Some popular commercial recognizers produce specific numerical values that are not in fact likelihoods.

be different. The output of the teams is an empirical probability distribution of the multimodal commands (i.e., pairs of speech and gesture), given the input feature sets of the members. Finally, the "committee" examines the results from the teams and produces a sorted n-best list of multimodal interpretations, for which the probabilistic estimates are greater than a supplied confidence limit. The surviving n-best lists of pairs of speech and gesture then can be filtered by a multimodal grammar rule and feature structure unification, which determines whether the pair forms a meaningful combination.

The MTC method assumes that a researcher first has conducted exploratory data analysis to find relevant features with which to train the member classifiers, which would be reflected in their posterior probabilistic classifications. With the advent of deep neural network systems (Salakhutdinov, 2014), the space of input features and member recognizers now can be explored automatically, with the features and weights at each level of the deep neural network learned without human intervention. In most current deep learning systems, more than three levels of processing are likely to be included.

To date, the use of feature structure unification and multimodal parsing has been successful for semantic multimodal integration when developing multimodal computer interfaces, partly because systems have been designed to support specific domains and styles of multimodal interaction. Further research is needed to see if this approach scales up for more multi-functional use, and also if a deep learning approach to statistical multimodal integration can fruitfully yield multimodal semantic interpretations.

We now turn to alternative methods for semantic multimodal integration.

Multimodal Finite State Transducer

Johnston and Bangalore (2000) provided a *multimodal finite state transducer* (FST) model for combining speech and gesture to produce a combined meaning, taking essentially a hybrid fusion approach. Briefly, the multimodal FST is a labeled directed graph, with two input streams for speech and gesture, and an output stream. Finite state rules attached to edges in the graph consume a word from the speech stream and a gesture symbol from the gesture stream to produce a fragment of a meaning representation on the output stream. When the transducer exits, the output stream contains the meaning representation. For term, see Table 8.3.

Figure 8.3 shows a small portion of such a transducer, taken from Johnston and Bangalore (2000), which was created by a context free grammar. Let us consider an example of how the FST operates for the expressions, "*email this department <pointing gesture> and this organization <pointing gesture>*." An edge in the graph uses ":" to separate the contents of the various streams. Starting in State 0, the automaton sees the word 'email' in the speech stream, ignores the Gesture stream (i.e., an epsilon or eps is found, meaning "nothing"), and emits the meaning fragment `'email([`

to the output stream, then transitions to State 1. The two transitions to State 2 search for deictic expressions"that" and "this" in the speech. The transition "**department:Gd:dept(**" to State 3 looks for the word "department" in the Speech stream, looks for a gesture **Gd** denoting a department in the Gesture stream, then emits "**dept(**" into the output stream. In order to handle a huge vocabulary of arbitrary locations and objects that can be selected in such a transducer, including the space of possible 3D coordinates, a set of "buffers" e_i is created that contain references to those entities. The number of buffers is limited by the number of gestures, rather than by the size of the vocabulary they contain. The transitions from State 3 to State 4 then combine the content of the gesture buffer e_i and move the contents to the output stream. The transitions from State 4 to State 5 and then to State 6 close off the meaning expression being generated by emitting "**)**" and "**])**", respectively. Finally, the transition from State 5 to State 1 looks for the word "and" in the Speech stream, and starts again (for "organization"). This FST operation on the streams shown in Figure 8.3 results in forming the meaning representation:

```
email([dept(e1), org(e2)])
```

Johnston and Bangalore (2000) stated that the FST is not restricted to this flat meaning representation, and that other types of meaning representation are possible. In a realistic scenario, the FST approach needs to combine and rank alternative interpretations of speech and gesture. It is claimed that this approach offers an efficient way to do so, because the gesture transitions can be folded into the n-gram language modeling of a speech recognition system, thereby modeling their co-occurrences. Thus, the same search algorithms used for speech recognition can be used for speech and gesture. To do so, the same learning algorithm that trains the edge weights in the hidden Markov models for speech recognition could weight the gestural transitions, resulting in a joint multimodal language model. In this approach, gesture would be recognized first, and its recognition would be used to prune speech hypotheses, implying a hybrid architecture as discussed in Chapter 7. However, the probabilities of speech and gesture co-occurrence would need to be trained over a multimodal corpus. Johnston and Bangalore (2000) reported a 23% relative error rate reduction for speech by using gestural information during recognition.

With respect to limitations, the FST illustrated here is oriented towards deictic pointing gestures that occur simultaneous with an utterance. A more expressive formalism would be required to handle the more complex temporal and spatial relationships discussed in Section 8.2. If new modalities are added to the system, the transitions in the FST need to be revised because their structure (i.e., the elements separated by ":") will need to be expanded. This is not required in the multimodal grammar framework, as long as the same feature structure labels are used for other modalities.

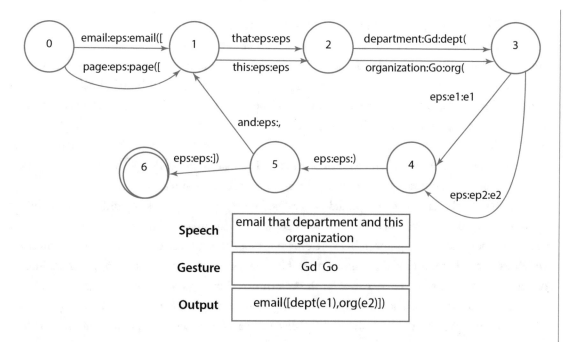

Figure 8.3: Three-stream multimodal finite state transducer. Based on a figure from Johnston and Bangalore (2000).

Event Logic Charts

Mehlmann and Andre (2012) emphasized that the multimodal integration mechanisms discussed above focus on discrete interaction, and therefore would be unsuitable for modeling many situations that produce a continuous output. For instance, imagine manipulating an object in 3D in a virtual reality environment, and seeing the output continuously, while speaking about the object to change some property (e.g., its color). The methods discussed above would require the gesture and speech to end before any output is produced, which they argue is not an acceptably responsive user interface for many applications.

   To overcome such limitations, the authors propose a *multimodal event logic* (see Table 8.3 for term), implementing a superset of Allen's temporal logic (Allen, 1983) operating over a knowledge base of events. Those events are populated by inputs from a variety of modalities in parallel. Unlike the FSTs discussed above that use simple presence of a symbol in a stream, statements in the event logic formalism are used on state transitions in a state chart automaton interpreter (Harel, 1987). State charts are a method to describe complex systems using finite state concepts in a more illuminating way through the use of embedding of diagrams, and the addition of concurrency that clarifies the system architecture.[10] In event logic charts, a state transition is taken if it can be shown that the transition's event logic expression can be proven to be a true statement about the knowledge base. For multimodal purposes, the knowledge base contains the ongoing history of multimodal events and streams. Such event logic expressions then describe relationships among events and intervals, for example that an interval of speech overlaps, is during, or is after an interval of gesture. The expressions combine information from different modes, and apply temporal and spatial constraints, as in multimodal grammars (Johnston, 1998). Motivated by similar real-time processing concerns, a formalism based on augmented transition networks (Woods, 1970) also has been proposed by Latoschik (2002) for use with multimodal virtual reality applications.

Different charts can be interpreted in parallel, for example for processing different modalities or controlling virtual characters (Mehlmann et al., 2012). This method has some of the benefits of the multimodal grammar approach in expressing multimodal combinations as event logic formulae, which can encode multimodal grammar rules. However, since it uses a parallel event chart interpreter rather than a serial chart parser as the rule-processing engine, it is capable of incremental parsing and fusion as data arrives asynchronously from multiple channels. The event logic state chart is more expressive than the simple FST discussed above, which incorporates simple tests for the presence of symbols in buffers or streams. The event logic chart approach is now part of the Social Signal Interpretation framework (Wagner et al., 2013), which provides a powerful toolkit that offers a graphical means to create a multimodal interpretation system, incorporating signal pre-processing and segmentation, classification, and both early and late fusion classifiers.

One drawback to this approach is that the state chart and its transitions need to be authored by hand, including various parameters, such as timeouts and thresholds. A potential next step would be application of machine learning techniques to capture the co-occurrence possibilities among the modalities, including weights and timeouts in the transition diagrams. Furthermore, the development of a general purpose incremental parsing and fusion engine could be a productive synthesis of the three approaches described above.

In summary, multimodal fusion architectures have generally operated at three levels. They involve early, intermediate/hybrid, and late fusion, corresponding to fusion of signal features, combining signals in one mode with classifications performed in another, and fusion of classifier decisions, respectively. Semantic multimodal integration architectures usually involve late fusion algorithms with a common meaning representation language that is populated by interpretations from each modality. The meaning combination algorithm may be a variant of unification. However, alternative multimodal fusion architectures have been based on finite automata, using a simple buffer approach or expressions written in a logical language. Late fusion and multi-level modular hybrid integration techniques generally have been the most fertile avenues for achieving high levels of robustness.

---

[10]   The World Wide Web Consortium has proposed State Chart XML (SCXML) (Barnett et al., 2012; World Wide Web Consortium, 2014) as a standard for expressing state charts.

Future multimodal signal and semantic processing could benefit from expanded use of large corpora, where available, and the application of machine learning and deep neural net learning techniques. In addition, more robust and usable systems could be achieved through adaptive processing, for example to handle the complex temporal processing requirements. Finally, multimodal processing techniques will need to be expanded along a number of dimensions for handling more complex multi-user collaborative input (Cohen et al., 2002).

8.3   EVALUATION OF MULTIMODAL INTEGRATION

During the development of multimodal systems, one focus of assessment has been on the demonstration of improved robustness over unimodal speech systems. To track this, researchers have calculated an overall multimodal recognition rate, although often summarized at the utterance level and with additional diagnostic information about performance of the system's component recognizers. This has provided a global assessment tool for indexing the average level of multimodal system accuracy, as well as the basic information needed for comparative analysis of multimodal vs. unimodal system performance.

However, multimodal research also has adopted more specialized metrics, such as a given system's rate of mutual disambiguation. This concept has been valuable for assessing the degree of error suppression that is achievable in multimodal systems. It also has provided a tool for assessing each input mode's ability to disambiguate errors in the other mode. This latter information has assisted in clarifying the (1) relative stability of each mode on average, (2) how effectively two modes work together to supply the complementary information needed to stabilize system performance, and (3) under what circumstances a particular input mode is effective at stabilizing the performance of a more fragile mode. In these respects, the mutual disambiguation metric has significant diagnostic capabilities beyond simply summarizing the average level of system accuracy. It is playing an active role in strategizing user-centered design for developing robust new multimodal systems (Oviatt, 2002). This latter topic will be addressed in the next section.

Table 8.1 shows an example of the error suppression achievable within a fusion-based multimodal architecture. It summarizes evaluation results from studies involving over 4,600 multimodal constructions by accented vs. native speakers, as well as during mobile vs. stationary use. The relative error suppression due to multimodal processing, compared with unimodal speech, ranged from 19–41%. Speech degraded significantly more for accented users and while mobile, both circumstances involving a noisy signal. However, these were precisely the cases for which mutual disambiguation of signals during multimodal processing yielded the largest improvements. That is, multimodal fusion produced the largest performance advantage for those users and usage contexts in which speech-only systems typically fail. One impact of this is to ensure more uniformly robust processing across users and conditions, in addition to improving average system reliability.

Table 8.1: Evaluation results from studies with accented vs. native speakers (left), showing that speech recognition degraded by 9.5% more for accented speakers.[11] However, the rate of mutual disambiguation of signals was 15% for this group, with gestural input retrieving failed speech recognition twice as often as for native speakers . Evaluation results for mobile vs. stationary users (right), showing that speech recognition degraded by 10% when mobile. The rate of mutual disambiguation of signals was 16% during mobile use, with gestural input retrieving failed speech recognition significantly more often than during stationary use [Note: Statistically significant results indicated by *]

Type of Language Processing	% Performance Difference for Accented Speakers		Type of Language Processing	% Performance Difference When Mobile	
Speech	-9.5% *		Speech	-10.0% *	
Gesture	+3.4% *		Gesture	—	
Multimodal	—		Multimodal	-8.0% *	
Type of MD Metric	Native Speakers	Accented Speakers	Type of MD Metric	Stationary	Mobile
Signal MD Rate	8.5%	15.0% *	Signal MD Rate	9.5%	16.0% *
Ratio of Speech Pull-Ups	.35	.65 *	Ratio of Speech Pull-Ups	.26	.34 *

In addition to improving recognition when signals are noisy, Table 8.2 shows that multimodal processing fortifies recognition when component signals are very brief, which can lead to ambiguity and failed interpretations. Monosyllabic speech accounts for a disproportionate number of speech recognition failures, because of the minimal acoustic signal information available for the speech recognizer to process. However, these relatively fragile constructions accounted for 85% of the cases in which a failed speech interpretation was retrieved during the mutual disambiguation process, which was significantly greater than the rate observed for multisyllabic utterances. For a more detailed analysis of these error pattern and resolution dynamics, see Oviatt (2002).

---

[11]   Interestingly, the reverse was true for native speakers, for whom more accurate recognition of speech fragments retrieved failed gesture recognition during mutual disambiguation.

Table 8.2 Evaluation results for brief monosyllabic vs. longer multisyllabic speech input, showing the prevalence of monosyllabic input, its high likelihood of being misrecognized, and the effectiveness of joint multimodal processing in handling this otherwise underspecified content. The far right column indicates that 85% of mutual disambiguation involving retrieval of failed speech occurred on monosyllabic input. [Note: Statistically significant difference present between monosyllabic and multisyllabic constructions]

	% Total Commands in Corpus	% Speech Recognition Errors	% MD with Speech Pull-Ups
1-Syllable	40%	58.2%	84.6%
2-7 Syllables	60%	41.8%	15.4%

When examining the rate of mutual disambiguation, all cases were assessed in which one or both recognizers failed to determine the correct lexical interpretation of the users' input, although the correct choice effectively was "retrieved" from lower down on an individual recognizer's n-best list to produce a correct final multimodal interpretation. The rate of mutual disambiguation per subject (MD_j) was calculated as the percentage of all their scorable integrated commands (N_j) in which the rank of the correct lexical choice on the multimodal n-best list (R_i^{MM}) was lower than the average rank of the correct lexical choice on the speech and gesture n-best lists (R_i^s and R_i^g), minus the number of commands in which the rank of the correct choice was higher on the multimodal n-best list than its average rank on the speech and gesture n-best lists, or:

$$MD_j = \frac{1}{N_j} \sum_{i=1}^{N_j} Sign\left(\frac{R_i^S + R_i^G}{2} - R_i^{MM}\right).$$

MD was calculated both at the signal processing level (i.e., based on rankings in the speech and gesture signal n-best lists), and at the parse level after natural language processing (i.e., based on the spoken and gestural parse n-best lists). Results reported in Table 8.1 replicated across both signal and parse-level MD. Scorable commands included all those that the system integrated successfully, and that contained the correct lexical information somewhere in the speech, gesture, and multimodal n-best lists.

Metrics are critically important as a forcing function for developing any new technology. Ideally, a collection of carefully crafted metrics is needed to provide intelligent guidance for high-quality system design. In the future, other new metrics will be needed that reflect concepts of central importance to the development of emerging multimodal systems.

8.4   PRINCIPLES FOR STRATEGIZING MULTIMODAL INTEGRATION

A large body of cumulative evidence now clarifies that a well-designed multimodal system that fuses two or more information sources can be an effective means of reducing recognition uncertainty (Abouelenien et al., 2014; Kaiser et al., 2003; Kolossa et al., 2009; Luettin et al., 2001; Oviatt, 2002; Park et al., 2014; Papandreou et al., 2009; Ross and Poh, 2009; Song et al., 2013). Performance advantages have been demonstrated for different modality combinations (e.g., speech and pen, speech and lip movements), in widely varied tasks (e.g., user's meaning during mobile search, speaker identification, emotion recognition, detection of persuasiveness and deception), and in different environments (e.g., mobile cell phone use, in car noise). Perhaps most importantly, the error suppression achievable with a fusion-based multimodal system can be very substantial, frequently in excess of 40% (Oviatt, 2002). As outlined in the last section, multimodal systems also can perform more stably in real-world usage contexts and for a larger variety of users (Oviatt, 2002). This section summarizes basic principles for strategizing when and how to fuse information sources within a multimodal system.

There are several key concepts that surface as important in the design of fusion-based multimodal systems, which take into consideration that there are (1) fertile research strategies for yielding improved robustness and also (2) special targets of opportunity. Each of these topics is addressed below.

In the majority of cases, these fusion strategies have been documented to improve system reliability:

- **Increase the number of input modes incorporated within the multimodal system**

This principle is effective because it supports effective supplementation and disambiguation of partial or conflicting information that may be present in any individual input mode. As one example, Kaiser et al. (2003) reported a 67% relative error rate reduction with gesture, speech, and head tracking in a multimodal virtual reality application. Figure 8.4 illustrates triple mutual disambiguation among three input signals during system processing. The correct multimodal interpretation combined the second n-best item for speech with the third n-best items for gesture and head tracking (i.e., estimating gaze at an object). See Section 9.5 for other examples of superior error suppression in systems that fuse three or more input sources.

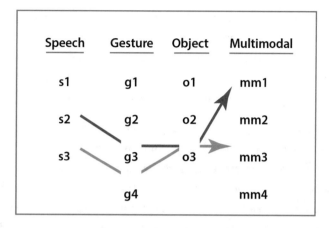

Figure 8.4: Mutual disambiguation among speech, gesture, and object recognition. Based on Kaiser et al. (2003).

- **Increase the heterogeneity of input modes combined within the multimodal system**

In order to bootstrap the joint potential of two or more input modes to achieve mutual disambiguation of partial or conflicting information during fusion, one strategy is to sample from a broad range of qualitatively different information sources. As discussed in Chapter 1, in multi-biometric systems it is widely recognized that fusing relatively uncorrelated information sources can produce larger magnitude error reductions.

- *Combine input modes that represent expressively rich information sources*

Touch, pointing devices, and basic sensors (e.g., GPS) can be used to support limited disambiguation of another more semantically rich input mode, such as speech. For example, if a user touches to select an input field before speaking information, the system's natural language processing can be constrained to a reduced set of possible interpretations (e.g., car rental return locations). This example would be a level 3 multimodal interface in terms of fusion (see Figure 1.1). However, two expressively rich input modes are required to achieve mutual disambiguation, which is possible in a level 4–6 multimodal interface (see Figure 1.1).

- **Integrate maximally complementary input modes**

In cases where a system fuses complementary modalities, it is possible to produce a highly synergistic blend in which the strengths of each mode can be capitalized upon and used to overcome weaknesses in the other (Cohen et al., 1989). As an example, in the multimodal speech and lip movement literature, natural feature-level complementarities have been identified between visemes and phonemes that serve to improve joint audio-visual speech intelligibility (Massaro and Stork, 1998). As another example, in multimodal speech and writing systems, location, and other spatial information can be indicated explicitly using pen input, whereas speech is better suited for specifying descriptions and temporal information (Oviatt, 1997; Oviatt et al., 1997).

An examination of error patterns and confusion matrices associated with alternative input modes can assist in discovering or confirming the presence of important complementarities. The most strategic multimodal design approach is to supplement an error-prone mode with a second one that can act as a natural complement and stabilizer in promoting mutual disambiguation. Successful identification of the unique semantic complementarities of a given pair of input modes can maximize mutual disambiguation and substantially reduce errors.

- **Develop multimodal processing techniques that retain information**

Whenever possible, it is important to develop multimodal signal processing, language processing, and architectural techniques that retain information and make it available during decision-level fusion. For example, alternative interpretations should be provided without being overly pruned from each of the component recognizers' n-best lists. Excessive pruning of n-best list alternatives (i.e., by setting probability thresholds in the recognizer's beam search too high) could result in eliminating the information needed for mutual disambiguation to occur. This is because the correct partial information must be present on each recognizer's n-best list in order for the correct final multimodal interpretation to be formed during unification.

The following are research strategies that are known to be relevant for successfully applying multimodal system design to targets of opportunity, which result in the greatest enhancement of robustness over unimodal system design:

- **Apply multimodal fusion when input is frequently expected to involve brief segments**

As described previously, brief segments of signal information are the most fragile and subject to error during recognition (e.g., monosyllabic acoustic content). They also are selectively improved during multimodal processing when additional information sources are combined that supplement and clarify their meaning.

- **Apply multimodal system design when input is expected to be noisy, whether due to challenging users, usage environments, or other factors**

When a recognition technology is known to be unreliable for a given user group or usage setting, such as the examples of accented and mobile speech discussed earlier, then a fusion-based multimodal system can both stabilize errors and improve average recognition accuracy. In some cases, mutual disambiguation can result in system robustness comparable to a non-risk case (e.g., native speaker, non-mobile usage).

In the above strategies, there is a central theme that emerges. Whenever information is too scant or ambiguous to support accurate recognition, a multimodal system can provide an especially opportune solution to fortify robustness. The key design strategies that contribute to enhanced robustness all are ones that add greater breadth and richness to the information sources that are fused. In general, the broader the information collection net that is cast, the greater the likelihood that missing or conflicting information will be resolved, leading to disambiguation of user input and improved robustness.

Table 8.3: Terminology for linguistic concepts
Disfluency refers to disruptions to the smooth flow of an otherwise coherent spoken utterance. There are different types of disfluencies, which can involve pausing, content corrections, non-lexical fillers ("uh"), and similar phenomena. Disfluencies also occur in other modalities, such as writing, and during other activity patterns such as manual gesturing.
Hyperarticulation refers to people's systematic adaptation of their speech toward hyper-clear features whenever they expect or experience a communication failure with their listener. Hyperticulate speech occurs during both interpersonal and human-computer exchanges, and it can include increased volume, duration, pitch and pitch range, clearer articulatory patterns, and other patterns. When interacting with spoken dialogue systems, user hyperarticulation is a major cause of system recognition failure, although it can be avoided by designing a multimodal interface.
Deixis refers to language terms for which the interpretation depends on contextual information, such as pointing to indicate the meaning of pronouns like "there," "this," or "here." Compared with unimodal spoken or textual language, deixis increases dramatically during multimodal communication. This is why multimodal expression of noun phrase references is greatly reduced.
Emblematic Gestures are culturally defined with a conventional and lexicalized meaning, such as spreading the fingers on a hand and touching the index finger to the thumb to make an "O" for "ok." Other examples include the gestures used by airport tarmac ground controllers.
Iconic Gestures visually depict concrete information that elaborates and complements the meaning of corresponding speech. For example, a speaker might separate their hands to indicate the size of an object they are describing.

Alphabetic Languages contain a standard and relatively compact set of basic written units (separate glyphs or letters), which roughly correspond to different sounds or phonemes in the spoken language. True alphabets contain consonants and vowels written as independent letters. In contrast, abjad alphabets do not express vowels, and abugidas indicate vowels with diacritics or graphic modification of consonants. Alphabetic languages typically use fewer total symbols (12–58), compared with syllabary (50-400) or logographic languages (thousands).

Diacritics are spatial elements or symbols used in many languages to disambiguate meaning (see examples for Hindi in Section 11.3), such as vowel choices. They are placed in a precise spatial relation to certain linguistic units, usually above or below them, which makes them difficult to accommodate on keyboards.

Romanization refers to the process of simplifying world languages by adopting a phonetically and semantically reduced form (e.g., pinyin instead of Mandarin). It involves using the Roman alphabetic to approximate pronunciation of the native language. Among the consequences are easier learnability, but increased ambiguity and reduced linguistic coverage and precision.

Linguistic Fluency refers to the facile ability to produce a large volume of linguistic content, such as words and abbreviations, which may increase or decrease when using different types of computer interfaces.

Nonlinguistic Fluency refers to the facile ability to produce a large volume of nonlinguistic representations, such as numbers, symbols, and diagrams, which may increase or decrease when using different types of computer interfaces.

Ontology refers to a partially-ordered hierarchical set of concepts types. A concept has properties and relations that distinguish one from another, and higher-level types of concepts subsume lower-level ones. A concept typically is linked to others with a taxonomic relation, such as "isa." Its properties are related to it by a "has-a" relation. Ontologies have been used to represent knowledge in computational systems, with well known ones including Cyc (Lenat and Guha, 1990) and KL-One (Brachman and Schmolze, 1985).

Feature Structures are attribute-value structures whose values can be filled with constant symbols, variables, or embedded feature structures. They are viewed within computational linguistics as partial structures that can be expanded by adding other consistent feature:value pairs. Note that the meaning of feature in linguistics and computational linguistics is different than that used elsewhere in this book in relation to signal processing.

Typed Feature Structures are feature structures whose terms are drawn from an ontology of types.

Unification is a recursive structure matching and combination operation that derives from logic programming and theorem-proving. In the context of multimodal integration, when partial meaning representation structures from two input modes are unified, they are filtered for inconsistencies and merged into a combined meaning representation during multimodal language processing.

Typed Feature-Structure Unification is a recursive structure matching method for determining whether two typed feature structures (FS1 and FS2) are consistent relative to an ontology and, if so, to produce a third (FS3) that includes the information in both. The "typing'" aspect of the unification process involves recursively comparing pairs of types from FS1 and FS2 to see if they are in a subsumption relationship in the ontology, and returning as part of FS3 the type that is their greatest lower bound. The algorithm also checks if corresponding feature values in FS1 and FS2 are consistent, i.e., they have identical atomic values, or one or both values are variables. The features in the resulting unified structure FS3 will take as values the consistent atoms or variable/value bindings from FS1 and FS2. Typed feature structure unification has been precisely analyzed and widely adopted within the field of computational linguistics (Copestake, 2000).

Chart Parser refers to a type of natural language parser that applies grammar rules to a database or "chart" of intermediate results that indicate which portions of a linear string of words has been covered by the application of various rules.

Multidimensional Chart Parser is a chart parser that is generalized to examine structures beyond simply a linear string of entities. For example, it could analyze spatial constructions in 2D or 3D, or structures in space and time. Such a parser often will have to specify constraints beyond the linear sequences of text and speech.

Multimodal Finite State Transducer refers to a finite state automaton that has more than one input stream (or "tape"), including one for each modality. It also produces an output (i.e., is a transducer).

Multimodal Event Logic Chart is a state chart automaton (Harel, 1987) whose state transitions use an event logic that describes and relates multimodal events, such as the occurrence of speech and gesture events. If the event logic statement on a state transition can be proven to be true over the database of events, the state transition can be taken. Multiple state charts can be interpreted in parallel to produce output continuously.

Mutual Disambiguation involves disambiguation of signal- or semantic-level information in one error-prone recognition modality by using partial information supplied by another modality. Mutual disambiguation can occur in a multimodal architecture with two or more expressively rich recognition-based input modes. It leads to recovery from unimodal recognition errors within a multimodal architecture, with the impact of suppressing errors that would otherwise be experienced by the user.

CHAPTER 9

Commercialization of Multimodal Interfaces

This chapter discusses the commercialization of a wide range of systems with multimodal interfaces, examining products that are either for sale or have been transitioned to customers. For these systems, we distinguish the type of multimodal interface and its main features, system functionality, and its processing and architectural features. We also discuss trends, major challenges, and future directions in developing these interfaces. In particular, new user input modes are described that are ripe for inclusion, which could increase the system's functionality, usability, and reliability. This chapter also outlines international standards and available toolkits that support developers in creating new prototypes and products quickly. Finally, much more than a high functioning system interface is needed to commercialize a product. This chapter discusses obstacles that have been encountered to adopting new multimodal technologies, and a case study of one such system currently being transitioned to a large government organization.

We have emphasized that multimodal systems are especially beneficial in mobile and field scenarios. The most pervasive mobile multimodal system is the cell phone (see Section 2.3), which is equipped with an ever increasing variety of sensors, including camera(s), microphone(s), touch screen/surface, accelerometer, gyroscope, fingerprint reader, and so forth. As Evans (2014) has said, "Each sensor is a business model." To date, the possible strategies for fusing modality and sensor information to optimize cell phone functioning and usability have been largely underexploited. One exception is the common use of touching or pressing to engage a recognition-based modality like speech. Another is the growing use of sensors, such as GPS location, to constrain the interpretation of meaning within a modality—such as "Show me *nearby* restaurants" during voice search. Indeed, there are many more business models that could be capitalized upon by strategizing more clever forms of multimodal fusion between active input modes, passive modes, and environmental sensors.

Even virtual keyboards on cell phones now are multimodal hybrid ones, as described in Chapter 1. For example, the popular Swype keyboard (Nuance, 2015a) for Google Android phones and Apple iPhones supports entering words either by speaking, gestural swiping (i.e., drawing a line connecting letters in a word), writing, or more traditional tapping on keys. Swype also is flexibly multilingual, permits code-mixing of languages, and includes intelligent predictive processing of the content entered.

Apart from cell phones, users' bodies now can be tracked in diverse field settings using systems based on Microsoft's Kinect™, Intel's RealSense™, and LeapMotion's™ gesture tracking device. The first two tools sense multimodally by combining microphone arrays with infrared and regular cameras to track users' speech, gestures, and body movements. Applications based on these tools are discussed further in Section 9.7.

This chapter considers applications that use a wide range of active input modalities, including:

- speech;

- sketch and handwriting;

- hand gestures;

- touch or multi-touch;

- pointing with mouse/stylus, or pressing buttons; and

- keyboard or virtual hybrid keyboard input.

Some applications also include passively sensed modalities, such as:

- gaze tracking, eye and eyelid position, blink rate;

- face tracking and emotion recognition;

- head and body position;

- gait and movement patterns; and

- paralinguistic information available in the signal of active input modes, such as speech rate, pitch, volume, and pausing that provide information about attitude, certainty, emotional state, truthfulness, etc.

The sections that follow describe examples of commercial multimodal interfaces for automotive, geospatial, virtual assistant, warehouse automation, entertainment, multi-biometric, education, and robotic systems.

9.1   AUTOMOTIVE INTERFACES[12]

Automotive manufacturers are rapidly implementing multimodal systems, typically ones that incorporate user input based on voice, buttons or knobs, and touch, with others on the horizon such as gesture, gaze, and facial data for alertness monitoring (Castronovo et al., 2010; Sezgin et al., 2009). Virtually all the major automobile manufacturers have implemented voice control of car navigation

---

[12]   Transportation systems more broadly have integrated multimodal-multisensor interfaces, including aircraft cockpits (Adacel, 2006; Lockheed, 2015a; Schutte, 2007). Automotive systems that are designed for use by the general population are presented here as an example, and one that is changing especially rapidly.

and entertainment systems, using spoken language processing from Microsoft, Nuance Communications, Voicebox Technologies, and others. In 2015, the Apple Car Play and Google Android Auto platforms will enable integrating personal smart phones into automobile interfaces that control its computer-based systems (Apple, 2015c; Google, 2015c).

From the viewpoint of user personalization and functionality, this presents attractive opportunities to access one's own music, contact list for phone calls, email with addresses needed to navigate, and so forth. However, with respect to overall multimodal interface design, it also raises questions about how best to integrate the various user input modalities and system recognizers available on both platforms. For example, initially dual speech recognizers may co-exist in some cars, one for voice access of virtual assistants via the phone, and another for controlling in-vehicle systems such as entertainment and navigation. A major question raised by introducing cell phone controls in the car concerns how best to design non-distracting and safe capabilities for a moving vehicle.

Automotive infotainment manufacturers such as Harman (2015) are implementing multimodal interfaces with the aim of increasing system reliability and lowering the user's cognitive load (Boagey, 2014). In addition to voice controls, many cars now have a touch-sensitive screen that accepts swiping gestures to control navigation and other functions. Data can be accessed from the user's smart phone (e.g., music, contacts, calendar) or their cloud-based accounts. Since touch gestures can create smudges on the display that impair visibility in some lighting conditions, Denso has incorporated the Leap Motion gesture control device into the dashboard. It enables a driver to control the radio and other functions by gesturing in front of the dashboard without touching anything (Denso, 2015).

As another alternative approach, Audi and BMW incorporate a touch-enabled dial that rotates to scroll among choices on the display (see Figure 9.1) or from a connected cell phone. Once the correct option is displayed on the in-vehicle screen, the dial can be pushed to select it. The touch-enabled surface of the dial on the Audi controller also enables character entry via finger tracing, as shown in Figure 9.1. The character entry option is especially attractive in countries like China, where the total character set for the language is very large. The above different approaches for manual input are just emerging. It is unclear how they compare with respect to accuracy of initial input, or impact on diverting users' visual attention off the road during entry and correction of input.

In-vehicle spoken dialogue systems are challenging to support largely because of the noisy car environment, including road noise, passenger cross-talk, and other sources. Voice recognition in vehicles has relied on the use of strategically placed microphone arrays with active beam-forming and echo cancellation, often built into the visor or an overhead console (Hetherington and Mohan, 2013). In comparison with in-vehicle systems, cell phone speech recognition tends to be more accurate for a variety of reasons. Cell phone speech recognizers have been based on training with much larger corpora of user queries. In addition, cell phone users can more easily adapt their location to reduce noise before speaking (e.g., stepping inside a building), and can effectively adjust microphone placement by how they hold the phone.

Figure 9.1: Audi A3 2015 multimodal user interface, which enables touch, rotation of the dial, and finger character entry on a touch-enabled screen.

In future integrated phone/car systems, when a phone is docked in the car, the microphones used will be the in-vehicle array. The cell phone's speech recognition capabilities will enter a "car mode" in which the acoustic models are tailored for the car environment. The set of applications available on the phone will be pared back to those deemed appropriate for the car by the manufacturer, altering the corresponding recognition vocabularies.

Another challenge for developing a high-performance dialogue system is to match it appropriately for in-vehicle tasks. Recent studies (Reimer et al., 2013) have found that voice control of entertainment functions was as fast or faster than using physical button controls, but it required more glances off the road. They also found that voice control of navigation required the lengthiest user interactions, risking driver distraction. This may simply be due to long confirmation dialogues. However, it also may be due to the massive vocabulary of streets and destinations, which can precipitate recognition errors, multiple correction attempts, and user hyperarticulation (Oviatt, 1996).

Driver fatigue has been implicated in 30–50% of driving accidents, and is an even greater concern for operators of heavy equipment, such as mining trucks (Barr et al., 2003; Caterpillar, 2008; Hagenmeyer, 2007; Reissman, 1996). Numerous multimodal systems are being developed to alert drivers to their state of drowsiness. These systems typically rely on analysis of drivers' head, face, and eyes (e.g., lid closure, blink rate, and velocity), and physiological measures (Dong et al., 2011). For example, Optalert™ has developed drowsiness detection glasses that monitor eye blinks 500 times per second (Optalert, 2015). Seeing Machines has developed the DSSTM multimodal gaze and head-tracking system (Seeingmachines, 2015), which monitors driver "microsleeps" and alerts the driver via audio and haptic sensors. In a wireless network context, such as a mining site, the system also alerts a control facility.

Many systems also monitor the vehicle itself, including steering wheel movement and lane departures. Pernix Pty Ltd. (2015) offers the ASTiD™ vehicle monitoring device that analyzes micro-movements of the steering wheel, and HaulCheck™ from AcuMine Ltd (2015) offers a device that measures lane departures and distance from obstacles. For passenger cars, trucks, and buses, Daimler has developed the Attention Assist™ (2015) device that was available in Mercedes vehicles in 2013. It monitors steering wheel movement for patterns indicating drowsiness, and can invoke automatic braking and other safety features. Drivers are alerted auditorily, as well as via a coffee cup icon displayed on the dashboard. Caterpillar has compared many of these devices, and recommends a multimodal interface to increase system reliability, speed of alerting, and overall safety (Caterpillar, 2008). For a comprehensive review of this topic, see Dong et al., 2011.

Currently, in-vehicle systems mainly represent level 1–3 multimodal interfaces, as summarized in Figure 1.1. For example, the driver's pressing on a steering wheel control can engage the car's spoken dialogue system. Then a request for gas stations along the route can display current options based on GPS location and direction of movement. In the future, in-vehicle systems may incorporate recognition of small finger gestures while the driver's hands remain on the steering wheel (Endres, et al., 2011; Pfleging et al., 2012). They also may jointly interpret gestures, speech, and facial emotional expressions using a late-fusion or hybrid architecture.

Of course, adding modalities is not the only way to improve recognition performance. In the future, better performance also could leverage dialogue, user, and physical contextual information. For example, during spoken interaction with the navigation system, GPS location could alter the statistical language model's probabilities for interpreting nearby destinations. Interpretation could be improved further by accessing the user's calendar for scheduled destinations (i.e., enabled by cell phone integration), as well as the current dialogue context.

Eventually, in-vehicle interfaces will incorporate out-of-the window information retrieval while a driver is navigating, such as "What is that building?" based on processing of voice, gestures, head position and eye gaze (Moniri and Muller, 2014; Kim and Misu, 2014). An additional future direction is multi-biometric driver authentication and personalization of car functions (e.g., seat and rear-view mirror positions). Dragon Drive from Nuance already provides voice biometrics to identify the driver through a spoken passphrase (Nuance, 2015b). However, a more transparent and secure approach could combine a steering wheel fingerprint reader, face recognition, iris pattern recognition, analysis of voice quality, and other information sources.

9.2   GEOSPATIAL AND DESIGN INTERFACES

There are numerous multimodal geospatial map systems, as well as spatially intensive ones that involve drawing, painting, computer-aided design, construction management, annotation of medical or intelligence/satellite images, and so forth. Multimodal interfaces that support such systems are described below. They typically include input using modalities such as pen, voice, touch and multi-touch, and gestures.

Sketch-Thru-Plan (STP) is a collaborative map-based multimodal planning system for military operations planning and command-and-control (C^2), which is currently being transitioned to the US military (Cohen et al., 2015). The users of a C^2 system include decision-makers, for example in the US Army and US Marine Corps (USMC), who engage in strategic and tactical planning. One of the essential C^2 planning tasks for militaries is allocation and positioning of resources, which can be indicated by symbols (e.g., military units, equipment) placed on a map system in the context of routes and landmarks. The symbol names and icon shapes are part of organizational doctrine learned by all soldiers, along with standardized procedures for deploying them.

In the past, entities have been positioned on a paper map by affixing Post-it notes with handwritten information. This non-digital work practice does not require any system training, but it fails to support sharing or integration of digital data (Cohen and McGee, 2004). In contrast, the currently deployed C^2 system (Command Post of the Future, CPOF) has a collaborative graphical interface (Greene et al., 2010). A major limitation of this interface is that it includes embedded menu hierarchies and fine-grained drag-and-drop interactions that are complex and slow, even when completing simple tasks (Cohen et al., 2015). One basic motivation for developing the Sketch-Thru-Plan (STP) system was to improve upon the CPOF graphical interface.

STP's multimodal interface incorporates speech, sketch, and handwriting, each of which can be used individually or combined with other input. A user can speak an entity name while sketching it as a point, line, or area. Figure 9.2 illustrates examples of user input and system feedback. A user can assign tasks to entities, such as specifying that a military unit should deliver supplies. In addition, a user can annotate entity attributes by speaking or writing further information about them. During this input, the system assists with planning by inferring and displaying possible tasks that an entity is likely to perform. With STP, users can create and position over 4,000 different symbols within the system's vocabulary using speech and/or drawing. After entering information, each type of user input is processed with a different recognizer. Speech input is recognized as a natural language expression that is parsed to produce a typed feature structure meaning representation, which then is unified with the one produced by the sketch recognizer. The STP system is a level-6 type of multimodal interface (see Figure 1.1), with the ability to fuse partial semantic information from two content creation modes.

Figure 9.2: A user speaks "Company boundary Bravo north, Charlie south" while drawing a horizontal line across the middle of the map. The system confirms with the symbols "B" and C," positioned above and below the user's line. The user then speaks "Objective Saddle," while encircling an area at the top of the map, which the system confirms with an icon and label (copyright Adapx, used with permission).

In addition to writing on a computer screen, STP can process writing on a large-size digital paper map using a digital pen to capture entire operations or when working in the field (Cohen and McGee, 2004). Pen input on the digital paper map also is translated into precise geospatial latitude and longitude coordinates. With this interface, users can input information the same way they do with non-digital work practice, except the information is captured and distributed digitally.

This digital pen input also can be co-processed with spoken input, thereby creating a tangible multimodal system (McGee et al., 2000; McGee and Cohen, 2001).

The cognitive science foundation of multimodal interaction with map systems was established using a high-fidelity system simulation (Oviatt, 2012), as discussed in Sections 3.1, 3.2, 3.6, and 6.1. This extensive proactive design resulted in a usable and easily learnable system, well-tailored to its users and usage context. It paved the way for building QuickSet, a prototype multimodal interface for initializing map simulations (Cohen et al., 1997), which was the predecessor of STP. Based on this experience, STP was productized in virtue of improved core technologies (e.g., speech and sketch recognizers, natural language processing), a 20-fold increase in vocabulary, integration with a state-of-the-art mapping system (i.e., ESRI's ArcGIS), incorporation of industry-standard interoperation frameworks, and interoperation with numerous systems used by the US military. The system was built after extensive prototyping, experimental testing with users, and participatory design with military domain experts (i.e., trainees, retirees, and active-duty soldiers).

During later-stage evaluations, user and system testing included iterative evaluation of the components, and tests in actual deployment environments (e.g., in noisy military vehicles, and at training ranges). *User juries* were conducted with over 150 active duty Army soldiers, who used STP to develop plans. Table 9.1 summarizes user evaluations based on a 5-point Likert-scale questionnaire that compared STP with the C^2 system with which users were familiar (CPOF, or the Army's vehicle C^2 system; Cohen et al., 2015). In addition to uniformly higher ratings, plan creation by expert CPOF users was 235% faster using the multimodal interface rather than with CPOF. The STP system has been used successfully by multiple organizations within the U.S. Army and USMC during military exercises, and the USMC is now integrating it into their C^2 software. Overall, the QuickSet and STP systems have received more proactive interface design and evaluation testing than perhaps any other multimodal interface ever built. For term, see Table 6.1.

Drawing and painting constitute completely different user "tasks," which are focused instead on the quality of artistic expression and visual renderings. Wacom Corporation (Wacom, 2015) developed the high-end Cintiq™ line of displays for personal computers, which support users and professional artists during drawing and painting. They can use bimanual input controls to touch or gesture with their non-dominant hand, while simultaneously using an electronic stylus with their dominant hand for content creation. For example, the user can perform industry-standard pinch/zoom, rotate, and other gestures to control the visual display, while brushing fine strokes with her other hand to create a painting. Bimanual manipulation enables greater flexibility in rapidly and expertly changing the display granularity, orientation, and other aspects so the artist can add or inspect sketched details. Wacom's product does not involve fusion of gestural processing with sketch or handwriting. However, sensors in the pen (e.g., pressure) combine with the content of pen input to render different artistic realizations, such as wider or more fine-grained brush strokes. That is, sensor input constrains the artistic expression of pen input. The STP system described above uses the Wacom display, but integrates its pen input with speech to create a fusion-based multimodal system for content creation.

Table 9.1: Summary of questionnaire results for STP vs. C^2 systems used by subjects

Organization	System Compared to STP	Number of Users	STP Easier to Use	STP Faster	STP Better	Prefer Speech/ Sketch
Division 1	Vehicle C^2 system	41	83%	88%	81%	90%
Division 2	Vehicle C^2 system	44	97%	97%	100%	87%
Division 3	Vehicle C^2 system	37	78%	89%	84%	87%
Overall		**122**	**87%**	**92%**	**89%**	**88%**
Division 2	CPOF	16	76%	94%	85%	88%
Division 3	CPOF	12	88%	79%	84%	100%
Division 4	CPOF	5	100%	100%	100%	100%
Overall		**33**	**84%**	**89%**	**87%**	**94%**

In contrast with the two successful commercial examples outlined above, Think3™ was an early multimodal computer-aided design (CAD) system available from 2001–2005. It enabled users to speak, draw with a mouse, and otherwise use a traditional graphical interface to create and update architectural or mechanical designs. One case study obtained a 23% speedup when using the multimodal interface, compared with using the same GUI without speech (Engineer Live, 2013; Price, 2004). This early product was not successful in the long run, in part because it tried to sell an entire CAD system, rather than a multimodal plug-in for an existing CAD system. However, Think3 did redesign the entire user interface to take advantage of speech. Others who built plug-ins did not engage in redesign for spoken input, so their interfaces were suboptimal GUI-speech blends. (Engineer Live, 2013).

9.3   VIRTUAL ASSISTANT INTERFACES

All the major cell phone companies (e.g., Amazon, Apple, AT&T, Blackberry, Google, LG, Microsoft, Samsung), and many other independent companies such as Nuance, Openstream, and Yahoo, have developed virtual software agents that assist users with making appointments, playing music, obtaining information, dialing the phone, and similar tasks. Deployed on cell phones, tablets, and wearable devices, many virtual assistants can be engaged with touch-to-speak input. They provide spoken responses and display visual information, which enables the user to touch on selections. Some virtual agents also are capable of conducting spoken interactions that involve follow-up queries (see examples in Section 2.3). We will not survey the similarities and differences among all currently available virtual assistants, which have been well characterized in product reviews. Instead, we concentrate here on describing their multimodal capabilities. Multimodal interaction with these assistants takes advantage of alternative input modes, such as speaking, typing, or touching, along with screen control via touch and gestures. Voice is recorded on the device, but transmitted to a remote recognition server that has been trained on billions of user utterances in many different natural languages. Recognition rates for spoken dialogue interactions have increased dramatically as more data is collected, and as vendors have begun deploying deep learning neural network technologies (Yu and Deng, 2015).

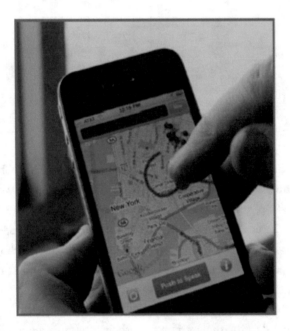

Figure 9.3: Speak4It user interface with combined speech and sketch input, which enables user queries and information retrieval about local businesses. From Ehlen and Johnston (2012). Copyright © 2012 ACM. Used with permission.

Unique among the virtual assistants was Speak4It™, a multimodal map-based assistant offered by AT&T for finding local services (Ehlen and Johnston, 2012). The local business search topic of this system dates back to the earliest prototype multimodal map systems (Oviatt, 1996; Moran et al., 1997), which enabled real-estate and tourist search, respectively. As an example, a user could say "Thai groceries in this area" and draw a circle around a map region. The system would fuse speech and sketch, dispatch a request to a backend webserver to retrieve the data, and then display the results on the phone's map. This multimodal interface is based on level-6 fusion (see Figure 1.1). It was informed by the same early proactive user testing as the QuickSet and STP systems, and tested on thousands of users. Running on Apple's iPhone and iPad, the assistant was available as a commercial product between 2010 and 2014, but has recently been taken off the market while AT&T licenses its speech and language technology to another firm. Speak4It and its capabilities, illustrated in Figure 9.3, are described in more detail in Section 2.3.

In addition to cell phone virtual assistants, numerous companies have developed virtual assistants that can operate on other internet-connected devices, such as PCs. For example, Nuance provides branded intelligent assistants to other firms, such as Tangerine Bank in Canada and Garanti Bank in Turkey, who use them as part of their advertising and customer service. The multimodal Enterprise Virtual Assistant™ (EVA) from Openstream coordinates interaction across multiple types of device (e.g., cell phone, tablet, PC). It also includes fusion of speech and pen-based touch. EVA is discussed further in Section 9.9.

Healthcare applications with multimodal technology are beginning to emerge (O'Hara et al., 2014). Physician dictation using speech recognition has long been a major application for Nuance and other speech vendors. However, they have yet to develop multimodal interfaces beyond push-to-talk, and correction of any errors (e.g., in dictated patient records) still is handled with re-speaking or with keyboard and mouse input. More recently, Sense.ly in Palo Alto (Sense.ly, 2015) has announced a product for telemedicine that enables remote patients to speak with a virtual assistant called "Molly" to describe their symptoms. The virtual assistant can sense and recognize the patient's body motions using a Microsoft Kinect device (see Section 9.7). Molly records speech while tracking the patient's body, and transmits these two data streams to recognizers that analyze speech, body parts, and body movements. The system also performs natural language processing during the nurse-patient dialogue. For example, Molly may ask the patient to point to where she is experiencing pain (see Figure 9.4). The Kinect software will track the patient's body, and recognize the body part to which the user points. The user's corresponding speech is also recognized and interpreted ("it hurts here"). The data from these interactive sessions may then be forwarded to a physician for a follow-up video call (e.g., via Skype).[13]

Future virtual assistants are expected to participate in more complex multimodal dialogues involving new input modes. They also will begin to include early and late fusion of different modalities (e.g., audio-visual recognition of users' facial expressions for detection of pain, frustration, etc.). In addition, virtual assistants will begin to provide more proactive user assistance. They will anticipate and offer to perform actions for users based on intention and plan recognition (Sukthankar et al., 2014). These capabilities will make use of personal data gleaned from the user's cell phone,

[13]   A sample video is available at: http://sense.ly/#prettyPhoto[group]/3/.

calendar, email, and other sources. Virtual agents will increasingly be physically embodied as robots, as discussed in the next section. See Section 10.5 for further discussion of emerging research topics related to virtual agents and robotic instantiations.

Figure 9.4: Nurse avatar "Molly" in the Sense.ly interface perceives the remote patient using a Kinect device. In response to Molly's question, "Where does it hurt?" (left), the system tracks the patient's arm to determine pointing at the right shoulder (right). Molly then asks, "What is wrong with your shoulder?" Courtesy of Sense.ly.

9.4   ROBOTIC INTERFACES

The robotics industry has primarily concentrated on applications in highly structured environments, such as factories and hospitals. In such places, robots either do not interact with humans during their operation (e.g., robotic welders), or respond to a few button pushes (e.g., pharmaceutical delivery robots in hospitals). With the introduction of the Roomba™ vacuum cleaner from iRobot, robots have been developed that operate alongside people in their homes. Still, such robots have minimal ability to interact with humans. However, major commercial developments have been ongoing in Japan to build humanoid robots for entertainment and education, as well as for assisting people, primarily the elderly and disabled.

Honda Robotics has been developing the Asimo™ humanoid robot since 1986 (see Figure 9.5), concentrating first on its ability to walk on two legs with human movement patterns. Currently, Asimo is 130 cm high, weighs 55 kg, can run at 9 km/h (5.6 miles per hour), jump, hop, climb stairs, and perform other human-like tasks (Honda, 2011). Recently, Asimo has been upgraded to incorporate multiple senses designed for interacting with people. Specifically, Asimo has two cameras for stereo vision, with which it performs face recognition among a set of known faces, object detection and tracking, and recognition of a small repertoire of human gestures (e.g., palm-outward "stop" gesture). It has a sense of touch in its hands and arms, which is useful for manipulation tasks like pushing carts, pouring drinks, and greeting humans. It attempts to track and predict nearby human movements to avoid collision. Finally, it has three microphones in its head, enabling it to orient to objects using audio-visual cues, and to capture voice for recognition (Nakadai et al., 2010).

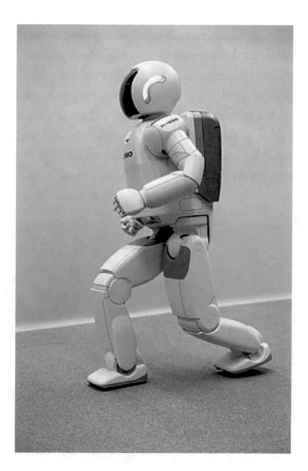

Figure 9.5: Honda Robotics' Asimo Robot. Courtesy of Honda.

In addition to giving many demonstrations, Asimo currently operates as a receptionist at Honda headquarters. A spinoff technology, Stride Management Assist, is an adaptation of Asimo's locomotion abilities in devices that assist people with walking (Nagajaran and Goswami, 2015). Stride Management Assist is now in testing by the National Center for Geriatrics and Gerontology in Japan and by the Rehabilitation Institute of Chicago.

Aldebaran Robotics in France and Softbank Mobile in Japan have collaborated on the development of Pepper™, a 1.2 m high social robot designed for interacting with humans (see Figure 9.6). It moves on an omnidirectional wheel base, has two arms, and its head contains four microphones, two cameras, a 3D depth sensor, and three touch sensors. It has a touch-screen display on its chest. Unlike most other robots, the focus of Pepper's development is emotion recognition and intelligence. It has been developed to respond intelligently to human emotions during conversation. It engages in recognition of users' facial expressions and speech quality, from which it determines emotional state. The multiple microphones enable Pepper to orient towards the direction of sounds. Speech recognition is conducted by a remote computer, which enables use of large vocabulary systems. Like other Aldebaran products (i.e., Nao robot), a software development kit enables customers to program the robot's behavior, for example to program various conversational strategies.

Pepper has so far been developed to converse with and entertain customers waiting in bank lobbies, including telling jokes. It also can described bank services for waiting customers. In addition, Nescafé Japan is using Pepper to sell products in their stores, engaging customers in conversation and displaying information on its touch-enabled tablet screen. Pepper is now being developed for consumer use. Section 10.5 outlines emerging trends in research on social robots.

Figure 9.6: Pepper, a social robot from Aldebaran Robotics and Softbank Mobile. Courtesy of Aldebaran.

9.5   MULTI-BIOMETRIC INTERFACES

One of the first industries to incorporate multimodality, albeit for the single but very important problem of identifying people, is the biometric industry. Typical use cases include physical access (e.g., entry to buildings, cars), criminal and civil applications, network entry (e.g., banking), cyber security, fraud prevention, airport security, and retail transactions. A number of systems incorporate multiple modalities such as iris or retina, DNA, fingerprint, finger or palm vein, face recognition, signature, and voice print (see Figure 9.7). This technology can be used to identify a given person from a massive database of people, or to verify that a given person is who they say they are. Ross and Poh (2009) provided a comprehensive review of the multi-biometric identification problem, including distinguishing different types of data (see Figure 9.7) and approaches to combining results from biometric analyzers.

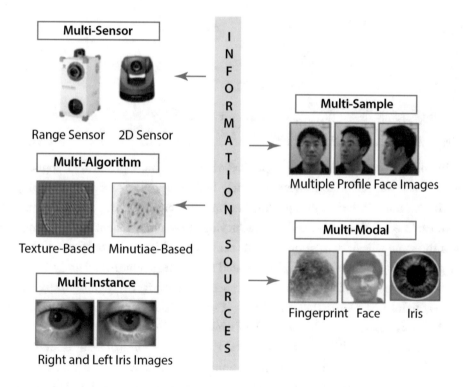

Figure 9.7: Multiple sources of biometric data, including multimodal data from qualitatively different sources (copyright European Association for Signal Processing (EURASIP), based on Ross (2007)).

Table 9.2 summarizes many companies that offer multimodal biometric products, including comparative information on the number and type of information sources upon which their products are based.

Table 9.2: Multimodal biometric companies, data sources incorporated in products, and multimodal fusion tools

Company	Iris	Fingerprint	Voice	Finger vein	Palm	Face	DNA
Anviz	X	X				X	
Crossmatch Technology	X	X			X	X	
IDTech360	X	X				X	
MorphoTrak	X	X		X	X	X	
M2Sys	X	X	X	X	X	X	X
NEC Biometrics				X	X	X	
Rayabin Co	X	X				X	
Smartmatic	X	X	X			X	
TechnoBrain	X					X	
WCC Smart Search and Match	Multimodal fusion architecture for 3rd-party biometric recognizers						

Multimodal biometrics has been a particularly active and sophisticated application area, largely because it is imperative to achieve extremely high levels of accuracy in identifying a given individual. It also must include "anti-spoofing" techniques that reject imposters. Biometric techniques have explored different strategies for achieving these aims, including analyzing multiple instances of the same type of data, samples of the same type of data collected from different sensor systems (e.g., cameras), multimodal data from related sources (e.g., multi-level analysis of face), and multimodal data from more diverse sources (e.g., speech quality, face recognition). As discussed in Chapter 1, research has demonstrated that the most substantial suppression of error rate occurs by fusing multiple uncorrelated types of data, each of which contributes complementary discriminative identification (Muncaster and Turk, 2006; Ross and Poh, 2009). As one of many examples, Sanchez and Kittler (2007) reported that a linear combination of classifiers results in a false acceptance rate of 12.67% using lip shape combined with speech, but drops to 0.29% based on five features—two facial features, lip shape, and two speech features. Likewise, false rejections dropped from 14% to 0%. These findings are consistent with the literature on multimodal error suppression and system robustness presented in Section 3.5. They have driven strong interest in building commercial multimodal biometric systems that combine multiple relatively uncorrelated modalities.

Multimodal biometric systems also have been sophisticated in the sense that they frequently combine a larger number of input modalities or other information sources, using a multi-algorithm or parallel fusion approach (Ross and Poh, 2009). They typically represent an advanced level 4 type of fusion, as summarized in Figure 1.1. It is common for these systems to incorporate some passively tracked behaviors or physical characteristics that are difficult to spoof (e.g., iris pattern, fingerprints, face recognition, gait, speech quality). See Chapter 7 for a related discussion of approaches to signal processing and advanced information fusion.

Future multimodal biometric systems will increasingly incorporate more sources of data, and ones that are easier to collect reliably and unobtrusively from a distance. For some applications, they will continuously verify user identification over time during use, especially for critical applications that represent targets for hijackers or thieves (e.g., pilot identification in remote cockpits, remote web-based banking or investment transactions). In the not too distant future, multi-biometrics will completely replace typed user passwords for many secure applications.

9.6   EDUCATIONAL INTERFACES

A number of educational applications have employed multimodal interaction. Chapter 3, especially Sections 3.6 and 3.7, emphasize why multimodal interfaces are especially advantageous for educational purposes.

Perhaps the most widely commercialized multimodal educational technology is interactive whiteboards or smartboards (Promethean, 2015; Smart, 2015). They are an excellent example of a hybrid interface that is tangible and multimodal, with pen, touch, and keyboard the primary input modalities. Some commercially available interactive whiteboards also support multi-touch and multi-person input (see Figure 9.8), supporting collaborative work. Their large-scale screens and active pen input mimic non-digital work practice in business and the classroom, which facilitate group attention and collaborative exchange. For example, pen input can be used to highlight, underline, or encircle information to focus a group's attention. It also can be used to flexibly annotate information, diagram or write formulas involving symbols and digits, or summarize content just discussed by the group. In addition, synchronized pen and gestural input can be used to illustrate and explain real-time dynamic processes, or to control the pace of video images and annotate key concepts while discussing them. These interfaces are attractive to teachers and students, and they have collaborative affordances that stimulate interactive exchange (Dawson, 2010; Giusti et al., 2011; Smith et al., 2005; Somekh et al., 2007; Winzenried et al., 2010).

Commercially available digital books also have proliferated rapidly in recent years. The highly competitive nature of the market has inspired different functionality and interface solutions, including keyboard-based input, and in other cases pen, touch, gestures and multimodal input. The Apple iPad supports multi-touch, gestural, and keyboard input. Multi-touch input permits a reader to control the visual display, such as flicking page corners to turn them. This interface also incorporates a screen reader for presenting contents auditorily, which improves accessibility for very young, blind and visually impaired readers (Apple, 2011). Pen input for annotation is not supported, and it is not yet widely available on digital books because of the technical challenges of updating inked content rapidly (Gormish et al., 2009). However, the commercially available LeapPad book includes a pen for writing and touching words, and spoken feedback that can be translated into other languages. In the future, more widespread incorporation of pen input into e-books would be advantageous for annotating, outlining, sketching, concept mapping, and reusing information during the active reading that is required of students in educational contexts.

Figure 9.8: Three students collaborate by simultaneously writing and pointing while they solve flight technology problems. Courtesy of Smart Technologies.

A third commercially active area in educational technology is digital pen and paper interfaces, which are based on Anoto technology (Adapx, 2015; Anoto, 2009). These tangible interfaces mimic familiar pen and paper physical tools, which assists in minimizing students' cognitive load (Oviatt et al., 2012). Digital paper is printed with the Anoto dot pattern that distinguishes the x,y coordinate locations on the paper and uniquely identifies each piece of paper. Digital pen input on the paper is captured by a camera in the tip of the pen, which records the coordinates and identity of the sheet of paper. The software that manages the digital pen data then associates the physical paper and ink coordinates with the application that printed it, thereby providing semantics for the contents written. Digital pen and paper interfaces also combine input and output modes multimodally. Most digital pens create written content, and provide both ink and vibro-tactile feedback. Some also can record, play back, or even recognize speech input (Leapfrog, 2010; Livescribe, 2014). As described in Section 3.7 and Chapter 11, digital pen and paper interfaces are capable of stimulating 10–40% improvement in students' basic cognition, compared with keyboard-based interfaces.

In the case of Livescribe's digital pen and paper interface, multimodal input includes writing, speech, and touch/tap. This particular pen also has a display on the side that provides visual feedback, as shown in Figure 9.9 (Livescribe, 2014). The Livescribe interface includes controls at the bottom of each printed page of digital paper. A student can use the pen to touch on a printed control that turns on or off speech recording, for example, or adjusts its volume.

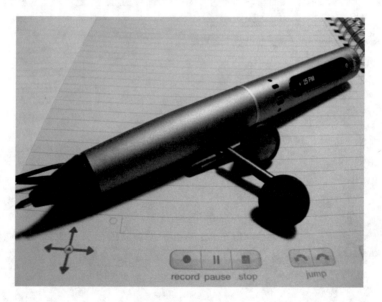

Figure 9.9: Livescribe digital pen that records writing and speech, with visual display on the side and earphones for listening to speech output. Digital paper notebook includes pen-tap controls at the bottom of each page for managing the interface and playing back speech. From Oviatt et al. (2012). Copyright © 2012. Copyright © 2012 ACM. Used with permission.

The Livescribe Pulse and Echo pens can record a user's writing and speech during lectures, interviews, and similar exchanges. The Livescribe software then can search inked content in a user's notes, and replay speech during a classroom lecture that co-occurred in time (Livescribe, 2014). The audio and synchronized digital ink data are stored in the pen and can be played back on a personal computer once the pen is docked or has transmitted via Bluetooth. Data also can be sent to various note-taking applications, such as Evernote and Microsoft OneNote. Both the handwriting and speech can be recognized by the system with results output as text, although most applications only perform handwriting recognition.

Recently, Livescribe pens have become integrated with cell phones for speech processing and transmission. This interface also has become more interoperable with other vendor software. Compared with pen-based laptops, digital pen and paper interfaces offer a more ultra-lightweight and inexpensive interface that is usable in a variety of field settings, as illustrated in Figure 9.10.

Figure 9.10: Student in the field filling out a form and marking on a map while collaborating with other students to collect environmental data using a digital pen and paper interface. From Oviatt (2013a). Copyright © 2013 Routledge Press. Used with permission.

9.7   ENTERTAINMENT AND GAMING INTERFACES

Since 2010 Microsoft has been shipping the Kinect™ tracking device as an inexpensive accessory to its XBox™ gaming computer, and recently as a standalone device for Microsoft Windows™ (Microsoft, 2015b, 2015c). Kinect is a multisensory device that computes three-dimensional images of objects by illuminating them with a pattern of infrared dots. Using an infrared camera, it computes the disparity of the projected dots from their expected positions, enabling it to produce a 3D depth map of the scene. Kinect software can track six people, two of them active, identifying up to 20 joint angles per active person. However, resolution is insufficient to track many details, such as individual fingers. Since it uses infrared light, Kinect must be used indoors with good lighting conditions. Kinect also includes a standard camera and a digitally steerable four-microphone array with echo cancellation for capturing far-field voices, as well as a teleconferencing capability.

Kinect provides a library of gesture recognition software, enabling gestures to provide continuous information that can be passively tracked. Gestures also can convey explicit commands to be executed by a system. However, co-occurring speech is required to make sense of some types of gesture, for example beat or iconic ones (Kopp et al., 2007). As explained in Section 4.3.4, speech and gesture frequently convey complementary information. Speech is best for describing future and past events, out-of-view entities and events, subsets of entities, attributes of entities, and similar information (Cohen and Oviatt, 1995). In contrast, gestures can convey actions and their attributes, such as speed, intensity, manner of movement, and so forth. As a result, many gesture-based applications could be improved by fusing the meaning from co-occurring spoken language.

Hundreds of commercial Kinect-based games have been built that track the user's body, recognize a set of gestures, and identify faces. Most games do not use voice, although some are beginning to emerge (e.g., Kinect Sports games). Kinect can also be added to standard Microsoft Windows for other non-gaming applications (for discussion, see Section 10.1). Finally, software development kits are publicly available, which has stimulated a large body of developers and researchers (Microsoft, 2015c; see Section 9.9).

Developers are now actively attempting to create products in domains other than entertainment (Johnson, 2014; DeVault et al., 2014). Future versions of Kinect applications, such as for robots, will likely incorporate fusion-based speech and gesture processing to expand their functionality. Applications also will expand more rapidly when the granularity of face- and body-tracking improves for analyzing finger movements, manual gestures, and facial expressions relevant to users' communications and state (see Section 9.9 on Intel's RealSense™ SDK with 3D gesture recognition software from SoftKinetic (Intel, 2015)).

9.8   WAREHOUSE AUTOMATION INTERFACES

Fifty percent of the labor in a small distribution center (i.e., less than 25 employees) is spent picking orders (Hanrahan, 2009). "Voice picking" is a solution technology for such warehouses and distribution centers, which involves voice input and manual interaction with a wearable computer (see Figure 9.11). In first generation voice picking systems, the computer provides audio instructions to mobile warehouse personnel about what items should be picked from the warehouse shelves for an order. First, the system asks the user to speak digits specifying an item's location in the warehouse, so that the product is properly identified. Then the system tells the user how many items to pick at that location. In response, the user speaks a confirmation of the number of items picked.

Figure 9.11: Multimodal warehouse application from Lucas Systems, with voice input via a wireless microphone to a handheld computer/scanner. Courtesy Lucas Systems.

For the first-generation systems, speaker-dependent speech recognition was used that communicated with a centralized speech server. However, the cost and complexity of server-based solutions was an impediment to market penetration for small distribution centers (Villaneuva, 2012). Recently, handheld and wearable computers have become sufficiently powerful to run speaker-independent recognizers to process the small prompted vocabularies during these elementary dialogues.

Second-generation systems incorporate voice as one input mode, along with bar-code scanning and an array of lights over the warehouse bins. Companies, such as BarCoding Inc., Lucas Systems, and Vocollect now have multimodal products (Lachenman, 2013). These support entry of item identification data using a handheld or ring-worn bar-code scanner, and in other cases a handheld display with buttons and stylus input (Slevin and May, 2011).

As with other commercial products discussed in this chapter, the trend in this large industry has been toward adopting multimodal interface solutions that provide greater functionality and flexibility (Zetes, 2009). Voice picking is only one function that needs to be accomplished in distribution centers. Others include receiving, price checking, and moving products between locations. In this application context, handhelds and especially wearables that combine bar code scanning, touch-screen selection, stylus, and voice input are advantageous. In the future, robotic agents potentially could more adeptly and inexpensively complete these routine warehouse tasks.

9.9   INTERNATIONAL STANDARDS AND COMMERCIAL TOOLKITS

In order to provide a means to combine modalities in an application, to facilitate interoperation among third party components, and to stimulate the formation of a multimodal ecosystem, the World Wide Web Consortium (W3C) established a working group to propose a Multimodal Interfaces and Architecture standard (Dahl, 2013; World Wide Web Consortium, 2014). Representatives from numerous companies were involved, including AT&T, France Telecom, Deutsche Telekom, Openstream, IBM, Intel, and others. Another goal was to be vendor neutral, so any vendor's components that met the specification would interoperate with others. Earlier research efforts on interoperation frameworks for multimodal interaction included the Open Agent Architecture (Cohen et al., 1994; Martin et al., 1999; Moran et al., 1997), the Adaptive Agent Architecture (Kumar et al., 2000), the Galaxy Communicator architecture (Seneff et al., 1999), and PAC-Amodeus (Nigay and Coutaz, 1995; Coutaz et al., 1995).

The architecture in Figure 9.12 is intended to handle active and passive modalities, as well as other sensors for input and output. In some cases, the passive modalities are used for authentication, as in multimodal biometrics. The key to the architecture is the language communicated by the components, the run-time environment, and the structure of the Interaction Manager. The modality components may in fact be local to a machine, or available on a centralized server. Thus, sensors themselves need to be able to send data through the architecture to the process that will analyze them. For example, a process that monitors a microphone on a cell phone may send the data to a networked server. There is a specification of an *Event Transport Layer* of LifeCycle Events, which requires the events to be transported reliably and in the order they were generated. Examples of such messages between a modality component and the Interaction Manager are StartRequest, CancelRequest, StartResponse,CancelResponse, and so forth. These events specify various types of fields, including metadata about the request. They also specify content data, such as a natural language parse. Such contents would be specified with the Extensible MultiModal Annotation language (EMMA), which is based on XML. Details of EMMA are described below. In addition to the basic architecture, the modality components need to be encapsulated so they can be easily plugged into the architecture.

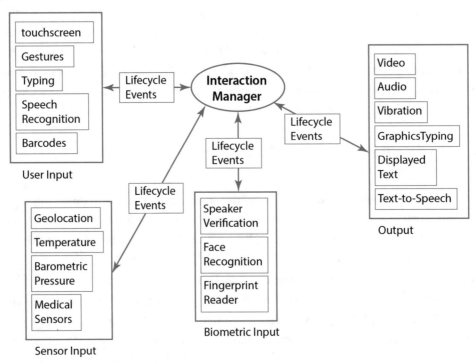

Figure 9.12: W3C architecture (copyright World Wide Web Consortium, source (Dahl, 2013) used with permission).

The Interaction Manager can be implemented as the developer desires, but the W3C notes that an emerging standard called State Chart XML would be suitable (World Wide Web Consortium, 2014). SCXML is an encoding of a State Chart in XML (Harel, 1987). For example, Mehlmann and Andre's Event Logic Chart (Section 8.2.2) multimodal integrator could be implemented in SCXML.

Schnelle-Walka et al. (2013) discussed various weaknesses with the W3C architecture. One is the inability of modality components to communicate with one another directly. A second is the implied tree structure of the interaction managers and modality components. The need for inter-component communication arises with closely synchronized modalities, such as audio-visual speech recognition during input (Potamianos et al., 2015) or synthesis of coordinated speech and lip motion for output (Massaro, 2004). The issue of overly restrictive communication among components is a result of an implicit pipelined architecture being superimposed on an XML web document framework. Similar concerns were dealt with in the Open Agent Architecture (Cohen et al., 1994; Martin et al., 1999; Moran et al., 1997) and Adaptive Agent Architecture (Kumar et al., 2000). The Open Agent Architecture was the basis for the Siri system that was ultimately sold to Apple Computer (Apple, 2015a). These approaches have components (i.e., "agents") advertise their capabilities with and communicate through a facilitator, which routes communication to components capable of handling them. High-bandwidth point-to-point connections between agents also could be arranged by the facilitator. Agents, such as those controlling devices like thermostats and TVs or websites, could connect to the facilitator at run-time, and forward their vocabulary and APIs, thus increasing the overall system capabilities. This facilitated architecture overcomes the problem of being too prescriptive in how a multimodal system should be built. However, unlike EMMA (see below), those systems did not stipulate the content of the messages that flowed among the agents. Such "service discovery" capabilities for multimodal systems are now being discussed within the W3C.

The Extensible MultiModal Annotation language (EMMA) is a W3C standard communication language for content transmitted by modality components. We refer the reader to a complete description of the W3C standard (Johnston et al., 2009), and simply discuss it briefly below.

The EMMA XML language is intended to provide a means to express interpretations based on user inputs, such as speech, natural language, handwriting, sketch, and so forth. It has tags to represent disjunctions, sequences, word lattices, and similar information. For example, the following might be the EMMA representation of an uncertain interpretation of "from Boston to Denver," where "Boston" might also be heard as "Austin."

```
<emma:emma version="1.0"

        xmlns:emma="http://www.w3.org/2003/04/emma"

        xmlns:xsi="http://www.w3.org/2001/XMLSchema-instance"

        xsi:schemaLocation="http://www.w3.org/2003/04/emma

          http://www.w3.org/TR/2009/REC-emma-20090210/emma.xsd"

        xmlns="http://www.example.com/example">

    <emma:one-of id="r1" emma:medium="acoustic" emma:mode="voice">

        <emma:interpretation id="int1">

            <origin>Boston</origin>

            <destination>Denver</destination>

            <date>03112003</date>
```

```
        </emma:interpretation>

    <emma:interpretation id="int2">

        <origin>Austin</origin>

        <destination>Denver</destination>

        <date>03112003</date>

        </emma:interpretation>

    </emma:one-of>

</emma:emma>
```

The XML representation indicates that the medium is acoustic, and the modality is voice. It indicates that there are alternative interpretations bracketed by the "one of" expression, which are then further specified. Of course, there are many attribute-value representations, such as the feature-structure representation described in Chapter 8. Another is JavaScript Object Notation (JSON), which uses delimiters (such as "{" and "}") to surround parts of the expressions. Many professionals have claimed that XML is appropriate for web page interactions, while JSON is appropriate for computer-computer interactions, and a debate remains in progress about the relative advantages of each viewpoint.

Although multimodal standards have been developed, few commercial systems appear to use them, except for Openstream who was a participating collaborator in their development. The reasons for not doing so are many. They include the long time required for a standard to be developed and adopted, the changes in software engineering practice during the standardization process, inadequacies in the standard, and the differing motivations of the various firms involved in formulating or ignoring the standards. Standards can be overly prescriptive because they are inspired by certain devices and use cases. Years later, other devices and uses emerge that require a different approach. In some cases, vendors think their own architecture is superior, and may even have patented it, so they have little motivation to share it with their competitors. Even for members of the W3C consortium committee who wrote the standard, they may not themselves be using it in cases where their multimodal capabilities were added to an existing system that did not originally comply with the standard. In such cases, it likely was easier to simply continue with their existing architecture. Finally, firms that are trying to establish a "lock" on the market would prefer that component vendors adopt their architecture and API, rather than enable full-scale interoperability, because platform superiority often is viewed as a key to commercial success.

A time-honored and successful way to proliferate a software platform is to offer a software development kit to developers. Three examples of commercial offerings that support multimodal interface development are Microsoft's Kinect™ (see Section 9.7), Intel's RealSense™, and Openstream's CueME™.

Microsoft has provided a free software-development kit (SDK) for Kinect that enables software engineers to use gesture and voice while interacting at a distance from a computer display (Microsoft, 2015c). The SDK provides methods for controlling and interpreting signals from the various sensors on the Kinect device, including depth, infrared, and visible light cameras, as well as a four-microphone array for far-field voice capture. Up to six people can be tracked at once, and the microphone array will focus on the loudest voice unless it is programmed to do otherwise. The SDK offers APIs for gesture definition and recognition, for voice recognition, as well as for skeletal tracking and face identification.

Unlike most SDKs, Microsoft also provides user interface guidelines, which briefly discuss motivations for building an alternative-mode multimodal application using Kinect. However, no explicit support is provided yet for building fusion-based multimodal speech/gesture applications. We expect that once strategic fusion-based applications are more prevalent in other sectors (e.g., on smart phones), the Kinect SDK may well also be upgraded to facilitate them. Since there are many interesting research projects now making use of Kinect (see Section 10.1), especially for robotics (Bohus and Horvitz, 2014), Microsoft also has released a developer's reference platform called Mobile Autonomous Robot using Kinect (MARK) (Microsoft, 2015d).

Intel has developed the RealSense™ SDK (Intel, 2015), a 2014 upgrade of their former Perceptual Computing SDK. It uses the RealSense device's 3D camera to provide face, head, eye movement, gesture, speech, and emotion recognition. Compared with Microsoft's Kinect (Microsoft, 2015b), it incorporates 3D gesture recognition software from SoftKinetic to perform more fine-grained hand and finger tracking. This includes micro-gestures that support touch-less interaction with objects on a display, as well as control of what is displayed (e.g., panning). It is designed for use within three or four feet of a computer screen, and the toolkit also supports speech input using Nuance's Dragon Assistant voice recognition software (Nuance, 2015c). The RealSense toolkit places an emphasis on gaming, education, and communication applications involving an immersive virtual experience. For example, 3D immersive Skype calls have been demonstrated that incorporate user-selected backgrounds, such as the office or beach. In another application, a user's fine-grained facial expressions, head, and eye movements were mirrored in the movements of a 3D virtual character. In a third demonstration, a developer used RealSense to build a music synthesizer for several instruments controlled by hand movements, gestures, and speech.

Openstream has developed and licenses CueMe™ (Openstream, 2015) a software development platform for multimodal systems based on the W3C international standard reference architecture (Dahl, 2013). It includes EMMA, an XML-based message content standard (Johnston et al., 2009). Using CueMe, Openstream and its customers have developed a series of multimodal applications, including mobile field-force automation, financial, pharmaceutical, and other applications. The CueMe software framework captures user input from a number of modalities, including speech, sketch, handwriting, keyboard, stylus, touch, GPS, bar-code scanners, and others. The input modalities are sent to an Interaction Manager server, per W3C standard, for late fusion and interpretation, which then invokes the back-end software. The IM can coordinate information presentation across multiple connected devices, including cell phones, tablets, and personal computers. CueMe has been used for common applications involving form filling, question answering, personal information management, annotation of drawings (using synchronized speech and sketch input), and other functionality. Openstream's Enterprise Virtual Assistant, called EVA, is built on top of CueME. Numerous corporations, including Walmart, Merck, Roche, and Bank of NY/Mellon, all have implemented multimodal applications based on CueMe and EVA.

9.10   ORGANIZATIONAL RESISTANCE TO ADOPTING NEW TECHNOLOGIES

The adoption of multimodal interface technologies for consumers is accelerating, while the transition has been slower for enterprises. Consumers are simply more adventurous and have less inertia in switching to new technologies and products. In contrast, large bureaucratic and risk-averse commercial and federal organizations have many sources of inertia, and many people in different roles involved in purchasing decisions. Numerous people have remarked on the difficulty of making technology transitions in such organizations. Among the classic obstacles that impede new technology adoption are cost, in-house IT staff who only are trained in the old technology, and resistance from employees who all need to cooperate on using the same technology.

Most famously, Moore (1999) identified the "Chasm" between early adopters and the late-adopting majority, where innovative technologies and technology companies often die. To bridge this chasm, he points out that one must first have a complete product with an obviously strong return on investment, not just a promising new technology concept, feature, or capability like a multimodal user interface. Given a whole product, people Moore calls "Visionary and Technology Enthusiast" customers may advocate for it because of its transformational impact and order of magnitude return on investment (Moore, 1999). However, the much larger group of "Pragmatists and Conservative" customers are more interested in a whole solution, including how it will be priced, maintained, and integrated successfully within organizations. Moore argues that the preferred way to cross the chasm and reach the larger market is to adopt a "D-Day approach," in which an initial use case is implemented in the target organization. Once successful, the product then is able to fan out and penetrate a larger market by referring to the initial use case. This technology transition strategy is one of risk reduction, because a demonstration of successful adoption by a similar organization reduces risk and can more easily be modeled.

Sketch-Thru-Plan (STP) is an example of an enterprise multimodal system that is in the process of "crossing the chasm" to adoption by the U.S. military. Advocates within the U.S. Marine Corps have understood the potentially large benefits of adopting a multimodal C^2 planning system, as indicated by evaluation results summarized in Section 9.2. As a result, they have begun augmenting their existing C^2 system with the STP interface, using a process that will ease this major transition for their users and IT organization. This initial use case within the Marines provides impetus for the larger U.S. Army to consider adoption. Although senior Army management has been supportive, their IT organization is reluctant to undertake the major effort needed to integrate the multimodal technology into their business practices, which have been directed at upgrading their existing systems to web-based technologies. This inertia is a classic response from a large bureaucracy, and from IT organizations in particular. Once another similar organization has adopted and vouches for STP, the question will be asked by decision-makers, "Why don't we have this ourselves?" This example emphasizes that enterprise adoption of new technology is a very slow and politically hazardous process. Moore's strategy is a wise approach to alleviating concerns about risk.

Multimodal interface technologies have proven the considerable benefits described in Chapter 3, resulting in commercialization by many companies selling to consumers and enterprises. The migration to multimodal interface technologies has been extensive and continues to accelerate for consumers, especially on smart phones, tablets, and automobiles. Their multimodal interfaces have steadily expanded the sensors and input modes available to users. Multimodal technology has become especially prominent in areas like automotive interfaces, virtual assistants, entertainment and games, and education. Commercialization of enterprise multimodal technologies also has been prominent, mainly in areas like warehouse automation, multi-biometrics, robotics, and geospatial systems. The large range of products involved spans wearable, cell phone, handheld, tablet, in-vehicle, desktop, and wall-size platforms. Multimodal-multisensor interfaces for these and other applications are expected to increase substantially in the next five years. Table 9.3[14] summarizes basic features of the commercial multimodal applications presented in this chapter.

---

[14]   This list is not intended to be exhaustive.

Table 9.3: Summary of commercial applications supporting multimodal interaction

Application Type	Geospatial	Education	Automotive	Warehouse	Games, Entertainment	Virtual Assistant	Multimodal Biometrics	Robotics
	Adapx Sketch-Thru-Plan, Think 3, Wacom	Anoto, Promethean, Livescribe Smart	All car makers, Tier1 suppliers (Delphi, Denso, Harman, etc.), Apple CarPlay, Google Android Auto	Honeywell/Vocollect, Lucas Systems, Barcoding Inc.	Microsoft Xbox, Forza Horizon	Apple's Siri, Google Now, Samsung's S, Microsoft's Cortana, Nuance's Nina, Speak4It, Voicebox, Openstream's EVA, Sense.ly	M2Sys, MorphoTrak, NEC, WCC, Safran (many others)	Aldebaran, Jibo, Robokind, Honda
Platforms	PC, tablet PC, digital pen /paper	Digital pen, Digitizing board	In-car electronics + cell phone	Wearable or mobile computer	Microsoft Kinect, Intel RealSense, LeapMotion	Cell phone, PC, tablet, wearables	Custom hardware, cellphone	Asimo, Jibo, Nao, Pepper, Robokind
Voice	X	X	X	X	X	X	X	X
Sketch	X	X	X		X	X		
Touch/Multi-touch	X	X	X	X		X		X
Hand gesture			E		X	X		X
Handwriting	X	X	X			X	X	
Mouse /stylus	X			X		X		
Gaze location and state (e.g., shut, blink)			X		E			X
Face tracking			X		X	E		X
Keyboard, buttons	X		X	X	X	X	E	
Head position			E		X	X		X
Torso Position			E		X	X		X
Eye position			E		E			X
Arm positions					X	X		X

Face recognition			E		X	X	X	X
Fingerprint			E			X	X	
Iris							X	
Finger Vein							X	
Palm Vein							X	
Gait							E	
Retina							E	

CHAPTER 10

Emerging Multimodal Research Areas and Applications

This chapter introduces several areas of concentrated multimodal research and application development that have emerged rapidly within the last decade. Rather than attempting to exhaustively cover all new areas, we present qualitatively different multimodal topics that jointly characterize their range of valuable functionality. In most cases, we also have selected topics not already discussed in Chapter 9. The one exception to this is virtual agents and robotic interfaces, which is of especially active commercial interest. The topics discussed below include tangible, ubiquitous, and wearable multimodal interfaces, multimodal affect recognition, multimodal learning analytics, multimodal accessible interfaces for disabled users, and multimodal virtual agents and robotic interfaces.

10.1 TANGIBLE, UBIQUITOUS, AND WEARABLE MULTIMODAL INTERFACES

Multimodal interfaces are well suited for instantiation in tangible real-world objects. The array of such interfaces has expanded, and many now are available commercially. From a design standpoint, tangible multimodal interfaces are hybrids that combine the advantages of two or more types of computer interface: ones that are embodied within tangible physicalized forms, and also that support human input and interaction involving multiple modalities. For example, early tangible multimodal interfaces supported interaction with graspable objects (McGee et al., 2000; Cohen and McGee, 2004), sometimes in simulated or virtual reality environments, and also control of robotic applications (for further discussion, see Section 10.5).

Some recent tangible multimodal interfaces begin to epitomize Weiser's vision of interfaces that "disappear" into everyday familiar objects in our environment, so we cease to be consciously aware or distracted by them (Weiser, 1991). Weiser talked about computer interfaces embedded in post-it notes and paper, "dynabooks," and electronic meeting boards. He contrasted these ubiquitous interfaces with earlier virtual reality systems:

> *"Virtual reality focuses an enormous apparatus on simulating the world rather than on invisibly enhancing the world that already exists."* –Weiser (1991, p. 20)

Consistent with Weiser's vision, Section 9.6 describes numerous tangible multimodal interfaces embedded in everyday objects that are now commercially available, including digital pen and paper interfaces, digital books, and interactive whiteboards.

Tabletop interfaces are another example of hybrid interfaces that are tangible, multimodal, and mimic existing artifacts. Tabletop interaction and interfaces have represented a very active area of research. They previously have included multi-touch, gestural, and virtual keyboard input, but newer prototypes now include pen input as well (Block et al., 2008; Brandl et al., 2008; Haller et al., 2010; Leitner et al., 2009; Liwicki and El-Neklawy, 2009). While multi-touch is useful for controlling aspects of the interface and display, high-resolution pen input is more useful for specifying application content, including marking or writing directly on displayed documents, photographs, moving images, and maps. Tabletop interfaces can reduce workload, increase participation and collaboration, and stimulate reflection in children (Shaer et al., 2011). They have been demonstrated as effective in cognitive-behavioral therapy with children who have autistic spectrum disorders (Battocchi et al., 2010; Giusti et al., 2011).

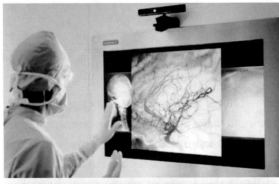

Figure 10.1: Kinect touch-less gestural interface for controlling medical imagery during surgery (top), and exercise application that encourages whole-body physical activity with postural feedback (bottom). Used with permission from Microsoft.

In support of ubiquitous interaction and natural multimodal movement patterns, Microsoft's Kinect and similar tools offer a relatively unobtrusive way to process 3-D motion recognition, face recognition, gesture recognition, speech recognition, and user identification, including of multiple people (Microsoft, 2015b). While developed initially for use with game consoles and applications (see Section 9.7), this technology is versatile and has spawned a wide variety of application directions, as shown in Figure 10.1, including medical, fitness and physical rehabilitation, advertising, robotics, interactive arts, and many research prototypes (Walker, 2012; Webster and Celik, 2014). Major advantages of this multimodal interface technology include that users can move freely, do not need to wear or trigger a physical device, and the technology is low cost and openly extensible for application development. Regarding limitations, it currently can process gross motor movements rather than fine-grained ones, nearby actions within ten meters that are free of occlusion, and activity in settings with adequate lighting.

Figure 10.2: User wearing Google glasses (left), with inset displaying subway information while mobile (right, top) and photo being taken while interacting with a child (right, bottom). Left: Courtesy of iStock. Right: Courtesy of the Associated Press and thejournal.ie. Used with permission.

Two of the newest directions in wearable multimodal interfaces are Google glasses and digital watches. Google glasses support multimodal touch, gesture, speech, camera capture, and sensor input (e.g., GPS, accelerometer), as well as multimedia timeline-based output. For example, a user may view an incoming email as a thumbnail photo with text, to which they can provide a spoken reply. Internet access is guided by a user's current GPS location while they are mobile.

Figure 10.2 illustrates a user wearing Google glasses (left). It shows examples of two displays inset in the glasses, one updating subway information while mobile (right, top) and another while taking a photo (right, bottom).

The need to minimize user distraction while mobile and wearing glasses requires a highly flexible multimodal interface. Commercial developers are just beginning to explore possible application functionality, and how to design a glasses-based mobile interface for safe mobile interactions. Other substantial challenges for this type of interface are social in nature (Dredge, 2014; Garfinkel, 2014; Starner, 2001), including (1) privacy concerns by those who assume the Google glasses user is recording them without consent and (2) disruption of natural en-face gaze patterns during social interaction. These factors risk contributing to erosion of interpersonal trust.[15] Like some virtual reality interfaces that require head-mounted displays, gloves, and body suits, Google glasses currently lack the degree of transparency described in Weiser's original concept of the "disappearing interface."

Smart watches with Internet connectivity are intended to be multi-functional mobile devices, like smart phones (with which they integrate), except they are wearable. Examples include the Samsung Galaxy Gear S and Apple Watch (Apple, 2015b; Samsung, 2015), both of which will become available in spring of 2015. Many of the applications they support overlap with smart phone functionality—including personal information management, voice dialogues with virtual assistants, music playback, mapping, making phone calls, timekeeping, and so forth.

Not surprisingly, smart watch interfaces are multimodal-multisensor ones like smart phones. For example, the Apple Watch is controlled with pressure-sensitive touch, gestures, speech, a "Digital Crown" winder, and sensors (e.g., accelerometer, heart-rate monitor). Raising the wrist engages the watch display via sensors. Sensors on the back of the watch monitor heart-rate for fitness and health applications. A "Digital Crown" winder on the side of the watch replaces gestural controls for the screen display (e.g., zooming). Pressure-sensitive touch can distinguish a tap from a press, which elicit different interface functions. It can also be used to draw input for transmission. Gestures, such as swiping across the watch display, causes "Glances," or brief updates of frequently accessed content (e.g., weather, messages). Finally, speech can be used, for example to conduct dialogues with Siri. Unlike the iPhone, there is no keyboard input, virtual or otherwise. In addition to visual and auditory output, the Watch can deliver haptic-vibratory feedback.

Likewise, the Samsung Galaxy Gear S smart watch has a multimodal-multisensor interface. It coordinates with Android phones, and supports user touch, speech, gestures, virtual keyboard, and sensors. With the Samsung watch, a gesture is used to turn on the watch display, and it incorporates heart-rate monitoring to support fitness and health applications. This watch has a considerably larger curved display, which can be used to take photos and make phone calls directly. Its

---

[15] In January 2015, Google announced that it is discontinuing sales of Google glasses in order to redesign them to overcome public criticism and better position their functionality.

larger size also enables using multi-touch gestures and virtual keyboard input in the same way as on smart phones.

Applications currently are being developed for the Apple Watch, including the ability to make automatic payments using Apple Pay and to interact with in-vehicle applications. For example, with a BMW self-parking car the user will be able to return to a parking garage, tap on their watch and say, "BMW, pick me up" (Quain, 2015). They also will be able to see what battery charge remains on their electric car. Other planned applications will focus on controlling objects that are part of the Internet of Things (IoT), which is expected to increase rapidly during the next five years.

This IoT ecosystem of related applications includes home appliances and entertainment, personal health monitoring and medical care, environmental monitoring and energy management, traffic monitoring and transportation planning, and other areas. These many applications represent a major expansion of end-user field and mobile functions, with a new emphasis on the control of distant objects and processes. They also involve heavier use of sensors and passive user input, which does not require explicit input from a user. Similar applications will run on smart phones, and it remains to be seen how the functionality of smart watches vs. smart phones ultimately will diverge in the marketplace.

One usability issue common across smart phones, smart watches, in-vehicle systems, and many others is the trend toward developing multimodal-multisensor interfaces that rely increasingly on passive sensors and input modes. Such interfaces risk unintended system consequences due to sensor false alarms. Unintended activation of system processes during false alarms can be nonintuitive, disorienting users and complicating error resolution. Other concerns involve potential intrusion of privacy and security. It is important that new multimodal-multisensor interfaces be designed to support transparent functioning. One prerequisite for achieving adequate user oversight is inclusion of active content creation modes in the interface.

10.2   MULTIMODAL AFFECT RECOGNITION

Computers now are being developed that detect and respond to human emotions in order to produce more engaging, nuanced, and impactful interactions. This research is part of the general movement toward human-centered ubiquitous computing in which computers sense activities and states within natural contexts. Most recently, affect detection techniques have been developed that rely on processing multimodal signals like speech, facial expressions, gestures, posture, physiological cues, and language to reliably detect users' affective state (Calvo and D'Mello, 2010; Zeng et al., 2009). In addition, new systems that produce affect use computational techniques to model how emotions arise from cognitive appraisals in different contexts. Such systems often express emotions using embodied interfaces with conversational agents or robots (Calvo and D'Mello, 2010). For example, Section 9.4 summarizes Pepper, the Japanese social robot that uses audio-visual information in human speech and faces to recognize emotion in humans with whom it is interacting.

Multimodal affect recognition is a multidisciplinary area based on cognitive science and psychological theories and models, computational processing techniques for different component technologies, linguistics and communication science, and related areas. For example, psychological research by Ekman and colleagues contributed the Facial Action Coding Scheme (FACS), the most commonly used system for coding emotional states by analyzing facial expressions. It evaluates fine muscle contraction and relaxation patterns in the face, and also movement patterns such as head nods (Ekman and Friesen, 1978). Facial emotions reflect change in the autonomic nervous system, and many basic emotional expressions are similar across cultures (Ekman, 1992, 1994).

Other classic psychological research has revealed how emotion influences the acoustic-prosodic qualities of speech (Scherer, 2003). Such work has contributed concepts and operational models that capture the speaker's emotional state, listener's attribution, and mediating acoustic cues. Although most empirical research on emotion has been atheoretical, discrete theories that originated in Darwin's work continue to prevail. They posit a small number of basic emotions, each of which is characterized by a specific physiological and behavioral response pattern. Ekman's work and most research on emotion in speech has adopted this general view (Ekman, 1992; Scherer, 2003). Psychological research on emotion also has contributed a better understanding that beyond "basic" emotions (e.g., anger, fear, sadness, joy, boredom), there are "families" of emotions (e.g., explosive rage, cold subdued anger) that contain significant variation (Scherer, 2003). These important qualifications have implications for those interested in developing more realistic affective technologies.

Recent research has been attempting to detect users' chronic affective state to diagnose health conditions like depression and post-traumatic stress syndrome (Scherer et al., 2014; Stratou et al., 2013). In robotics, detection of emotion enables more flexible responding with at-risk fragile seniors, autistics, and other clinical populations. One especially active area of affective computing is educational technologies, including intelligent tutoring systems, games, and related areas. Considerable research has focused on classifying students' affective state as a reflection of motivation and readiness to learn, often with the aim of adapting problem difficulty level or types of system assistance (Woolf et al., 2009; Zakharov, 2007). In other cases, like Affective AutoTutor, the system automatically detects negative affective states in students that could prevent learning, such as frustration, confusion, or boredom (Calvo and D'Mello, 2010). Affective AutoTutor processes certain features of students' discourse, facial expressions, gross body movements, and contextual information. This system includes a pedagogical agent that responds to students by adapting its speech, verbal content, and facial expressions. Compared with a control tutor that did not respond affectively, this system has demonstrated improved learning in lower-performing students, although not in higher-performing ones (Calvo and D'Mello, 2010).

One major challenge in developing more accurate identification of human emotions is the lack of realism and ecological validity of many emotion databases, which involve posed or simulated emotions rather than spontaneous ones (Scherer, 2003). This has limited many systems to only handling exaggerated expressions involving prototypical emotions, rather than more realistic or blended ones. However, very recent work on emotion recognition is beginning to focus on more naturally occurring behaviors. When more natural and subtle emotion must be processed, unimodal acoustic recognition often degrades. This has stimulated expansion of research on emotion recognition using combined multimodal cues (Zeng et al., 2009). Other major challenges include adequately representing realistic blended emotions, the temporal dynamics of changing emotional states, and selecting appropriate methods for feature representation of emotional states. A series of workshops called Audio-Visual Emotion Challenge (AVEC) has been providing an increasingly difficult corpus for testing of emotion recognition algorithms by the research community (Schuller et al., 2012).

In addition to health and educational applications, integration of better emotion recognition is beginning to have an impact on social robotics, as discussed in Section 9.4. Emotion recognition also would be a valuable capability for guiding improved dialogue interaction with virtual assistants on smart phones and in car systems. Section 9.1 described emerging technology capabilities for recognizing drivers' state of alertness. Future automotive systems also could benefit by knowing if a driver is extremely angry or agitated, or if they are frustrated or confused during a dialogue exchange with the in-vehicle virtual assistant.

10.3   MULTIMODAL LEARNING ANALYTICS AND EDUCATION

Multimodal learning analytics is an emerging field within learning analytics (Baker and Yacef, 2009) that analyzes combined natural communication modalities such as speech, writing, gesturing, facial expressions, gaze, and physical activity patterns (Oviatt, 2012; Worsley and Blikstein, 2010). A primary objective of multimodal learning analytics is to identify domain expertise and changes in expertise accurately, quickly, and objectively, and also to examine learning-oriented precursors. Another aim is to analyze coherent signal, activity, and lexical patterns in order to provide a more meaningful "systems perspective" on learning, and potentially to uncover entirely new learning-oriented phenomena. Multimodal learning analytics has the potential to improve our understanding of how students learn, and to create better resources for supporting learning with new curricula and digital tools. In particular, multimodal learning analytic techniques can guide the design of promising educational technologies (e.g., pen, multimodal, tangible) that are not limited by keyboards (Oviatt, 2013b). They are expected to yield more sensitive, reliable, and richly contextualized metrics of learning behaviors and domain expertise, as well as ones that can be analyzed more unobtrusively and automatically in field settings such as classrooms.

There are many advantages of multimodal learning analytic techniques, compared with keystroke-based learning analytics. First, whereas learning analytics examines students' keystroke input only during technology-mediated learning, multimodal learning analytics can be used to analyze expressively rich communication modalities during both interpersonal and computer-mediated learning exchanges. This is important because learning occurs in both contexts, and a baseline involving interpersonal learning is required in order to evaluate the effectiveness of new educational interfaces. Second, the dominant educational technology platform worldwide is mobile cell phones with multimodal input capabilities, not technology with keyboard-based interfaces. Learning analytics techniques that rely on click-stream analysis therefore are limited in their utility, and will become increasingly obsolete as cell phones with multimodal input are increasingly adopted. Third, multimodal learning analytic techniques can track multiple expressively powerful communication modalities that provide a particularly informative window on human thought and learning. For example, diagrammatic and symbolic representations that students sketch and write while solving math problems provide valuable insights into their mental models and problem solution progress. Likewise, spoken dialogue among collaborating students can elucidate ideas under consideration before they commit to action.

Research in this area has been stimulated by a series of international data-driven grand challenge workshops held in conjunction with the annual *International Conference on Multimodal Interaction*.[16] It also has been enabled by the Math Data Corpus, which contains high-fidelity time-synchronized multimodal data recordings of collaborating student groups while they worked together to solve mathematics problems varying in difficulty (Oviatt et al., 2013). Figure 10.3 illustrates five time-synchronized visual data streams during actual data collection. In this corpus, short-term longitudinal data were collected on each students' multimodal communication and activity patterns, including close-talking speech, digital pen input, and camera-based input on facial expressions, gestures, and physical movement patterns. This database includes extensive ground-truth coding of students' performance, speech transcriptions, and the representational content of writing. More recent datasets now are available in Spanish and for language-based tasks.

New multimodal learning analytics research has revealed that student activity patterns can be highly predictive of domain expertise, independent of any content analysis. Based on analysis of the Math Data Corpus, expert students were four-fold more active in contributing group problem solutions, whether these solutions were correct or not (Oviatt and Cohen, 2013). This difference between expert and non-expert students in problem-solving initiative was greatest on the most difficult problems, as illustrated in Figure 10.4. In addition, recent signal-level analyses of students' digital pen writing strokes have achieved high accuracy in classifying students as math domain experts vs. non-experts. Machine learning analysis of the average distance and duration of individual

---

[16]   For information on the Multimodal Learning Analytics Data-Driven Grand Challenge Workshops, see:
http://icmi.acm.org/2014/index.php?id=challenges.

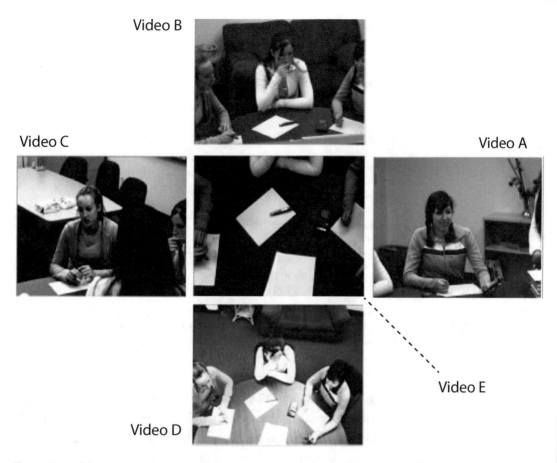

Figure 10.3: Multi-stream multimodal data collection during collaborative math problem solving, which involved twelve synchronized audio, visual, and digital pen input sources for developing multimodal learning analytics predictors From Oviatt et al. (2013). Copyright© 2013 ACM. Used with permission.

pen strokes while students solved math problems correctly predicted domain experts 91.7% of the time (Oviatt et al., in press). Once again, this analysis of pen signal features did not require any content analysis. Another discovery is that valuable predictive information about domain expertise is present in all modalities. It has been detected based on spoken language (e.g., technical math terms), visual input (e.g., calculator use), and handwriting dynamics (Ochoa et al., 2013). A fourth finding is that multimodal data analysis distinguishes domain experts from non-experts more reliably than unimodal analysis. Table 10.1 shows that multimodal analysis of student activity patterns (i.e., who initiated the majority of group problem solutions) based on combined speech and writing successfully identified the dominant domain expert in a group 100% of the time, which exceeded unimodal rates (Oviatt and Cohen, 2013). Since this performance did not require any analysis of written or spoken content, it would be easier to implement for learning analytics purposes in the near term.

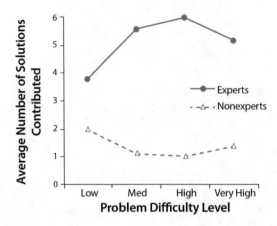

Figure 10.4: Average number solutions contributed for problems varying in difficulty by domain experts vs. non-experts in mathematics From Oviatt (2013b). Copyright© 2013b ACM. Used with permission.

Multimodal learning analytics is an example of a big data initiative that has emphasized the need for high-quality data, rather than simply large-volume data. Converging multimodal data is both denser and richer, and capable of yielding prediction results in less time. It also can track students' learning status more continuously than a single source of information, since any individual data source typically is intermittent and may even be sparse. Research has been developing new hybrid methods for combining machine learning with empirical science techniques to improve the interpretability and transparency of learning analytics predictors.

Future research will require collecting larger datasets that involve tracking student learning in different content domains, in situated learning contexts, and over longer time periods. New datasets also will be required for students representing different cultural-linguistic groups. In addition, more powerful hybrid engineering techniques will be needed that can produce more accurate results based on interpretable parameters. Finally, substantial future work needs to focus on participatory design with teachers, students, educational policy-makers, and other stakeholders of future learning analytics systems. The aim of this participatory design is to ensure that new technical capabilities are able to provide valuable functionality, high accuracy, and adequate transparency and privacy so that they are widely adopted and avoid adverse consequences.

Recognition of emotion and domain expertise both contribute to a system's ability to accurately index users' status. These and other valuable sources of contextual information about a user (e.g., personality) will improve technology's ability to adapt and provide personalized support during various activities. In addition, multimodal data analytics will emerge as a valuable tool not only for evaluating learning during education, but also in many other application areas. Analysis of richly informative multi-stream, multimodal data will push the boundaries of the current "big data" trend by expanding this theme to focus on high-quality data, not just large volumes of it.

Table 10.1: Likelihood of successfully predicting the dominant math domain expert out of three students in a session based on their written, spoken, and multimodal input, including simply initiating answers vs. contributing correct answers

	Written Answers	Oral Answers	Multimodal Oral + Writing
Contributes Most Answers	40%	90%	100%
Contributes Most *Correct* Answers	70%	90%	100%

10.4   MULTIMODAL ACCESSIBLE INTERFACES

As discussed in Sections 3.1 and 4.3.3, there are large individual differences in users' preference to interact using different modalities, and in their dominant multimodal integration and synchronization patterns. In this regard, users with disabilities simply represent natural variation within the diversity of the larger population. According to the World Health organization, approximately 15% of individuals worldwide have a disability of some kind (Ladner, 2012). With increasing lifespans, this percentage will increase as people develop sensory, cognitive, and mobility limitations typical of the senior years. For individuals who live long enough, most will experience some type of disability. As discussed earlier, we also all experience temporary "disability" when mobile contexts make it impossible to use a particular modality for some period of time. Given this reality, disability is a common and growing occurrence as users age and expand their use of technology in mobile settings. Therefore, design for universal access is an imperative.

Multimodal interfaces satisfy the concept of universal design, which involves designing interfaces in a way that can be used by the vast majority of people regardless of abilities (Ladner, 2010). They enable disabled users to flexibly configure and use an interface to solve their own accessibility limitations, by selecting which input modes to use on the multimodal interface. Adaptable personalization systems, such as SUPPLE++, also could be combined with a basic multimodal interface to automatically generate appropriate system output for disabled users. In particular, SUPPLE++ adapts output for users with varying motor and vision abilities (Gajos et al., 2007).

One delightful impact of the rapidly expanding commercialization of multimodal interfaces on cell phones has been the development of more accessible interfaces and applications for disabled groups, including blind and deaf users (Ladner, 2012). Smart phones are now being realized as multi-functional accessibility devices (Ladner, 2012). This has depended critically on prerequisites involving their alternative input modes (e.g., speech, touch, keyboard, digital pen), output modes (e.g., speech, vibration, visual), multiple sensors (e.g., camera, GPS, accelerometer), and expansion of the cellular data network and high bandwidth capabilities. For example, some smart phones now can perform optical character recognition (OCR) so blind users can take photographs of pages with text, which then can be digitized and read aloud using text-to-speech technology. Through programs like Mobile Accessibility, new Android cell phone applications have been developed as navigational aids for the blind, including using text-to-speech to indicate current location, approximate address, street signs, walking directions, and so forth (Mobile Accessibility, 2014). To support successful navigation of walking routes, one Android application called PhoneWand processes blink input with vibration and orientation feedback. Others have been developed to support reading text while in field settings. These interfaces depend on gestural control of a screen reader, combined with mobile OCR that involves user guidance based on tactile and audio feedback (Mobile Accessibility, 2014). A variety of other smart phone applications now support pragmatic functions for the disabled, such as bar code reading to assist with shopping, color identification for the color blind, and face detection to automatically frame photos for the visually impaired (Mobile Accessibility, 2014).

In some cases, new work on interaction design has made input modes more accessible to disabled users. For example, blind users can use touch input with systems such as Slide Rule, Perkinput, and VoiceOver, the iPhone's screen reader (Ladner, 2012). Using Slide Rule, a blind user can touch the screen, and information about the objects touched is read aloud. The blind user then can double tap an object to activate it as part of a touch or multi-touch application. Gestural controls also are available for paginating and browsing information in lists. Slide Rule was designed to make basic phone functions available, such as calling, email, and music playback (Kane et al., 2008).

In contrast, Perkinput uses multi-point touch for actual text entry. Essentially, each finger either touches the screen or not to convey a six-bit Braille encoding of text, with accompanying audio feedback (Azenkot et al., 2012). Perkinput is usable on touch-screen phones, such as the Apple iPhone. In other cases where touch surfaces are not available, input tools like the Talking Tactile Pen has been developed by Touch Graphics Inc. (Touch Graphics, 2014). Using this interface, printed codes can be photographed using the camera in the tip of a Livescribe digital pen (Livescribe, 2014). The digital pen then uses text-to-speech to speak information according to directions on the printed code (Ladner, 2012).

During the last ten years, video telephony has begun supporting real-time exchange of signed language by deaf users, including commercial products like Skype. In 2010, FaceTime became available on mobile iPhones with front-facing cameras, as illustrated in Figure 10.5, which has been adopted by deaf users worldwide (Ladner, 2012). To facilitate phone calls between deaf and hearing communicators, a longer-term challenge is real-time automatic translation of sign language (Ong and Ranganath, 2005).

Figure 10.5: Two deaf users engage in a visual sign language conversation using FaceTime on the iPhone. Courtesy of AppAdvice, http://appadvice.com/appnn/2010/07/video-relay-calling-facetime-assists-deaf.

One major advantage of the newer multimodal interfaces on smart phones is that they can now replace previous special purpose devices (Ladner, 2012). They offer durable and supported commercial platforms for consolidating multiple accessibility applications. In the future, it would be advantageous to have multimodal accessibility interfaces designed with the full participation of disabled end users, so they can apply their unique expertise to improving accessibility technology (Ladner, 2010).

10.5 MULTIMODAL VIRTUAL AGENTS AND ROBOTIC INTERFACES

Hundreds of research projects worldwide have developed conversational software characters, or Embodied Conversational Agents (ECAs). Their functionality varies widely, including establishing social rapport (Bickmore and Picard, 2005; Gratch et al., 2007), providing counseling and healthcare (DeVault et al., 2014), information retrieval and management (Bohus and Horvitz, 2009, 2014; Wahlster, 2006), educating normally developing and disabled students in science and languages (Massaro and Cohen, 1990; Oviatt et al., 2004b; Johnson, 2014), and many other areas. Typically, people speak to a screen-based character that responds with spoken language, facial expressions and gestures, and an accompanying graphical display showing information. In this section, we discuss examples of animated character research that support multimodal user input, and the topics they investigated.

SmartKom was a major research effort in Germany that explored multimodal interaction with virtual agents in three different environments: kiosk, mobile phone, and the home (Reithinger et al., 2003; Wahlster, 2003, 2006). This ambitious research project is especially noteworthy for its wide range of interface modalities and usage contexts. The system featured multiple input and output modalities, including speech and touch input, hand gesture recognition, and emotion recognition based on facial expressions. It also incorporated multimodal biometrics based on hand shape, signature, and voice using a decision-fusion approach (Grashey and Schuster, 2006). SmartKom's virtual character could speak, point, and provide graphical displays. This system incorporated both early and late multimodal fusion methods. For example, early fusion was used for acoustic and lip motion analysis, but late fusion for semantic multimodal integration (Engel and Pfleger, 2006). SmartKom's meaning representation used a variant of XML, which formed the foundation for

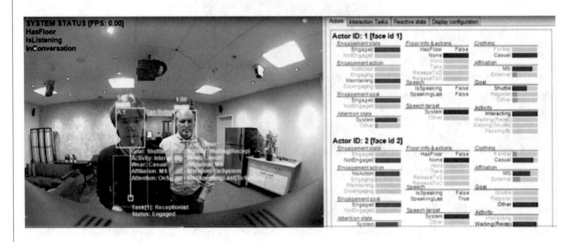

W3C EMMA international standards discussed in Section 9.9.

Figure 10.6: View from conversational agent of two approaching conversants, with system state shown on the right. Used with permission from Microsoft.

At Microsoft, Bohus and Horvitz (2009) developed a "talking head" virtual agent that can engage multiple people in conversation. This research has focused on flexible multi-party dialogue interaction in a naturalistic field environment, including coordination of nonlinguistic and linguistic cues, such as the state of engagement, who has the conversational "floor," conversants' clothing, affiliation, etc. It has targeted three tasks, including a receptionist who schedules transportation, a trivia game played with passersby, and a meeting scheduler. The system senses its users with a four-microphone array and a stereo camera. Based on these data, it identifies conversants, determines when it is being addressed, and then conducts a spoken dialogue during which it tracks users' faces, heads, body location and movements. During the conversation, the character's head and eyes can orient towards and away from its addressees, providing naturalistic cues as it coordinates turn taking. Figure 10.6 shows a system view of two people who are approaching it to initiate a conversation. The system's real-time conversation-tracking data are shown on the right.

SimSensei Kiosk is a virtual human interviewer, which was designed to support patients with post-traumatic stress (DeVault et al., 2014). The virtual character shown in Figure 10.7 incorporates spoken language understanding and vision-based head, gaze, and face tracking of a user. The system uses this information to recognize the user's emotional state (e.g., anger, disgust). The SimSensei character is able to engage a user in a multimodal dialogue, from which it also extracts different types of user speech acts and the positive or negative emotional valence any user utterances. This project represents newer research integrating emotion recognition into the design of conversational characters (see also Section 10.2). It also illustrates the application of conversational agent technology to medical diagnostics and mental health care.

Figure 10.7: SimSensei conversational agent that functions as a behavioral health coach. From DeVault et al. (2014). Copyright© 2014 IFAAMAS. Used with permission.

As discussed in Section 9.4, robots have been developed for a large variety of purposes, primarily accomplishing physical tasks. Social robotics emphasizes communicating and maintaining a relationship with human users, which frequently includes a multimodal interface. Social robotic "tasks" typically are situated in a social-conversational or entertainment context. For example, several recent research projects have focused on bartender robots that can deliver drinks while conversing with customers (Giuliani et al., 2013; Keizer et al., 2014).

Social robots often are intended to interact with children, senior citizens, families, or disabled users (Fasola and Mataric, 2012). As discussed in Section 9.4, Asimo was designed to support mobility-impaired users. Robokind, a humanoid robot with a highly expressive face that includes blinking, eyebrow and lip movements, was designed to support research with autistic users (Robokind, 2015). The area of social robotics is expanding rapidly due to recent advances in commercial robot platforms, which has enabled end users and researchers to develop robots that have many sensors (e.g., microphone arrays, cameras, infra-red, and other sensor capabilities). Some of these platforms have been based on Kinect sensors, integrating speech recognition, person finding, and verbal and nonverbal dialogue capabilities. Platforms and software development kits have become more widely available, including Aldebaran's robots (see below) and Microsoft's MARK SDK (Mobile Autonomous Robots using Kinect; Microsoft, 2015d).

There are various commercial robot platforms for research that offer multisensory perception, but it typically is the responsibility of the developer to build the robot architecture and implement multimodal fusion. Aldebaran's Nao robot (see Figure 10.8 and Section 9.4) is one research platform that is based on a highly articulated humanoid robot with four directional microphones, two cameras, and three touch sensors (Aldebaran, 2015a). Numerous research projects (e.g., Bohus and Horvitz, 2014) have involved multimodal human-robot interaction using Nao as a base platform. Aldebaran and Softbank Mobile also now offer the larger Pepper robot as a platform, which moves on wheels and includes a display screen (Aldebaran, 2015b). Pepper enables development of speech, computer vision, touch, and emotion recognition. In 2015, Pepper's natural language capabilities will be augmented with the IBM Watson system (TechTimes, 2015). Finally, a new research robot called Romeo currently is being developed by a European consortium, and built by Aldebaran. It likewise will enable development of speech, vision, and emotion recognition (Aldebaran, 2015c).

Considerable research in social robotics has investigated person identification, based on face and voice recognition (Perzanowski et al., 2001; Stiefelhagen et al., 2007). Such research has also focused on recognition of human gestures, head pose, gaze, and conversational spoken language (Droeschel et al., 2011; Sidner and Lee, 2007; Sidner et al., 2006; Stiefelhagen et al., 2007). As an example, ARMAR III was capable of multimodal person identification, which is based on early fusion of audio and visual information (Stiefelhagen et al., 2007). ARMAR III also performed multimodal processing of users' speech and gestures, based on late semantic integration. Like virtual agent research, research on social robots has examined the verbal and non-verbal communicative signals that are needed for a robot to track users' engagement during conversation, including head nods, face tracking, and spoken language (Bohus and Horvitz, 2014; Okuno et al., 2001; Sidner et al., 2006; Sidner and Lee, 2007; Traum and Morency, 2010). Recently, it also has examined various issues related to emotion recognition (Alonso-Martin et al., 2013).

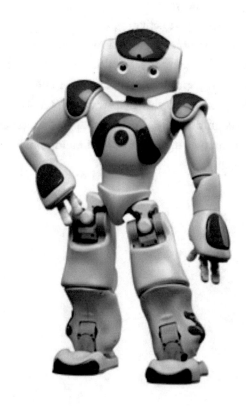

Figure 10.8: Aldebaran Nao robot. Courtesy Aldebaran Robotics.

The Jibo robot will be introduced commercially in 2016. It is an example of a social robot intended to function as a family companion and virtual assistant (Breazeal, 2015). Jibo is stationary, but can autonomously rotate its head, camera, and display. It is designed for face tracking and recognition, body tracking, speech and touch recognition, natural language processing, and emotion recognition. It will respond to questions and offer proactive help using spoken output and by displaying information on its screen. The screen is larger than a cell phone's, which is designed to support entertainment and educational applications for children and others. Like other recent robots and animated characters, Jibo will be connected to the Internet for supplying information, entertainment, and communication services. It also will use the Internet to access servers for speech recognition and natural language processing. Jibo will support remote audio-visual telephony between an individual and a group, including tracking its users' faces and turning its camera to look at a speaker or addressee, thereby creating the impression of attentiveness (Breazeal, 2015).

As devices become increasingly small, wearable, and ubiquitous in the environment, they require human interfaces with an expanded repertoire of multimodal-multisensor interactive capabilities. These pervasive computational systems are beginning to support us in a wider range of field and mobile settings, during less restrictive activities, and to accomplish more powerful multi-functionality. They also can function less obtrusively, and minimize our cognitive load associated with managing them. The development of multimodal-multisensor interfaces, especially consolidated on smart phone devices, has produced a spurt of progress in accommodating individual differences for disabled users and others. As discussed in this chapter, new interfaces now are emerging that can adapt to users' emotional and cognitive state. The next chapter discusses requirements for developing more expressively power computer interfaces beyond multimodality, as well as their impact on human cognition and performance.

CHAPTER 11

Beyond Multimodality: Designing More Expressively Powerful Interfaces

Multimodal interfaces are a major component in the evolution of more expressively powerful input to computers, as illustrated in Figure I.1. From a communications perspective, expressively powerful interfaces support users' ability to convey information involving different modalities, representations, and linguistic codes. Since language is a carrier of thought, more expressively powerful interfaces are capable of directly and substantially stimulating human cognition. The long-term aim of work on designing more expressively powerful computer interfaces is the development of a new generation of computer interfaces that are far more effective thinking tools (Oviatt, 2013a).

Chapter 3 discussed evidence (see Sections 3.4 and 3.6) showing that a multimodal interface can reduce users' task-critical errors and speed up performance. A flexible multimodal interface also enables users to self-manage and reduce their own cognitive load while working on tasks that vary in difficulty. The next sections (11.1 and 11.2) summarize recent research results documenting that interface support for expressing multiple representations also substantially facilitates human cognition and performance, including improving appropriate idea production, correct problem solving, and accurate inferential reasoning. Interfaces that support multiple representations, including spatial ones, also can minimize the performance gap between low- and high-performing users. Section 11.2 provides explanatory background on why this facilitation occurs. It also summarizes general principles for designing more expressively powerful computer input that is capable of substantially stimulating human cognition.

The final section of this chapter (11.3) discusses future work that is needed to design computer interfaces that are better able to fluidly and unambiguously express most world languages. It describes how and why the keyboard is a major impediment to expressing native languages that are not Roman alphabetic ones (e.g., Mandarin, Hindi), a problem that becomes especially acute on smaller platforms such as cell phones.

This chapter also outlines what is at stake, from the viewpoint of human cognition and performance, in successfully developing improved computer interfaces for conveying multiple linguistic codes.

11.1 IMPACT OF INTERFACE SUPPORT FOR EXPRESSING MULTIPLE REPRESENTATIONS

Recent work has revealed that the expressive power of input modes like a digital pen, whether used alone or as part of a multimodal interface, can exert a substantial influence on improving:

- divergent idea generation;

- convergent problem solving; and

- accurate inferential reasoning.

The reason for this is that pen interfaces can be used to express multiple types of representation (e.g., words, numbers, symbols, diagrams), and also to shift rapidly among them while working. Pen interfaces are especially well suited for specifying spatial content (e.g., diagrams), which is widely considered to be the foundation of thought (Johnson-Laird, 1999). They provide a single input tool that can be used to shift easily among different representations so a person's attention remains focused while working on a task. For example, while solving a math problem a person may begin by diagramming to clarify their understanding of a problem, then writing formulas with numbers and symbols, and finally labeling their answer with words. This expressive power and fluidity in conveying qualitatively different representations makes pen input an ideal for tool during thinking and reasoning tasks. Since multimodal interfaces inherit the performance advantages of their component modalities, a multimodal interface that incorporates pen input accrues these same advantages.

11.1.1 IDEATIONAL FLUENCY

In one research study, high school students were asked to produce appropriate ideas related to biology while they used different computer interfaces and non-digital tools. Figure 11.1 illustrates sample problems, which required producing as many hypotheses as students could to explain the data. In this controlled within-subject study, students expressed more total nonlinguistic content (e.g., numbers, symbols, diagrams) when using a pen interface, compared with using either a non-digital pen or keyboard (Figure 3.4, left). More strikingly, they also generated 38.5% more appropriate biology hypotheses. Regression analyses revealed that knowing students' level of nonlinguistic communication predicted 72% of the variance in their ability to produce appropriate ideas (Figure 3.5, left; Oviatt et al., 2012).

In contrast, when the same students used keyboard input they produced more linguistic content, such as words and abbreviations (Figure 3.4, right). In this case regression analyses revealed that students' higher rate of linguistic communication actually predicted a decline in their ability to generate ideas (Figure 3.5, right). In fact, knowing students' level of linguistic communication predicted 62% of the variance in their inability to produce appropriate biology hypotheses. For further background on these studies, see Oviatt et al. (2012).

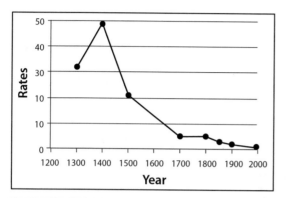

Problem 1. The figure above shows changes in the homicide rate for men in England between 1200 and 2000. List as many hypotheses as you can for why the homicide rate fell so much during this time period.

Problem 2. Above is a picture of a human foot (right) and a chimpanzee foot (left). List as many hypotheses as you can regarding how the function of human vs. chimp feet could have led to these differences in appearance.

Figure 11.1: Examples of hypothesis idea-generation tasks in science. From Oviatt et al. (2012). Copyright© 2012 ACM. Used with permission.

11.1.2 PROBLEM SOLVING

In another study on problem solving, low- and high-performing high school students solved 13% more biology problems correctly when they used a digital pen and paper interface, compared with a keyboard one (Oviatt and Cohen, 2010b). Figure 11.2 shows a sample problem. Analyses confirmed that when students made diagrams or other spatial marks[17] before solving a science problem, this nonlinguistic content was associated with 25–36% higher problem-solution scores, compared with matched problems in which they did not (Oviatt et al., 2012). Figure 11.3 summarizes these findings.

---

[17]   In addition to making structured diagrams, students often used the pen to make more elemental marks on problem visuals while preparing to work on a problem. For example, they circled relevant information, drew lines between related concepts, and other self-organizational pen marking in advance of solving a problem.

Meredith has attached earlobes (homozygous) and Lucas has detached earlobes (homozygous). Their son, George, has attached earlobes. George has four children, 50% with attached earlobes and 50% with detached earlobes.

Given that attached earlobes is a dominant trait:

What genotype is George's wife Susan?

Figure 11.2: Example of genetic inheritance problem-solving task. From Oviatt et al. (2012). Copyright© 2012 ACM. Used with permission.

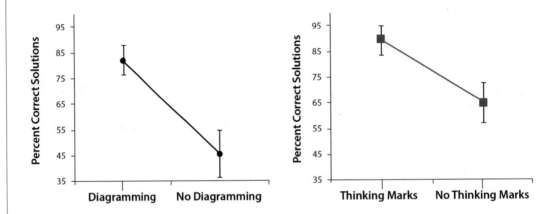

Figure 11.3: Scores on matched problems when students did vs. did not make a diagram (left), and when they did vs. did not make marks on problem visuals (right). From Oviatt et al. (2012). Copyright© 2012 ACM. Used with permission.

11.1.3 INFERENTIAL ACCURACY

Another research study investigated inferential reasoning in undergraduates. It assessed whether a pen interface elicits more diagramming, and also more correctly formed diagrams, compared with using a non-digital pen. Figure 11.4 illustrates a sample inference problem. As illustrated in Figure 11.5, the results confirmed that the same students constructed more total Venn diagrams, and also more correctly formed Venn diagrams, when using a pen interface rather than a non-digital pen (Oviatt et al., 2012). In addition, the pen interface stimulated +9.4% more correct inferences about the content displayed in these diagrams, compared with when the same students used a non-digital pen (Oviatt et al., 2012). When students constructed multiple diagrams rather than just a single one, inference accuracy increased an additional +9.3%. Regression analysis revealed that the frequency of diagramming significantly helped students to suppress scoping errors (e.g., overgeneralizations), the most common type of inference error. The impact was that increased diagramming improved students' total inference accuracy.

In summary, the affordances of pen interfaces invited specific activity patterns (i.e., constructing more spatial diagrams), which encouraged visual inspection of the diagram contents. This led to more refined thinking about the correctness of related inferences, which improved their inference accuracy. Figure 11.6 illustrates the chain of activity—ideation refinement, in which pen interfaces stimulated diagramming activity that directly assisted in clarifying thinking and reasoning.

Problem 1.
All banana slugs are yellow.
Some banana slugs are bright yellow.
None of the poisonous animals are banana slugs.

Figure 11.4: Example of three-statement inference problem, from which students had to summarize as many valid conclusions as they could that derive from this information. From Oviatt et al. (2012). Copyright© 2012 ACM. Used with permission.

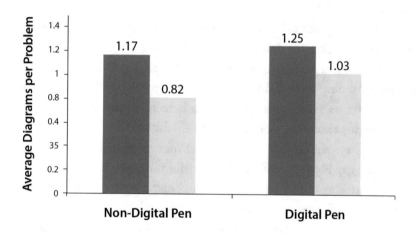

Figure 11.5: Average number of total diagrams and correctly drawn Venn diagrams when the same students solved inference problems using a digital pen vs. a non-digital pen

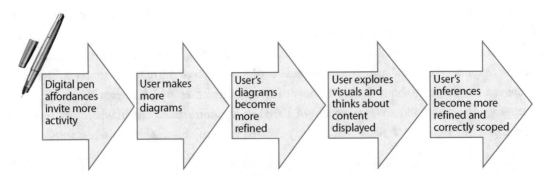

Figure 11.6: Chain of activity—ideation refinement, in which using a pen interface elicited more active diagramming, more correctly formed Venn diagrams, and more accurate inferences about the displayed content, compared with using a non-digital pen. From Oviatt et al. (2012). Copyright© 2012 ACM. Used with permission.

11.1.4 BEYOND AVERAGE: REDUCING THE PERFORMANCE GAP BETWEEN USERS

When designing new computer tools, it's important to look beyond averages and ensure that an interface has a positive impact for different groups. Research has shown that introducing a new computer tool can be a greater handicap for low-performing individuals than high-performing ones, which risks expanding the existing performance gap (Oviatt, 2013a). When designing an interface that facilitates cognition, one specific aim is to minimize the existing *performance gap* between low- and high-performing users. See Table 4.2 for terms.

Recent studies have shown that interfaces that minimize cognitive load also tend to minimize the performance gap between low- and high-performing groups (Oviatt, 2013a). In addition, interface support for making spatial constructions can assist low performers with solving problems, which can reduce the performance gap. Compared with high performers, studies show that low performers make twice as many elemental marks on problem visuals when preparing to solve a problem—such as circling relevant information. This helps them to organize their understanding of the problem so they can approach solving it (Oviatt and Cohen, 2010a). Pen interfaces, and multimodal ones that incorporate them, support spatial constructions and also reduce cognitive load. As a result, these types of interface can minimize the performance gap between groups more effectively than a keyboard-based interface, while also elevating all students' average performance.

11.2   EXPLANATORY THEORY AND INTERFACE DESIGN PRINCIPLES

One important theme in this research is the critical role of spatial constructions in stimulating human thought. An apt diagram can make information more visually available to think about, especially if it is well matched with a task domain and it makes alternative possibilities visually explicit (Bauer and Johnson-Laird, 1993). Diagrams can facilitate visual comparison, focus attention on relevant information, alleviate the need to manipulate symbolic linguistic content, reduce related cognitive load, and other support for thinking and reasoning about information (Larkin and Simon, 1987). As described by Larkin and Simon:

> *"Diagrams automatically support a large number of perceptual inferences, which are extremely easy for humans"* —Larkin and Simon (1987, p. 98).

An additional key issue is that pen interfaces leave a durable ink trace, which supports memory and reflective reasoning about information (Oviatt, 2013a).

Another important theme is that pen interfaces have affordances that elicit high rates of nonlinguistic content, especially spatial drawing and marking, which is effective at mediating and clarifying thought. From a theoretical perspective, Affordance theory predicts that the physical similarity of pen interfaces with non-digital pens elicits perceptually based expectations of similar communications functionality. This includes broad coverage of all types of representation, but especially nonlinguistic content such as diagramming and marking. In addition, people's main use of computer interfaces is for communications, and they communicate at a higher rate when using a digital tool than a comparable non-digital one (Oviatt et al., 2012; Oviatt, 2013a).

Consistent with Activity theory, the results also confirm that an interface that increases communication of representations well matched with a task can facilitate parallel improvement in thinking and reasoning about its content. This view reflects Vygotskian theory that:

> *Language directly mediates, guides, and refines thought.*

The impact is that language, and representational content more broadly, can stimulate all types of human cognition, including ideational fluency, problem solving, and inferential reasoning. The above factors are at the root of explaining why human thinking and reasoning is so well supported by pen interfaces, as well as multimodal ones that incorporate them.

In summary, more expressively powerful interfaces for conveying multiple representations (e.g., pen, multimodal) can substantially stimulate cognition beyond the level supported by either keyboard interfaces or non-digital tools, which are the most common alternatives in use today. The magnitude of improvement in appropriate idea generation, correct problem solving, and accurate inferential reasoning in different studies has ranged from 9–38%. These results have been generalized widely across different user populations (e.g., ages, ability levels), content domains (e.g., science, math, everyday reasoning), types of cognition, computer hardware, and evaluation metrics. Table 11.1 summarizes fourteen general principles for designing more expressively powerful computer input, which can directly stimulate cognition (excerpted from Oviatt, 2013a).

11.3   FUTURE DIRECTIONS: INTERFACE SUPPORT FOR EXPRESSING WORLD LINGUISTIC CODES

Multilingual interfaces have been the focus of many worldwide research initiatives, especially in regions such as the European Union. Traditionally, work in this area has centered on topics involved with processing of text-based user input, including translation and application development, rather than the more basic issue of designing a computer interface that supports expressing one's native language. Especially on platforms like cell phones, which are primarily used for communications, users could benefit substantially from simply being able to express themselves more fluently in their native language. This section discusses the performance bottleneck that is posed by keyboard input for expressing most world languages, which cannot be resolved using the current approach of Unicode mappings for adapting the keyboard to different world languages. For detailed background on the cognitive and performance limitations of keyboard interfaces and Unicode mappings for supporting world languages, see Oviatt (2013a, Chapter 2).

Perhaps the most consequential direction for developing more expressively powerful computer interfaces involves redesigning them for major world languages that are not Roman *alphabetic* ones. Existing keyboard interfaces currently undermine access to computing for native communicators of these world languages, or approximately 80% of people (Lewis, 2009; Oviatt, 2013a). This includes communicators of Mandarin, Hindi, and other dominant world languages.

Many languages that are not Roman alphabetic ones are complex, spatially intensive (i.e., *diacritics*), and include a large number of linguistic units that require many-to-one mappings with each key on a keyboard interface. For example, Hindi has 600 consonant-vowel (CV) units, 20,000 CCV units, and complex vowel diacritics and ligature systems (Dey et al., 2009). Using a keyboard to directly express an Indic language like Hindi, typically using InScript (InScript, 2014), can require 3–4 keystrokes to enter a single character. It then often requires selecting among five to seven vowel and ligature distinctions from a pop-up window to disambiguate meaning. There also are two to three full keyboard layout levels, which a user must toggle among to locate characters when typing. Figure 11.7 illustrates an input sequence required when typing one sentence. Using such computer input is lengthy, non-intuitive, increases cognitive load and errors, reduces memory for information, and is a barrier to learning and adopting computers at all (Hamzah et al., 2006; Joshi et al., 2004; Oviatt, 2013a). Table 8.3 defines italicized terms.

In the case of Japanese, Figure 11.8 shows that a user must mentally convert native language representations into phonetic and then alphabetic characters before typing them. Homophone lists often are much lengthier than for Indic or Chinese languages, running as long as 20–60 choices. It has been calculated that selecting the intended word from a homophone list can consume up to 70% of total input time when expressing Japanese (Hamzah et al., 2006). In Hamzah and colleagues' empirical work, a within-subject quantitative comparison was conducted of typing vs. handwriting during both transcription and note-taking tasks. When input was handwritten, Japanese users were significantly faster, and made fewer errors and corrections to their input. They also made fewer concept omission errors during note-taking, compared with typing their input. In fact, their handwritten input contained a striking 14-fold fewer errors and corrections than keyboard input (Hamzah et al., 2006).

Figure 11.7: InScript QWERTY keyboard layout for directly typing Devanagari Hindi script on a cell phone. When typing "*The monkey stole the peppers off the balcony,*" a user must disambiguate meaning five times for vowel and ligature distinctions. To enter the first word, she types the keys shown in order. The pop-up window on white squares displays ligature choices that she then must select among as an extra step during typing.

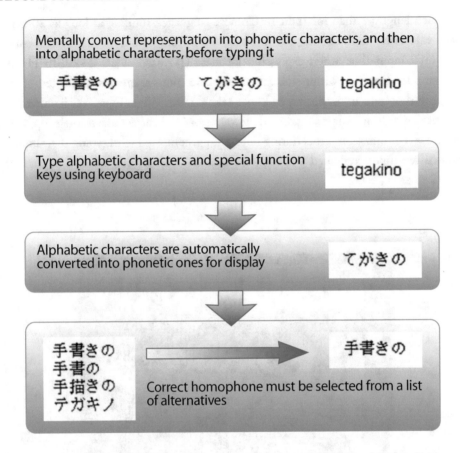

Figure 11.8: Multi-step process of Japanese input using keyboard. From Oviatt (2013a). Copyright© 2013a Routledge Press. Used with permission.

In recent decades, another impact of keyboard input on computers has been rapid *Romanization* of world languages. This major trend has involved shifting from one's native language to a simplified Romanized version when using a computer (e.g., pinyin for Mandarin). Romanization uses the Roman alphabet to approximate pronunciation of the native language, and involves adopting a phonetically and semantically reduced version of it. For example, in India people are increasingly using transliteration software such as Google and Baraha (Baraha, 2014; Google, 2014) to input Romanized Indic languages. Romanization reduces linguistic coverage and precision, which leads to ambiguities when using a computer to express the native language. Often, a reader must reconstruct the intended meaning from context, which causes higher mental load. The increased use of Romanized languages results in skill loss and attrition of worldwide heritage languages, which threatens a corresponding loss of the valuable cultural knowledge they transmit. To date, research is lacking on the cognitive impact of using computer interfaces for expressing transliterated languages.

Due to the major difficulties imposed by keyboard mappings for languages that are not Roman alphabetic ones, the cognitive advantage of using a more expressively powerful computer interface rather than the keyboard would far exceed the 9–38% discussed above in studies with English speakers. New multimodal interfaces could be redesigned to better accommodate expressing these complex and spatially intensive world languages. In addressing this issue, one major task will be to support active content creation modes that are alternatives to the keyboard, such as pen and speech input. Since these input modes already are available on many cell phone platforms, interface redesign could focus on integrating them to optimize fluent and unambiguous language expression for target languages. Section 6.3 describes the type of advanced prototyping methods that will be required to advance solutions on this important topic. For further reading on this topic, see Oviatt (2013a).

Table 11.1: Fourteen principles for designing expessively powerful thinking tools—excerpted from Oviatt (2013a, Chapter 12)
1: Interfaces with different input capabilities prime qualitatively different types of communicative activity; for example, keyboard interfaces stimulate increased linguistic fluency, but pen interfaces prime more nonlinguistic fluency.
2: Interfaces play a major role in mediating, guiding, and refining human cognition, including idea generation, problem solving, and inferential reasoning; the magnitude of impact depends on their ability to stimulate increased communicative or physical activity, and on how well matched they are with a task domain.
3: Computer interfaces have affordances that can elicit more total communicative activity than analogous non-digital tools, in part because their main functionality is perceived to be communications.
4: Interfaces that support more expressively rich communication also stimulate mental effort required to produce ideas more fluently, solve problems more correctly, and make more accurate inferences about information.
5: Interfaces that support more expressively rich communication have greater expressive precision for constructing and manipulating mental representations that are required to mediate accurate thought.
6: Interfaces that support constructing and manipulating spatial representations, and creating permanent images for visual reference, facilitate focusing attention, visual comparison, extracting inferences, and adopting different viewpoints, which aid in productive thinking across domains.

7: Interfaces that support communicative flexibility, including shifting between different representations, modalities, and linguistic codes, facilitate perspective shifting during problem solving; this reorganization of information prevents functional fixedness, stimulates insight, improves the quality of solutions, and increases conceptual change.

8: Interfaces that support communicative flexibility enable self-managing cognitive load; This permits reserving mental resources for solving harder problems, improving the quality of their solutions; it also supports accommodating individual and situational differences in cognitive load.

9: Interfaces associated with higher extraneous cognitive load reduce performance (e.g., keyboard interfaces), as reflected in numerous cognitive and performance metrics, including high-level self-regulation.

10: Interfaces that mimic existing work practice, communication patterns, and non-digital tools (e.g., digital pen and paper) leverage automated skills that conserve users' attention and working memory resources, reducing their cognitive load in a way that improves performance.

11: Interfaces that mimic existing non-digital tools (e.g., digital pen and paper) have affordances that facilitate more rapid adoption than other technologies; they also can elicit higher usage rates than an analogous non-digital tool, especially when digitization adds new functionality.

12: Interface affordances can transparently but powerfully prime novel exploratory behaviors, new learning, and transfer of learning, if they are well matched with a task domain.

13: Interfaces that stimulate high rates of novel or exploratory activity, whether through physical manipulation or communication and social interchange, will stimulate the highest rates of learning—as evident behaviorally and in activity-dependent neural change.

14: Interfaces that contextualize learning in relevant physical and social contexts (e.g., conversational interfaces), and especially mobile ones that support variability in these contexts, will stimulate higher levels of exploratory learning and transfer of learning.

CHAPTER 12

Conclusions and Future Directions

Multimodal interfaces have eclipsed keyboard-based interfaces as the dominant computer interface worldwide, driven largely by expansion of mobile devices in developing regions. Within the next five years, the number of smart phones with mobile broadband is expected to increase from two to six billion, which will be accompanied by a dramatic expansion of related applications. This major trend will continue to drive the development of new multimodal-multisensor interfaces and their commercialization. As discussed in Chapter 10, this expansion will include a variety of new field and mobile applications involving wearables, virtual assistants, social robotics, in-vehicle interfaces, education, entertainment, and many other areas. It also will include ones in which smart phones become the preferred platform for monitoring and controlling distant physical objects via the Internet. The trend toward cell phone integration with other devices and systems (e.g., watches, wristbands for fitness tracking, in-vehicle control of car systems) will become another major factor driving the development of multimodal interfaces.

At the same time, multimodal interfaces will directly support the multi-functionality of mobile devices and their applications, as originally predicted by Oviatt and Cohen (2000, p. 52):

> *"In the area of mobile computing, multimodal interfaces will promote... the multi-functionality of small devices, in part due to the portability and expressive power of input modes."*

As a particular interface becomes more multi-functional and complex, a single modality simply cannot support users effectively across all tasks and usage situations. Consequently, multimodal interfaces will further enlarge and accelerate market expansion of mobile devices, such that multimodality and mobility co-evolve. During this process, mobile devices can be expected to transform both the human interface and the overall technology industry.

As discussed throughout this book, multimodal interfaces are a major building block in the movement to establish more expressively powerful computer interfaces. Such interfaces support people's ability to communicate fluently using multiple modalities, representations, and linguistic codes, which can substantially stimulate human cognition and performance. Since cell phone penetration currently is lowest in developing regions, the primary future factors driving multimodal interface development will not only be mobility and support for multi-functional devices, but also the need to accommodate majority world languages around the globe. As pressure intensifies to satisfy this objective, global design teams will need to develop multimodal interfaces for expressing majority world languages that are not Roman alphabetic ones, which represent 80% of communicators worldwide.

Recent tangible and ubiquitous multimodal interfaces are beginning to epitomize Weiser's vision of interfaces that "disappear" into everyday familiar objects in our environment. These new interfaces are hybrids that support more natural multimodal interaction with physicalized computer systems, often wearable ones that are instantiated in familiar real-world objects like watches, wrist bands, pens, paper, books, tables, and whiteboards. The advantage of these interfaces is their transparency to users and ability to leverage existing activity patterns, which minimizes users' cognitive load. Interface tools with these properties are easy to learn, and they support high levels of performance. One long-term interface design direction will be to combine emerging tangible interfaces that support multimodal input with ones that simultaneously sense users' affect, cognitive load, health status, learning progress, and similar information in order to adapt system responding to users' status.

In addition to the proliferation of tangible and wearable multimodal interfaces, new multimodal-multisensor interfaces on smart phones and other mobile devices are being developed to monitor and control distant physical objects via the Internet. The ecosystem of related applications includes personal health monitoring and medical care, environmental monitoring and energy management, traffic monitoring and transportation planning, control of home appliances and entertainment, and other areas. Applications related to the Internet of Things are expected to increase rapidly during the next five years. They represent further expansion of field and mobile usage patterns. They also involve heavier use of sensors and passive user input, which does not require explicit input from a user. The development of multimodal-multisensor interfaces that rely too heavily on passive triggers, without adequate human control via active input modes, is potentially hazardous for a variety of reasons. Among the main concerns are privacy, security, and unintended system consequences due to sensor false alarms. It is essential that new multimodal-multisensor interfaces be designed to support transparent functioning and adequate human oversight of the target system. One key prerequisite for achieving these aims is inclusion of active content creation modes in the user interface.

One major challenge for the design of future multimodal systems, especially ones that leverage large volumes of public and private data (e.g., multimodal learning analytics, medical records, airport surveillance, speech to in-home appliances exported for recognition), is assurance that the privacy, dignity, and rights of participating users will be protected. As systems become more richly multimodal and usage patterns more mobile, there is risk of violations that could be deeply intrusive and damaging to individuals. In fact, there already is copious evidence that both corporate and government entities are developing computational systems for their own financial and political gain, while ignoring and rationalizing serious erosion in individual's privacy rights (Lewis, 2014). It therefore is imperative that technology designers, citizen groups, and other stakeholders engage in participatory design of new multimodal systems to ensure that technology policy protects society's privacy, educational opportunities, employment, insurability, and other basic human rights.

One delightful impact of the rapidly expanding commercialization of multimodal interfaces on cell phones has been support for more accessible interfaces and applications. We finally are beginning to realize more powerful multimodal mobile interfaces that can improve the lives of users who are disabled by helping them to navigate, communicate, and perform routine activities while leading active lives in their community. Cell phones offer more durable commercial platforms for consolidating multiple accessibility applications, which are beginning to replace expensive special purpose devices. People who live long enough all will experience some type of disability. The demographics of aging populations worldwide make it imperative that we design an extensive collection of self-care technologies. Effective design for universal access and globalization will require adopting end-user participatory methodologies that include disabled and culturally diverse team members, which goes beyond simply including them as test subjects. This type of advanced interface design will require developing new curricula for computer and information science graduate schools.

In the next decade, multimodal interfaces will enable virtual assistants and social robots to assist people in homes, schools, hospitals, nursing homes, and many other settings. This will include assistance to frail elderly, disabled, and ill individuals. It therefore will be imperative for assistant systems to recognize nonverbal and verbal cues to people's cognitive and social-emotional status, so that cooperative interaction and the intended assistance can ensue. To achieve this, assistant systems will need to analyze human language, posture, gaze, prosody, and facial expressions in the context of ongoing interactions and dialogue. They also will need to recognize and facilitate multi-person interactions involving family members, hospital staff, and others. These collaborative and assistive behaviors will require some degree of intent recognition for individuals and groups, at least in given application contexts (Cohen and Levesque, 1991; Grosz and Sidner, 1990). Perhaps most importantly, assistive systems will need to successfully gain trust so they can engage in sometimes intimate joint actions with humans, such as carrying and toileting them, preventing falls, and so forth.

Commercialized multimodal interfaces already incorporate many input options such as speech, touch and multi-touch, gestures, stylus, sensors, and virtual keyboards. A major challenge in the future will be to strategize more advanced multimodal interfaces that can fuse these information sources in novel ways to achieve improved system reliability and usability. The development of multimodal-multisensor fusion strategies currently remains underexploited, although it is expected to yield considerable advantages for new commercial products. In addition to designing more advanced level 4–6 fusion-based multimodal systems, as shown in Figure 1.1, future interfaces will begin fusing multiple content creation and passively tracked modes that extend capabilities beyond level 6. In particular, passively tracked information, such as facial expressions and voice quality, will add valuable information that is needed for some applications to understand a person's attitude, emotional status, energy level, current health, and other information.

With respect to achieving a new level of robustness or hybrid vigor, future multimodal systems will depend critically on the availability of large multimodal databases, because they are fundamentally data-intensive systems. Like multi-biometric systems, they will gradually expand beyond bimodal fusion to incorporate a larger number of information sources, and also more heterogeneous and semantically rich ones. Future multimodal systems could benefit considerably from greater incorporation of machine learning and especially deep neural net learning techniques, as well as from the development of new multi-level, flexibly modular, hybrid architectures for processing and fusing information. Advances in all of these areas could substantially improve multimodal systems' ability to accurately interpret users' language, actions, and intentions in a wide array of different situations.

In designing future architectures for multimodal interfaces, important insights clearly can be gained from biological and cognitive principles of sensory integration, multisensory perception, and their adaptivity during purposeful activity. One challenge will be to translate recent findings from multisensory perception and neuroscience into guidelines for developing well integrated multimodal interfaces. This will require a clearer theory-based understanding of the conditions under which super-additivity effects can be expected, rather than interference between modalities. It also will require understanding how to design adaptive multimodal interfaces to handle large individual differences in both multisensory perception and multimodal communication. Adaptive multimodal-multisensor interfaces that incorporate a broad range of information have the potential to achieve improved robustness, and to support entirely new functionality. They also have the potential to perform flexibly as multi-functional and personalized mobile interfaces. As they evolve, adaptive multimodal interfaces will become capable of relatively human-like sensory-perceptual capabilities. This is likely to include predicting user needs, performing self-diagnostic functions, actively recruiting information from different sources when needed to interpret user activities, and many other future directions.

Bibliography

Abouelenien, M., Pérez-Rosas, V., Mihalcea, R., and Burzo, M. (2014) Deception detection using a multimodal approach. *Proceedings of the 16th International Conference on Multimodal Interaction*, New York:ACM Press, 58–65. DOI: 10.1145/2663204.2663229. 100

Abry, C., Lallouache, M. T., and Cathiard, M. A. (1996) How can coarticulation models account for speech sensitivity to audio-visual desynchronization? In Stork, D.G. and Hennecke, M.E. (eds.), *Speechreading by Humans and Machines: Models, Systems and Applications*, New York: Springer Verlag, 247–255. DOI: 10.1007/978-3-662-13015-5_19. 39

Accumine Ltd. (2015) HaulCheck. http://www.acumine.com/_Products/HaulCheck.php. 111

Adacel (2006) http://www.adacel.com/press/innews/8_25_06_Benefits_Speech_Recognition_Enabled_Cockpit.pdf, accessed 3/31/2015. 108

Adapx Inc. (2015) http://www.adapx.com, (retrieved 2/13/2015). 124

Adjoudani, A. and Benoit, C. (1995) Audio-visual speech recognition compared across two architectures. *Proceedings of the Eurospeech Conference*, Vol. 2, Madrid, Spain,1563–1566. 10, 21

Aldebaran Robotics (2015a) Nao Robot. https://www.aldebaran.com/en/humanoid-robot/nao-robot, retrieved (2/11/2015). 154

Aldebaran Robotics (2015b) Pepper Robot. https://www.aldebaran.com/en/a-robots/who-is-pepper, retrieved (2/11/2015). 154

Aldebaran Robotics (2015c) Project Romeo. http://projetromeo.com/, (retrieved 2/11/2015). 154

Alibali, M., Kita, S., and Young, A. (2000) Gesture and the process of speech production: We think, therefore we gesture. *Language and Cognitive Processing*, 15:593–613. DOI: 10.1080/016909600750040571. 23

Allen, J. F. (1983) Maintaining knowledge about temporal intervals. *Communications of the ACM*, 26(11): 832–843. DOI: 10.1145/182.358434. 95

Allwood, J., Dhakhwa, S., Regmi, B., and Shrestha, P. (2011) Multimodal corpus using multimodal dictionary in Lohorung. *Proceedings of the International Conference on Speech Database and Assessments*, Hsinchu Taiwan, October, 2011, 109–114. 56

Almor, A., (1999) Noun-phrase anaphora and focus: The informational load hypothesis. *Psychological Review*, 106:748–765. DOI: 10.1037/0033-295X.106.4.748. 84

Alonso-Martín, F., Malfaz, M. Sequeira, J., Gorostiza, J. F., and Salichs, M. A. (2013) A multimodal emotion detection system during human–robot interaction. *Sensors* 13:15549–15581. DOI: 10.3390/s131115549. 155

Alpaydin, E. (2010) *Introduction to Machine Learning*. Second Edition, Cambridge, MA:MIT Press. 69

Anastasio, T. and Patton, P. (2004) Analysis and modeling of multisensory enhancement in the deep superior colliculus. *The Handbook of Multisensory Processing*, Calvert, G., Spence, C., and Stein, B. (eds.), Cambridge, MA:MIT Press, 265–283. 30

Anderson, M. and Green, C. (2001) Suppressing unwanted memories by executive control. *Nature*, l. 410, 366-369. DOI: 10.1038/35066572. 47

Anoto (2009) from http://www.anoto.com, Retrieved May 1, 2009. 124

Apple Computer (2015c) Car Play. https://www.apple.com/ios/carplay/ (retrieved 2/12/2015). 109

Apple Siri (2015a) https://www.apple.com/ios/siri/ (retrieved February 18, 2015). 14, 131

Apple (2011) http://www.apple.com/ipad/ (retrieved March 2, 2011). 124

Apple (2014) http://support.apple.com/kb/HT4992 (retrieved July 31, 2014). 14

Apple Watch (2015b) http://www.apple.com/watch/overview/ (retrieved January 26, 2015). 142

Arbib, M. (2003) The evolving mirror system: A neural basis for language readiness. *Language Evolution*, ed. by M. Christiansen and S. Kirby, Oxford, UK: Oxford University Press, 182–200. DOI: 10.1093/acprof:oso/9780199244843.003.0010. 27

Argyle, M. (1972) Nonverbal communication in human social interaction. Hinde, R. (ed.), *Nonverbal Communication*, Cambridge, UK: Cambridge University Press, 243–267. 39

Arthur, A., Lunsford, R., Wesson, M., and Oviatt, S.L. (2006) Prototyping novel collaborative multimodal systems: Simulation, data collection and analysis tools for the next decade. *Proceedings of the 8th ACM International Conference on Multimodal Interfaces (ICMI'06)*, New York:ACM, 209–226. DOI: 10.1145/1180995.1181039. 55

Atrey, P. K., Hossain, M. A., Saddik, A. E., and Kankanhalli, M. S. (2010) Multimodal fusion for multimedia analysis: a survey. *Multimedia Systems*, 16: 345–379. DOI: 10.1007/s00530-010-0182-0. 63

Azenkot, S., Wobbrock, J., Prasain, S., and Ladner, R. (2012) Input finger detection for nonvisual touch screen text entry in Perkinput. *Proceedings of Graphics Interface 2012 (GI '12), Canadian Information Processing Society*, Toronto, Canada, 121–129. 150

Baddeley, A., (1986) *Working Memory*. New York: Oxford University Press. 48, 49

Baddeley, A., (1992) Working memory. *Science*, 255:556–559. DOI: 10.1126/science.1736359. 23

Baddeley, A. (2003) Working memory: Looking back and looking forward. *Nature Reviews*, 4: 829–839. DOI: 10.1038/nrn1201. 23, 48

Baddeley, A. D. and Hitch, G. J. (1974) Working memory. In *The Psychology of Learning and Motivation: Advances in Research and Theory*, Vol. 8, Bower, G. A. (ed.), New York:Academic Press, 47–89. DOI: 10.1016/S0079-7421(08)60452-1. 47

Baker, R. and Yacef, K. (2009) The state of educational data mining in 2009: A review and future visions. *Journal of Educational Data Mining* (JEDM), 1:3–17. 145

Bangalore, S. and Johnston, M. (2000) Integrating multimodal language processing with speech recognition. In B. Yuan, T. Huang and X. Tang (Eds.). *Proceedings of the International Conference on Spoken Language Processing (ICSLP'2000)*, Vol. 2, Beijing: Chinese Friendship Publishers, 126–129.

Bangalore, S. and Johnston, M. (2009) Robust understanding in multimodal interfaces. *Computational Linguistics*, 35(3):345–397. DOI: 10.1162/coli.08-022-R2-06-26. 13, 14

Baraha (2014) http://www.baraha.com. (retrieved January 18, 2014). 166

Barnett, J., Akolkar, R., Auburn, R.J., Bodel, M., Burnett, D.C., Carter, J., McGlashan, S., Lager, T., Helbing, M., Hosn, R., Raman, T.V., Reifenrath, K., and Rosenthal, N. (2012) *State Chart XML (SCXML): State Machine Notation for Control Abstraction*. World Wide Web Consortium. 96

Barr, L., Howarth, H., Popkin, S., and Carroll, R. J. (2003) *A Review and Evaluation of Emerging Driver Fatigue Detection Measures and Technologies*. Volpe Center, U.S. Department of Transportation. 111

Battocchi A., Ben-Sasson A., Esposito G., Gal E. Pianesi F., Tomasini D., Venuti P., Weiss P. L., and Zancanaro M. (2010) Collaborative puzzle game: A tabletop interface for fostering collaborative skills in children with autism spectrum disorders. *Journal of Assistive Technologies*, 4(1):4:14. DOI: 10.5042/jat.2010.0040. 140

Bauer, M. and Johnson-Laird, P. (1993) How diagrams can improve reasoning. *Psychological Science*, 4(6):372-378. DOI: 10.1111/j.1467-9280.1993.tb00584.x. 163

Beaudouin-Lafon, M. and Mackay, W. (2012) Prototyping tools and techniques. *The Human-Computer Interaction Handbook: Fundamentals, Evolving Technologies and Emerging Applications* (revised 3rd edition), Jacko, J. (ed.), Boca Raton, FL:CRC Press, 1081–1102. DOI: 10.1201/b11963-55. 53

Benoit, C. (2000) The intrinsic bimodality of speech communication and the synthesis of talking faces. In Taylor, M. Neel, F. and Bouwhuis, D., (eds.), *The Structure of Multimodal Dialogue II*. Amsterdam: John Benjamins, 485–502. DOI: 10.1075/z.99.32ben. 39

Benoit, C., Guiard-Marigny, T., Le Goff, B., and Adjoudani, A. (1996) Which components of the face do humans and machines best speechread? In Stork, D.G. and Hennecke, M.E., (eds.), *Speechreading by Humans and Machines: Models, Systems, and Applications: Vol. 150 of NATO ASI Series. Series F: Computer and Systems Sciences*, Berlin: Springler-Verlag, 315–325. DOI: 10.1007/978-3-662-13015-5_24. 34

Benoit, C. and Le Goff, B. (1998) Audio-visual speech synthesis from French text: Eight years of models, designs and evaluation at the ICP. *Speech Communication*, 26, 117–129. DOI: 10.1016/S0167-6393(98)00045-4. 8, 10

Benoit, C., Martin, J.-C., Pelachaud, C., Schomaker, L., and Suhm, B. (2000) Audio-visual and multimodal speech-based systems. *Handbook of Multimodal and Spoken Dialogue Systems: Resources, Terminology and Product Evaluation*, Gibbon, D. Mertins, I. and Moore, R. (eds.), Dordrecht:Kluwer, 102–203. DOI: 10.1007/978-1-4615-4501-9_2. 8, 9, 10

Berk, L. E. (1994) Why children talk to themselves. *Scientific American*, 271(5):78–83. DOI: 10.1038/scientificamerican1194-78. 50

Bernstein, L. and Benoit, C. (1996) For speech perception by humans or machines, three senses are better than one. *Proceedings of the International Conference on Spoken Language Processing, (ICSLP 96)* Vol. 3, New York: IEEE Press, 1477–1480. DOI: 10.1109/ICSLP.1996.607895. 10, 30

Bers, J., Miller, S., and Makhoul, J. (1998) Designing conversational interfaces with multimodal interaction. *DARPA Workshop on Broadcast News Understanding Systems*, 319–321. 10

Bertelson, P. and deGelder, B. (2004) The psychology of multimodal perception. In *Crossmodal Space and Crossmodal Attention*, Spence, C. and Driver, J., (eds.) Oxford, UK:Oxford University Press, 141–177. DOI: 10.1093/acprof:oso/9780198524861.003.0007. 29, 30, 33

Bertolami, R. and Bunke, H. (2006) Early feature stream integration versus decision level combination in a multiple classifier system for text line recognition. *IEEE International Conference on Pattern Recognition*, 845–848. DOI: 10.1109/ICPR.2006.466. 66, 70

Bickmore, T. and Picard, R. (2005) Establishing and maintaining long-term human-computer relationships. *ACM Transactions on Computer Human Interaction* (ToCHI), 59(1): 21–30. DOI: 10.1145/1067860.1067867. 151

Black, J., Isaacs, K., Anderson, B., Alcantara, A., and Greenough, W. (1990) Learning causes synaptogenesis, whereas motor activity causes angiogenesis in cerebellar cortex of adult rats. *Proceedings of the National Academy of Sciences*, 87:5568–72. DOI: 10.1073/pnas.87.14.5568. 52

Block, F., Haller, M., Gellersen, H., Gutwin, C., and Billinghurst, M. (2008) VoodooSketch: Extending interactive surfaces with adaptable interface palettes. *Proceedings of the 2nd International Conference on Tangible and Embedded Interaction*, New York:ACM Press, 55–58. DOI: 10.1145/1347390.1347404. 140

Boagey, R. (2014) Multi-Modal HMI: The future of in-car interaction. *Automotive World*, October, 2014. 109

Boersma, P. and Weenink, D. (2015) Praat: doing phonetics by computer [Computer program]. Version 5.4.08, retrieved 24 March 2015 from http://www.praat.org/. 57

Bohus, D. and Horvitz, E. (2014) Managing human-robot engagement with forecasts and... um... hesitations. *Proceedings of 16th International Conference on Multimodal Interaction*, Istanbul, Turkey, New York:ACM Press, 2–9. DOI: 10.1145/2663204.2663241. 151, 154, 155

Bohus, D. and Horvitz, E. (2009) Dialog in the open world: Platform and applications. *Proceedings of the 11th International Conference on Multimodal Interfaces—Machine Learning for Multimodal Interaction*, Cambridge, MA, New York:ACM Press, 31–38. DOI: 10.1145/1647314.1647323. 151, 152

Bohus, D., Saw, C.W., and Horvitz, E. (2014) Directions robot: In-the-wild experiences and lessons learned. *Proceedings of the 13th International Conference on Autonomous Agents and Multiagent Systems (AAMAS 2014)*, Paris, New York:ACM Press, 637–644. 133

Bolt, R. A. (1980) Put-that-there: Voice and gesture at the graphics interface. *Computer Graphics*, 14 (3):262–270. DOI: 10.1145/965105.807503. 7, 8

Bowers, C. A., Vasquez, M., and Roaf, M. (2000) Native people and the challenge of computers: Reservation schools, individualism, and consumerism. *American Indian Quarterly*, Spring 2000, 24(2):182–199. 61

Brachman, R. J. and Schmolze, J. (1985) An overview of the KL-ONE knowledge representation system, *Cognitive Science*, 9(2):171-216. DOI: 10.1016/S0364-0213(85)80014-8. 104

Brand, M., Oliver, N., and Pentland, A. (1997) Coupled hidden Markov models for complex action recognition. *Proceedings of Computer Vision and Pattern Recognition*, San Juan, Puerto Rico, 994–999. DOI: 10.1109/CVPR.1997.609450. 72

Brandl, P., Forlines, C., Wigdor, D., Haller, M., and Shen, C. (2008) Combining and measuring the benefits of bimanual pen and direct-touch interaction on horizontal surfaces. *Conference on Advanced Visual Interfaces*, 154–161. DOI: 10.1145/1385569.1385595. 140

Breazeal, C. (2002) *Designing Sociable Robots.* Cambridge, MA:MIT Press.

Breazeal, C. (2015) Personal communication. http://www.jibo.com, (retrieved 2/11/2015). 155, 156

Bregler, C. and Konig, Y. (1994) Eigenlips for robust speech recognition. *Proceedings of the International Conference on Acoustics Speech and Signal Processing (IEEE-ICASSP)* Vol. 2, New York:IEEE Press, 669–672. DOI: 10.1109/ICASSP.1994.389567. 10

Bregman, A. S. (1990) *Auditory Scene Analysis.* Cambridge MA:MIT Press,. 41

Brooke, N. M. and Petajan, E. D. (1986) Seeing speech: Investigations into the synthesis and recognition of visible speech movements using automatic image processing and computer graphics. *Proceedings International Conference Speech Input and Output: Techniques and Applications,* 258:104–109. 7, 10

Burgoon, J., Stern, L., and Dillman, L. (1995) *Interpersonal Adaptation: Dyadic Interaction Patterns.* Cambridge, UK: Cambridge Univ. Press. DOI: 10.1017/CBO9780511720314. 46

Busso, C., Deng, Z., Yildirim, S., Bulut, M., Lee, C. M., Kazemzadeh, A., Lee, S., Neumann, U., and Narayanan, S. (2004) Analysis of emotion recognition using facial expressions, speech and multimodal information. *Proceedings of the 6th ACM International Conference on Multimodal Interfaces,* State College, Pennsylvania, New York:ACM Press, 205–211. DOI: 10.1145/1027933.1027968. 66

Calvert, G., C. Spence, and B.E. Stein, (eds.) (2004) *The Handbook of Multisensory Processing,* Cambridge. MA.:MIT Press. 8, 23, 28, 30, 41

Calvo, R. and D'Mello, S. (2010) Affect detection: An interdisciplinary review of models, methods and their applications. *IEEE Transactions on Affective Computing,* 1(1):18–37. DOI: 10.1109/T-AFFC.2010.1. 143, 140

Card, S., English, W.K., and Burr, B. (1978) Evaluation of mouse, rate-controlled isometric joystick, step keys, and text keys for text selection on a CRT. *Ergonomics,* 21: 601–613. DOI: 10.1080/00140137808931762. 7

Carpenter, R. (2005) *The Logic of Typed Feature Structures with Applications to Unification Grammars, Logic Programs and Constraint Resolution.* Cambridge, UK:Cambridge University Press. DOI: 10.1017/CBO9780511530098. 90

Cassell, J., Sullivan, J., Prevost, S., and Churchill, E. (eds.) (2000) *Embodied Conversational Agents, Cambridge.* MA:MIT Press. 7, 10

Castronovo, A. Mahr, A., Pentcheva, M., and Müller , C. (2010) Multimodal dialog in the car: Combining speech and turn-and-push dial to control comfort functions. *Proceedings of*

Interspeech 2010, Makuhari, Japan, International Speech Communications Association, 510–513. 108

Caterpillar (2008) *Operator Fatigue Detection Technology Review.* https://safety.cat.com/cda/files/771871/7/fatigue_report_021108.pdf, (retrieved 3/3/2015). 111

Chen, C. (ed.) (2015) IEEE Transactions on Multimedia. *IEEE Society journal*, http://ieeexplore.ieee.org/xpl/RecentIssue.jsp?punumber=6046, (retrieved Jan. 12, 2015). 1

Chen, L. and Harper, M. (2009) Multimodal floor control shift detection. *Proceedings of the 7th ACM International Conference on Multimodal Interfaces*, New York :ACM, 15–22. DOI: 10.1145/1647314.1647320. 12

Cheyer, A. (1998) MVIEWS: Multimodal tools for the video analyst. *Proceedings of the 3rd International Conference on Intelligent User Interfaces (IUI'98)*, New York: ACM Press, 55–62. DOI: 10.1145/268389.268399. 10

Choudhury, T., Clarkson, B., Jebara, T., and Pentland, S. (1999) Multimodal person recognition using unconstrained audio and video. *Proceedings of the 2nd International Conference on Audio-and-Video-based Biometric Person Authentication*, Washington, DC. , 176–181. 11

Cohen, M. M. and Massaro, D. W. (1993) Modeling coarticulation in synthetic visual speech. In Magnenat-Thalmann , M. and Thalmann, D., (eds.), *Models and Techniques in Computer Animation.* Tokyo: Springer-Verlag, 139–156. DOI: 10.1007/978-4-431-66911-1_13. 7, 10

Cohen, P. R., Cheyer, A., Wang, M., and Baeg, S. C. (1994), An open agent architecture. *Proceedings of the AAAI Spring Symposium Series, AAAI Technical Report SS-94-03*, Menlo Park:Association for the Advancement of Artificial Intelligence, 1–8. 129, 131

Cohen, P. R., Coulston, R., and Krout, K. (2002) Multimodal interaction during multiparty dialogues: Initial results. *Proceedings of the 4th International Conference on Multimodal Interfaces*, New York:IEEE Press, 448–453. DOI: 10.1109/ICMI.2002.1167037. 97

Cohen, P. R., Dalrymple, M., Moran, D. B., Pereira, F. C. N., Sullivan, J. W., Gargan, R. A., Schlossberg, J. L., and Tyler, S. W. (1989) Synergistic use of direct manipulation and natural language. *Proceedings of the Conference on Human Factors in Computing Systems (CHI'89)*, New York: ACM Press, 227-234. (Reprinted in Maybury and Wahlster (eds.), (1998) *Readings in Intelligent User Interfaces*, San Francisco: Morgan Kaufmann, 29–37.) DOI: 10.1145/67449.67494. 9, 40, 83, 101

Cohen, P. R., Johnston, M., McGee, D., Oviatt, S., Pittman, J., Smith, I., Chen, L., and Clow, J. (1997) Quickset: Multimodal interaction for distributed applications. *Proceedings of the*

5th ACM International Multimedia Conference, New York: ACM Press, 31–40. DOI: 10.1145/266180.266328. 8, 10, 114

Cohen, P. R., Kaiser, E., Buchanan, C., Lind, S., Corrigan, M., and Wesson, M. (2015) Sketch-Thru-Plan: A multimodal interface for command-and-control. *Communications of the ACM*, 58(4), 56–65. 20, 112, 114

Cohen, P. R. and Levesque, H. J. (1991) Teamwork, *Noûs* 25(4), Special issue on cognitive science and artificial intelligence, 87–512. Reprinted in: Knowing, Reasoning, and Acting: Essays in honor of Hector J. Levesque, G. Lakemeyer, and S. McIlraith (eds.), Tributes Series, Vol. 16, College Publications, London, UK, 2011, 137–156. 171

Cohen, P. R. and McGee, D. (2004) Tangible multimodal interfaces for safety-critical applications. *Communications of the ACM*, Jan. 2004, 47(1):41–46. DOI: 10.1145/962081.962103. 8, 112, 113, 139

Cohen, P. R., McGee, D. R., and Clow, J. (2000) The efficiency of multimodal interaction for a map-based task. *Proceedings of the Language Technology Joint Conference (ANLP-NAACL 2000)*, Stroudsburg, PA:Association for Computational Linguistics Press, 331–338. DOI: 10.3115/974147.974193. 20

Cohen, P. R. and Oviatt, S. L. (1995) The role of voice input for human-machine communication. *Proceedings of the National Academy of Sciences*, 92(22), Washington, D. C.:National Academy of Sciences Press, 9921–9927. DOI: 10.1073/pnas.92.22.9921. 18, 127

Cohen, P. R., Swindells, C., Oviatt, S., and Arthur, A. (2008) A high-performance dual-wizard infrastructure supporting speech and digital pen input. *Proceedings of the 10th ACM International Conference on Multimodal Interfaces (ICMI'08)*, ACM: New York, 137–140. DOI: 10.1145/1452392.1452419. 55

Comblain, A. (1994) Working memory in Down's Syndrome: Training the rehearsal strategy. *Down's Syndrome: Research and Practice*, 2(3):123–126. DOI: 10.3104/reports.42. 51

Condon, W. S. (1988) An analysis of behavioral organization. *Sign Language Studies*, 58:55–88. DOI: 10.1353/sls.1988.0007. 11

Copestake, A. (2000) Appendix: Definitions of typed feature structures. *Natural Language Engineering*, 6(1):109–112. 90, 105

Corballis, M. (2002) *From Hand to Mouth: The Origins of Language*. Princeton, NJ:Princeton University Press. 27, 28

Corballis, M. (2003) From hand to mouth: The gestural origins of language. *Language Evolution*, Christiansen, M. and Kirby, S. (eds.), Oxford, UK: Oxford University Press, 201–218. DOI: 10.1093/acprof:oso/9780199244843.003.0011. 27, 28

Coutaz J., Nigay L., and Salber D. (1995) Agent-based architecture modelling for interactive systems. *Critical Issues in User Interface Engineering*, Palanque, P. and Benyon, D. (eds.), Heidelberg:Springer-Verlag, 191–209. DOI: 10.1007/978-3-642-02574-7_70. 129

D'Esposito, M. (2008) Working memory, the dysexecutive syndrome. *Handbook of Clinical Neurology*, Vol. 88, Ch. 11, Goldenberg, G. and Miller, B. (eds.), Amsterdam: Elsevier B.V., 237–248. 49

Daffner, K. and Searl, M. (2008) The dysexecutive syndrome. *Handbook of Clinical Neurology*, Vol. 88, Ch. 12, Goldenberg, G. and Miller, B. (eds.), Amsterdam: Elsevier B.V., 249–267. 49

Dahl, D. A. (2013) The W3C multimodal architecture and interfaces standard. *Journal on Multimodal Interfaces* 7(3):171–182. DOI: 10.1007/s12193-013-0120-5. 129, 130, 133

Dahl, G., Yu, D., Deng, L., and Acero, A. (2012) Context-dependent pre-trained deep neural networks for large-vocabulary speech recognition. *IEEE Transactions on Audio, Speech, and Language Processing*, 20(1): 30–42. DOI: 10.1109/TASL.2011.2134090. 67

Dahlbäck, N., Jëonsson, A., and Ahrenberg, L., (1992) Wizard of Oz studies—why and how. In Gray, W. D., Hefley, W. E. and Murray D., (eds.). *Proceedings of the 1st International Conference on Intelligent User Interfaces*, New York: ACM Press, 193–200. DOI: 10.1145/169891.169968. 53, 54

Daimler Benz (2015) *Attention Assist*. http://www.daimler.com/technology-and-innovation/safety-technologies/prevention, (retrieved 2/12/2015). 111

Dalal, N. and Triggs, B. (2005) Histograms of oriented gradients for human detection. *Proceedings of IEEE Computer Society Conference on Computer Vision and Pattern Recognition (CVPR'05)*, 1, 886–893. DOI: 10.1109/CVPR.2005.177. 75

Dalal, N., Triggs, B., and Schmid, B. (2006) Human detection using oriented histograms of flow and appearance. *Proceedings of European Conference on Computer Vision* (ECCV'06), Part II, Lecture Notes in Computer Science, Leonardis, A., Bischof, H. and Pinz, A. (eds.), Heidelberg:Springer Verlag, 428–441. DOI: 10.1007/11744047_33. 75

Darves, C. and Oviatt, S. (2004) Talking to digital fish: Designing effective conversational interfaces for educational software. In *Evaluating Embodied Conversational Agents*, Ruttkay, Z. and Pelachaud, C., (eds.), Dordrecht :Kluwer, 7:271–292. 36

Darwin, C. (1896) *The Descent of Man and Selection in Relation to Sex*. New York: D. Appleton and Company. 27

Davis, K., Biddulph, R., and Balashek, S. (1952) Automatic recognition of spoken digits. *Journal of the Acoustical Society of America*, 24(6):627–642. DOI: 10.1121/1.1906946. 7

Davis, S. and Mermelstein, P. (1980) Comparison of parametric representations for monosyllabic word recognition in continuously spoken sentences. *IEEE Transactions on Acoustics, Speech and Signal Processing*, 28(4):357–366. DOI: 10.1109/TASSP.1980.1163420. 67

Dawson, P. (2010) Networked interactive whiteboards: rationale, affordances and new pedagogies for regional Australian higher education. *Australasian Journal of Educational Technology*, 26(4):523–533. 123

DeGusta, M. (2012) Are smart phones spreading faster than any technology in human history? *MIT Technology Review*, May 9, 2012. 12

Denecke, M. and Yang, J., (2000) Partial information in multimodal dialogue. *Advances in Multimodal Interfaces—Third International Conference, Lecture Notes in Computer Science (Book 1948)*, Beijing, China, Berlin:Springer-Verlag, 624–633. DOI: 10.1007/3-540-40063-X_81. 11

Deng, L., Seltzer, M. Yu, D. Acero, A. Mohamed, A., and Hinton, G. (2010) Binary coding of speech spectrograms using a deep auto-encoder. *Proceedings of Interspeech*, Chiba, Japan, International Speech Communications Association, 1692–1695.

Denso Corporation (2015) https://www.behance.net/gallery/13504771/Gesture-Motion-In-Dash-Car-Music-Player, (retrieved 2/12/2015). 109

DeVault, D., Artstein, R., Benn, G., Dey T., Fast, E., Gainer, A., Georgila, K., Gratch, J., Hartholt, A., Lhommet, M., Lucas, G., Marsella, S., Morbini, F., Nazarian, A., Scherer, S., Stratou, G., Suri, A., Traum, D., Wood, R., Xu, Y., Rizzo, A., and Morency, L-P. (2014) SimSensei kiosk: A virtual human interviewer for healthcare decision support. *Proceedings of the 13th International Conference on Autonomous Agents and Multiagent Systems (AAMAS 2014)*, Paris, New York: ACM Press, 1061–1068. 127, 151, 153

Dey, P., Sitaram, R., Ajmera, R., and Bali, K. (2009) Voice keyboard: Multimodal Indic text input. *Proceedings of the 11th International ACM Conference on Multimodal Interfaces*, New York:ACM Press, 313–318. DOI: 10.1145/1647314.1647380. 164

Dimond, T. (1957) Devices for reading handwritten characters. *Proceedings of Eastern Joint Computer Conference: Computers with deadlines to meet, IRE-ACM-AIEE '57*, 232–237. 7

Dixon, N. F. and Spitz, L. (1980) The detection of auditory visual desynchrony. *Perception*, 9:719–721. DOI: 10.1068/p090719. 29

Dong, Y., Hu, Z., Uchimura, K., and Murayama, N. (2011) Driver inattention monitoring system for intelligent vehicles: A review. *IEEE Transactions On Intelligent Transportation Systems* 12(2):596–614. DOI: 10.1109/TITS.2010.2092770. 111

Draganski, B., Christian, G., Kempermann, G., Kuhn, G., Winkler, J., Büchel, C., and May, A. (2006) Temporal and spatial dynamics of brain structure changes during extensive learning, *Journal of Neuroscience*, 26(23), 6314–6317. DOI: 10.1523/JNEURO-SCI.4628-05.2006. 51

Dredge, S. (2014) Google hits back at the Google glass haters in 'top ten myths' blog post. *The Guardian*, March 20, 2014. 142

Droeschel, D., Stückler, J., Holz, D., and Behnke, S. (2011) Towards joint attention for a domestic service robot—person awareness and gesture recognition using time-of-flight cameras. *Proceedings of IEEE International Conference on Robotics and Automation (ICRA)*, Shanghai, China, New York:IEEE Press, 1205–1210. DOI: 10.1109/ICRA.2011.5980067. 154

Dumas, B., Solórzano, M., and Signer, B. (2013) Design guidelines for adaptive multimodal mobile input solutions. *Proceedings of the 15th International Conference on Human-Computer Interaction with Mobile Devices and Services (MobileHCI 2013)*, Munich, Germany, New York:ACM Press. DOI: 10.1145/2493190.2493227. 15

Dunbar, R. (2003) The origin and subsequent evolution of language. *Language Evolution*, Christiansen, M. and Kirby, S., (eds.), Oxford, UK:Oxford University Press, 219–234. DOI: 10.1093/acprof:oso/9780199244843.003.0012. 27

Duncan, L., Brown, W., Esposito, C., Holmback, H., and Xue, P. (1999) Enhancing virtual maintenance environments with speech understanding. Boeing M&CT TechNet. 11

Duncan, R. M. and Cheyne, J. A. (2002) Private speech in young adults: Task difficulty, self-regulation, and psychological predication. *Cognitive Development*, 16, 889–906. 50

Dupont, S. and Luettin, J. (2000) Audio-visual speech modeling for continuous speech recognition. *IEEE Transactions on Multimedia*, 2(3), New York: IEEE Press, 141–151. DOI: 10.1109/6046.865479. 10

Ehlen, P. and Johnston, M. (2013) A multimodal dialogue interface for mobile local search. *Proceedings of the 15th International Conference on Intelligent User Interfaces*, New York:ACM, 63–64. DOI: 10.1145/2451176.2451200. 14

Ehlen, P. and Johnston, M. (2012) Multimodal interaction patterns in mobile local search. *Proceedings of 2012 ACM Conference on Intelligent User Interfaces*, New York:ACM Press, 21–24. DOI: 10.1145/2166966.2166970. 116

Ekman, P. (1992) Facial expressions of emotion: New findings, new questions. *American Psychological Society*, 3(1):34–38. DOI: 10.1111/j.1467-9280.1992.tb00253.x. 34, 144

Ekman, P. (1994) Strong evidence for universals in facial expressions: A reply to Russell's mistaken critique. *Psychological Bulletin*, 115:268–287. DOI: 10.1037/0033-2909.115.2.268. 144

Ekman, P. and Friesen, W. (1978) *Facial Action Coding System: A Technique for the Measurement of Facial Movement*. Palo Alto, CA:Consulting Psychologists Press. 34, 70, 144

Encarnacao, L. M. and Hettinger, L. (eds.) (2003) perceptual multimodal interfaces (special issue). *IEEE Computer Graphics and Applications*, New York:IEEE Press. 11

Endres, C., Schwartz, T., and Muller, C. (2011) "Geremin": 2D Microgestures for Drivers Based on Electric Field Sensing. *Proceedings of the 16th International Conference on Intelligent User Interfaces*, New York:ACM Press, 327–330. DOI: 10.1145/1943403.1943457. 111

Engel, R. and Pfleger, N. (2006) Modality fusion. In *SmartKom: Foundations of Multimodal Dialogue Systems*. Wahlster, W. (ed.), Heidelberg:Springer-Verlag, 223–235. DOI: 10.1007/3-540-36678-4_15. 152

Engelbart, D. (1962) Augmenting human intellect: A conceptual framework. *SRI Project Summary Report 3578*, AFOSR-3223. 7

Engineer Live (2013) *Speech Recognition Technology Can Dramatically Improve Productivity*. February 21, 2013, http://www.engineerlive.com/content/15114, (retrieved 2/12/2015). 115

Englert, R. and Glass, G. (2006) Architecture for multimodal mobile applications. *20th International Symposium on Human Factors in Telecommunication* (HFT 2006), Sophia Antipolis, France: ETSI. 13, 15

Ernst, M. and Banks, M. (2002) Humans integrate visual and haptic information in a statistically optimal fashion. *Nature*, 415:429–433. DOI: 10.1038/415429a. 30, 32

Ernst, M. and Bulthoff, H. (2004) Merging the sense into a robust whole percept. *Trends in Cognitive Science*, 8(4):162-169. DOI: 10.1016/j.tics.2004.02.002. 30

Evans, B. (2014) Mobile is eating the world, Slide 14, 2014. http://a16z.com/2014/10/28/mobile-is-eating-the-world/ (retrieved 2/11/2015). 13, 14, 107

Fasola, J. and Mataric, M. (2012) Using socially assistive human–robot interaction to motivate physical exercise for older adults. *Proceedings of the IEEE* 100(8): 2512–2526. DOI: 10.1109/JPROC.2012.2200539. 154

Fay, N., Garrod, S., Roberts, L., and Swoboda, N. (2010) The interactive evolution of human communication systems. *Cognitive Science*, 34:351–86. DOI: 10.1111/j.1551-6709.2009.01090.x. 46

Ferchmin, P. and Bennett, E. (1975) Direct contact with enriched environment is required to alter cerebral weight in rats. *Journal of Comparative and Physiological Psychology*, 88:360–67. DOI: 10.1037/h0076175. 52

Fillmore, C. J. (1968) The case for case. In Bach, E. W. and Harms, R. T. (eds.), *Universals in Linguistic Theory*. Austin, TX: Holt, Rinehart and Winston, 1–88. 88

Fillmore, C. J. (1977) The case for case reopened. In Cole, P. and Sadock, J. M. (eds.),*Syntax and Semantics Volume 8: Grammatical Relations*. New York:Academic Press, 59–81. 88

Fillmore, C. J. and Baker, C. F. (2009) A frames approach to semantic analysis. In Heine, B. and Narrog, H. (eds.), *The Oxford Handbook of Linguistic Analysis*. Oxford, UK:Oxford University Press, 313–340. DOI: 10.1093/oxfordhb/9780199544004.013.0013. 77, 88

Flanagan, J. and Huang, T. (eds.) (2003) Multimodal human computer interfaces (special issue). *Proceedings of IEEE*, 91(9), Sept. 2003. 11

Fouse, A. (2013) Navigation of time-coded data. Ph.D. dissertation, University of California at San Diego. 57

Fridlund, A. (1994) *Human Facial Expression: An Evolutionary View*. New York:Academic Press. DOI: 10.1002/ajhb.1310080402. 34

Friedman, B., Kahn, P., and Borning, A. (2006) Value sensitive design and information systems. *Human Computer Interaction and Management Information Systems: Foundations*, Zhang, P. and Galletta, D., (eds.), Armonk N.Y: M.E. Sharpe, 348–372. DOI: 10.1002/9780470281819.ch4. 61

Fuster-Duran, A. (1996) Perception of conflicting audio-visual speech: An examination across Spanish and German. In Stork, D.G. and Hennecke, M.E. (eds.), *Speechreading by Humans and Machines: Models, Systems and Applications*, New York: Springer Verlag, 135–143. DOI: 10.1007/978-3-662-13015-5_9. 39

Gajos, K., Wobbrock, J., and Weld, D. (2007) Automatically generating user interfaces adapted to users' motor and vision capabilities. *Proceedings of the 20th Annual ACM Symposium on User Interface Software and Technology (UIST 2007)*, New York:ACM Press, 231–240. DOI: 10.1145/1294211.1294253. 149

Garfinkel, S. (2014) *Glass, Darkly*. MIT Technology Review, Feb. 17, 2014; http://www.technologyreview.com/review/524576/glass-darkly/. (retrieved July 21, 2014). 142

Garg, A., Pavlović, and Rehg, J. (2003) Boosted learning in dynamic Bayesian networks for multimodal speaker detection. *Proceedings of the IEEE*, 91(9):1355–1369. DOI: 10.1109/JPROC.2003.817119. 69, 92

Gatica-Perez, D., Lathoud, G., Odobez, J-M., and McCowan, I. (2005) Multimodal multispeaker probabilistic tracking in meetings. *Proceedings of the 7th ACM International Conference on Multimodal Interfaces*, New York: ACM, 183–190. DOI: 10.1145/1088463.1088496. 12

Gaver, W. (1991) Technology affordances. *Proceedings of the SIGCHI Conference on Human Factors in Computing Systems*, New York:ACM Press, 79–84. DOI: /10.1145/108844.108856. 43, 44

Genesereth, M. and Nilsson, N. (1976) *Logical Foundations of Artificial Intelligence*. San Francisco, CA:Morgan Kaufmann Publishers. 87

Germesin, S. (2009) Agreement detection in multiparty conversation. *Proceedings of the 11th International Conference on Multimodal Interfaces*, New York: ACM, 7–14. DOI: 10.1145/1647314.1647319. 12

Ghahramani, Z. (2001) An introduction to hidden Markov models and Bayesian Networks. *International Journal of Pattern Recognition and Artificial Intelligence*, 15(1):9-42. DOI: 10.1142/S0218001401000836. 78

Gibson, J. (1977) The theory of affordances. In *Perceiving, Acting and Knowing*, Shaw, R. and Bransford, J. (eds.), Hillsdale, N.J.:Erlbaum 3:67–82. 43

Gibson, J. (1979) *The Ecological Approach to Visual Perception*. Boston:Houghton Mifflin. DOI: 10.1002/bs.3830260313. 43

Giles, H., Mulac A., Bradac, J., and Johnson, P. (1987) Speech accommodation theory: The first decade and beyond. *Communication Yearbook 10*, McLaughlin, M.L., ed. London, UK:Sage Publ., 13–48. 46

Giuliani, M., Petrick, R., Foster, M. E., Gaschler, A., Isard, A., Pateraki, M., and Sigalas, M. (2013) Comparing task-based and socially intelligent behaviour in a robot bartender. *Proceedings of the 15th International Conference on Multimodal Interaction*, Marina del Rey, CA, New York:ACM Press, 263–270. DOI: 10.1145/2522848.2522869. 154

Giusti, L., Zancanaro, M., Gal, E., and Weiss, P. (2011) Dimensions of collaboration on a tabletop interface for children with autism spectrum disorder. *Proceedings of the SIGCHI Conference on Human Factors in Computing Systems*, New York: ACM Press, 3295–3304. DOI: 10.1145/1978942.1979431. 123, 140

Goldberg, H. (1914) Controller, United States Patent 1,117,184, December 28, 1914. 7

Goldin-Meadow, S. (2003) *The Resilience of Language: What Gesture Creation in Deaf Children Can Tell us About How Children Learn Language*. New York:Psychology Press. 46

Goldin-Meadow, S., Nusbaum, H., Kelly, S.J., and Wagner, S. (2001) Explaining math: Gesturing lightens the load. *Psychological Science*, 12(6):516–522. DOI: 10.1111/1467-9280.00395. 22, 51

Google (2015a) Now Voice Search. http://www.androidcentral.com/google-now-voice-search-edges-out-siri-and-cortana-search-comparison, (retrieved January 16, 2015). 14

Google (2015b) *Project Ara.* https://www.youtube.com/watch?v=0He3Jr-fZh0, retrieved Jan. 28, 2015. 15

Google (2015c) *Android Auto.* http://www.android.com/auto/. retrieved 2/12/2015. 109

Google transliteration (2014) http://www.google.com/inputtools/. (retrieved Jan. 18, 2014). 166

Gormish, M., Piersol, K., Gudan, K., and Barrus, J. (2009) An e-writer for documents plus strokes. *Proceedings of the 9th ACM Symposium on Document Engineering*, New York:ACM Press, 157–160. DOI: 10.1145/1600193.1600229. 124

Grant, K. and Greenberg, S. (2001) Speech intelligibility derived from asynchronous processing of auditory-visual information. *Workshop on Audio-Visual Speech Processing (AVSP-2001)*, Scheelsminde:Denmark, 132–137. 84

Grashey, S. and Schuster, M. (2006) Multimodal biometrics. In *SmartKom: Foundations of Multimodal Dialogue Systems*, Wahlster, W. (ed.), Springer-Verlag, Heidelberg. DOI: 10.1007/3-540-36678-4_12. 152

Gratch, J., Wang, N., Gerten, J., Fast, E., and Duffy, R. (2007) Creating rapport with virtual agents. *Proceedings of the 7th International Conference on Intelligent Virtual Agents*, Paris, France, Berlin:Springer. DOI: 10.1007/978-3-540-74997-4_12. 151

Gray, E. (1888) Telautograph, United States Patent 386,815, July 31, 1888. 7

Greene, H., Stotts, L., Patterson, R., and Greenburg, J. (2010) *Command Post of the Future: Successful Transition of a Science and Technology Initiative to a Program of Record.* Defense Acquisition University. 112

Greeno, J. (1994) Gibson's Affordances. *Psychological Review*, 101(2), 336–342. DOI: 10.1037/0033-295X.101.2.336. 43, 44

Grosz, B. J. and Sidner, C. (1990) Plans for Discourse. In *Intentions in Communication*, Cohen, P. R., Morgan, J., and Pollack, M. E., (eds.), Cambridge, Massachusetts: MIT Press. 171

Gupta, A. and Anastaskos, T. (2004) Dynamic time windows for multimodal input fusion. *Proceedings of INTERSPEECH'04: 8th International Conference on Spoken Language Processing, International Speech Communications Association*, 1009–1012. 39

Hadar, U., Steiner, T. J., Grant, E. C., and Clifford Rose, F. (1983) Kinematics of head movements accompanying speech during conversation. *Human Movement Science*, 2:35–46. DOI: 10.1016/0167-9457(83)90004-0. 34

Hagenmayer, L. (2007) Development of a Multimodal, Universal Human-Machine-Interface for Hypovigilance-Management-Systems. Ph.D. Thesis, University of Stuttgart, Institute for Human Factors, Dept. of Mechanical Engineering. 111

Haller, M., Leitner, J., Seifried, T., Wallace, J., Scott, S., Richter, C., Brandl, P., Gokcezade, A., and Hunter S. (2010) The NiCE Discussion Room: Integrating paper and digital media to support co-located group meetings. *Proceedings of the SIGCHI Conference on Human Factors in Computing Systems*, New York:ACM Press, 609–18. DOI: 10.1145/1753326.1753418. 140

Hamzah, M., Tano, S., Iwata, M., and Hashiyama, T. (2006) Effectiveness of annotating by hand for non-alphabetic languages. *Proceedings of the SIGCHI Conference on Human Factors in Computing Systems*, New York:ACM Press, 841–850. DOI: 10.1145/1124772.1124896. 164,165

Hanrahan, D. (2009) Multi-modal picking technology provides ROI for small to mid-size order fulfillment processes, Parcel, 9/22/2009, retrieved (1/28/2015). 127

Harel, D. (1987) Statecharts: A visual formalism for complex systems. *Science of Computer Programming*, 8(3):231–274. http://dx.doi.org/10.1016/0167-6423(87)90035-9. 95, 105, 130

Harman International (2015) http://www.harman.com/EN-US/Newscenter/Documents/HARMAN_TECH%20BOOKLET_010312_Fin.pdf, (retrieved 3/3/2015). 109

Hauptmann, A. G. (1989) Speech and gestures for graphic image manipulation. *Proceedings of the Conference on Human Factors in Computing Systems (CHI'89)*, Vol. 1. New York: ACM Press, 241–245. DOI: 10.1145/67449.67496. 17, 20

Hetherington, P. and Mohan A. (2013) *The Essentials of Automotive Hands-Free Systems, White Paper, Electronic Design,* http://electronicdesign.com/communications/essentials-automotive-hands-free-communications, 1/2/2013. (retrieved 2/12/2015). 109

Holzapfel, H., Nickel, K., and Stiefelhagen, R. (2004) Implementation and evaluation of a constraint-based multimodal fusion system for speech and 3D pointing gestures. *Proceedings of the International Conference on Multimodal Interfaces*, State College, Pennsylvania, IEEE, 175–182. DOI: 10.1145/1027933.1027964. 90

Holtzblatt, K. (2012) Contextual design, *The Human-Computer Interaction Handbook: Fundamentals, Evolving Technologies and Emerging Applications* (revised 3rd edition). (ed. by J. Jacko), Boca Raton, FL:CRC Press, chap. 43, 983–1002. 53

Holzman, T. G. (1999) Computer-human interface solutions for emergency medical care. *Interactions*, 6(3):13–24. DOI: 10.1145/301153.301160. 19

Honda Robotics (2011) *Asimo Running 9 km/hr* http://world.honda.com/ASIMO/video/, (retrieved 2/12/2015). 119

Hsueh, P. and Moore, J. (2007) Automatic decision detection in meeting speech. *Machine Learning for Multimodal Interaction, Lecture Notes in Computer Science LNCS 4892*, Berlin: Springer, 168–179. DOI: 10.1007/978-3-540-78155-4_15. 12

Huang, X. and Oviatt, S. (2006) Toward adaptive information fusion in multimodal systems. *Proceedings of the 2nd Joint Workshop on Machine Learning for Multimodal Interaction (Edinburgh, UK, 2005)*, Lecture Notes in Computer Science Volume 3869, Renals, S. and Bengio, S., (eds.), Berlin:Springer-Verlag, 15–27. DOI: 10.1007/11677482_2. 39

Huang, X., Oviatt, S. L., and Lunsford, R. (2006) Combining user modeling and machine learning to predict users' multimodal integration patterns. *Proceedings of the 3rd Joint Workshop on Machine Learning for Multimodal Interaction, Springer Lecture Notes in Computer Science*, Renals, S., Bengio, S., and Fiscus, S. (eds.), Berlin:Springer-Verlag GmbH, 50–62. DOI: 10.1007/11965152_5. 39, 69

ITU World Telecommunication (2013) The World in 2013, ICT facts and figures 2014 http://www.itu.int/en/ITU-D/Statistics/Documents/facts/ICTFactsFigures2013-e.pdf, (retrieved June 27, 2014). 12, 13

InScript (2014) http://ildc.in/inscriptlayout.html, (retrieved Jan. 18, 2014). 164

Intel RealSense (2015) https://software.intel.com/en-us/perceptual-computing-sdk, (retrieved February 4, 2015). 57, 127, 133

Iyengar, G., Nock, H., and Neti. C. (2003) Audio-visual synchrony for detection of monologues in video archives. *Proceedings of the International Conference on Multimedia and Expo (ICME'03)*,New York:IEEE Explore, 329–332. DOI: 10.1109/ICASSP.2003.1200085. 8

Iverson, J. and Goldin-Meadow, S. (1998) Why people gesture when they speak. *Nature*, 396:228. DOI: 10.1038/24300. 29

Jahnke, H. T. (2008) Indigenous perspectives on the ethical review processes of university ethics committees in Aotearoa/New Zealand. *Proceedings of the American Educational Research Association Conference*, New York, New York, March 2008. 61

Jain, A., Hong, L. and Kulkarni, Y. (1999) A multimodal biometric system using fingerprint, face and speech. *2nd Int'l Conference on Audio- and Video-based Biometric Person Authentication*, Washington D.C., 182–187. 11

Jain, A. and Ross, A. (2002) Learning user-specific parameters in a multibiometric system. *Proceedings of the IEEE International Conference on Image Processing (ICIP)*, New York:IEEE Press,57–60. DOI: 10.1109/ICIP.2002.1037958. 11

Jain, A. and A. Ross, (2004) Multibiometric systems. *Communications of the ACM*, 47(1):34–40. DOI: 10.1145/962081.962102. 33

James, K. and Engelhardt, L. (2012) The effects of handwriting experience on functional brain development in pre-literate children, *Trends in Neuroscience and Education*, 1–11. 51

James, K. and Swain, S. (2010) Only self-generated actions create sensori-motor systems in the developing brain. *Developmental Science*, 1–6. DOI: 10.1111/j.1467-7687.2010.01011.x. 51

Johnson, L. (2014) Using virtual role-play to prepare for cross-cultural communication. *Proceedings of the 5th International Conference on Applied Human Factors and Ergonomics (AHFE)*, Ahram, T., Karwowski, A. and Marek, T., (eds.), Krakow, Poland, Amsterdam:Elsevier. 127, 152

Johnson-Laird, P. (1999) *Space to Think, Language and Space*. Bloom, P., Peterson, M., Nadel, L. and M. Garrett, (eds.), MIT Press: Cambridge MA., 437–462. 158

Johnston, M. (1998) Unification-based multimodal parsing. *Proceedings of the COLING-ACL Conference*, Stroudsburg, PA:Association for Computational Linguistics, 624–630. DOI: 10.3115/980845.980949. 11, 90, 96

Johnston, M., Baggia, P., Burnett, D., Carter, J., Dal, D A., McCobb, G., and Raggett D. (2009) *EMMA: Extensible MultiModal Annotation Markup Language*. World Wide Web Consortium. 131, 133

Johnston, M. and Bangalore, S. (2000) Finite-state multimodal parsing and understanding. *Proceedings of the 38th Annual Meeting of the Association for Computational Linguistics*, Stroudsburg, PA:Association for Computational Linguistics, 369–375. DOI: 10.3115/990820.990874. 72 , 93, 94, 95

Johnston, M., Cohen, P. R., McGee, D. R., Oviatt, S. L., Pittman, J. A., and Smith, I. (1997) Unification-based multimodal integration. *Proceedings of the 35th Annual Meeting of the Association for Computational Linguistics*, Stroudsburg, PA:Association for *Computational Linguistics*, 281–288. DOI: 10.3115/976909.979653. 11, 90

Joshi, A., Parmar, V., Ganu, A., Mathur, G., and Chand, A. (2004) Keylekh: A keyboard for text entry in Indic scripts. *Proceedings of the SIGCHI Conference on Human Factors in Computing Systems*, New York:ACM Press, 928–942. DOI: 10.1145/985921.985950. 164

Juang, B. and Rabiner, L. (2005) Automatic speech recognition – A brief history of the technology development. *Encyclopedia of Language and Linguistics*, Second Edition, New York:Elsevier Publishers. 7

Jurafsky, D. and Martin, J. H. (2009) *Speech and Language Processing*. 2nd ed., Upper Saddle River, NJ:Prentice Hall, Inc. 69, 78, 89, 90

Kaiser, E., Olwal, A., McGee, D., Benko, H., Corradini, A., Cohen, P. R., and Feiner, S. (2003) Mutual disambiguation of 3D multimodal interaction in augmented and virtual reality. *Proceedings of the 5th International Conference on Multimodal Interfaces*, New York:ACM Press, 12–19. DOI: 10.1145/958432.958438. 91, 100, 101

Kane, S., Bigham, J., and Wobbrock, J. (2008) Slide Rule: Making mobile touch screens accessible to blind people using multi-touch interaction techniques. *Proceedings of the 10th International ACM SIGACCESS Conference on Computing Accessibility*, New York:ACM Press,73–80. DOI: 10.1145/1414471.1414487. 150

Kaplan, R. M. and Bresnan, J. (1995) Lexical-functional grammar: A formal system for grammatical representation. *Formal Issues in Lexical-Functional Grammar*, Dalyrmple, M., Kaplan, R. M., Maxwell, J. and Zaenen, A., (eds.) Stanford, CA:CSLI Press. 89, 90

Kay, A. C. (1977) Microelectronics and the Personal Computer. *Scientific American* 237(3):230–244. DOI: 10.1038/scientificamerican0977-230. 7

Kay, M. (1973) The MIND System. In *Natural Language Processing*, Rustin, R. (ed.,) New York:Algorithmics Press, 155–188. 90

Kegl, J., Senghas, A., and Coppola, M. (1999) Creation through contact: Sign language emergence and sign language change in Nicaragua. In M. DeGraff (ed.), *Language Creation and Language Change: Creolization, Diachrony and Development*, Cambridge Ma.: MIT Press, 179–237. 46

Keizer, S., Foster, M. E., Wang, Z., and Lemon, O. (2014) Machine learning for social multiparty human-robot interaction. *ACM Transactions on Interactive Intelligent Systems*, 4(3), 14:1–14:3. DOI: 10.1145/2600021. 154

Kendon, A. (1980) Gesticulation and speech: Two aspects of the process of utterance. Key, M. (ed.), *The Relationship of Verbal and Nonverbal Communication*,The Hague: Mouton, 207–227. 7, 11, 29, 34, 39

Kersey, A. and James, K. (2013) Brain activation patterns resulting from learning letter forms through active self-production and passive observation in young children. *Frontiers in Psychology*, vol. 3, article 567, 1-15. DOI: 10.3389/fpsyg.2013.00567. 51

Kim, Y-H. and Misu, T. (2014) Identification of the Driver's Interest Point using a Head Pose Trajectory for Situated Dialog Systems. *Proceedings of the 16th International Conference on Multimodal Interaction*, New York:ACM Press, 92–95. DOI: 10.1145/2663204.2663230. 112

King, A. J. and Palmer, A. R. (1985) Integration of visual and auditory information in bimodal neurons in the guinea-pic superior colliculus. *Experimental Brain Research*, 60:492–500. DOI: 10.1007/BF00236934. 29

Kipp, M. (2014) ANVIL: The video annotation research tool. In *The Oxford Handbook of Corpus Phonology*, J. Durand, Gut, U., and Kristoffersen G., (eds.) chapter 21, 420-436. 56

Kittler, J., Hatef, M., Duin, R. ,and Matas, J. (1998) On combining classifiers. *IEEE Transactions on Pattern Analysis and Machine Intelligence*, 20(3):226–239. DOI: 10.1109/34.667881. 63, 72, 91, 92

Kleim, J., Vij, K., Kelly, J., Ballard, D., and Greenough, W. (1997) Learning-dependent synaptic modifications in the cerebellar cortex of the adult rat persist for at least 4 weeks. *Journal of Neuroscience*, 17:717–721. 52

Kobsa, A., Allgayer, J., Reddig, C., Reithinger, N., Schmauks, D., Harbusch, K., and Wahlster, W. (1986) Combining deictic gestures and natural language for referent identification. *COLING'86: Proceedings of the 11th International Conference on Computational Linguistics*, Stroudsburg, PA:Association for *Computational Linguistics*, 356–361. DOI: 10.3115/991365.991471. 7, 9

Koffka, K. (1935) *Principles of Gestalt Psychology*. Harcourt, Brace and Company, NY. 41, 42

Kohler, W. (1929) *Dynamics in Psychology*. Liveright, NY. 41, 42

Kohler, E., Keysers, C., Umilta, M., Fogassi, L., Gallese, V, and Rizzolatti, G. (2002) Hearing sounds, understanding actions: Action representation in mirror neurons. *Science*, 297:846–848. DOI: 10.1126/science.1070311. 29

Kolossa, D., Zeiler, S., Vorwerk, A., and Orgimeister, R. (2009) Audiovisual speech recognition with missing or unreliable data. *Proceedings of Auditory-Visual Speech Processing*, Theobald, B-J., and Harvey, R. W. (eds.), International Speech Communication Association, 117–122. 71, 100

Koons, D., Sparrell, C., and Thorisson, K. (1993) Integrating simultaneous input from speech, gaze, and hand gestures, *Intelligent Multimedia Interfaces*, Maybury, M. (ed.), Cambridge, MA: MIT Press. 257–276. 11

Kopp, S., Tepper, P., and Cassell, J. (2004) Towards integrated microplanning of language and iconic gesture for multimodal output. *Proceedings of the 6th ACM International Conference on Multimodal Interfaces*, New York: ACM, 97–104. DOI: 10.1145/1027933.1027952. 11

Kopp, S. , Tepper, P., Striegnitz, K., Ferriman, K., and Cassell, J. (2007) Trading spaces: Humans and humanoids use speech and gesture to give directions. In: *Conversational Informatics:*

an Engineering Approach, Nishida T. (Ed), Wiley Series in Agent Technology, Hoboken, NJ:John Wiley and Sons: 133–160. DOI: 10.1002/9780470512470.ch8. 68, 91, 127

Krizhevsky, A., Sutskever, I., and Hinton, G. (2012) ImageNet classification with deep convolutional neural networks. *Neural Information Processing Systems 25*, Neural Information Processing Systems (NIPS) Foundation, 1097–1105. 67

Kumar, S., Cohen, P. R., and Levesque H. J. (2000) The adaptive agent architecture: Achieving fault-tolerance using persistent broker teams. *Proceedings of the 4th International Conference on MultiAgent Systems*, New York:IEEE Press,159–166. DOI: 10.1109/ICMAS.2000.858448. 129

Lachenman, J. (2013) Multi-modal voice applications in the food and beverage DC. *Food Logistics*, August 23, 2013, http://www.foodlogistics.com/article/11123073/voice-directed-warehouse-applicationsspeech-recognitionbarcode-scanning, (retrieved 2/12/2015). 128

Ladner, R. (2010) *Accessible Technology and Models of Disability, Design and Use of Assistive Technology: Social, Technical, Ethical, and Economic*. Oishi, M. M. K., Mitchell, I. M., Van der Loos, H. F. M. (eds.), New York:Springer-Verlag, 25–31. DOI: 10.1007/978-1-4419-7031-2. 151

Ladner, R. (2012) Communication technologies for people with sensory disabilities. *Proceedings of the IEEE*, 100(4): 957–973. DOI: 10.1109/JPROC.2011.2182090. 149, 150, 151

Lalanne, D., Evequoz, F., Rigamonti, M., Dumas, B., and Ingold, R. (2008) An ego-centric and tangible approach to meeting indexing and browsing. *Machine Learning and Multimodal Interaction, Lecture Notes in Computer Science LNCS 4892*, Popescu-Belis, A., Renals, S. and Bourlard, H., (eds.), Berlin: Springer, 84–95. DOI: 10.1007/978-3-540-78155-4_8. 12

Lalanne, D., Lisowska, A., Bruno, E., Flynn, M., Georgescul, M., Guillemot, M., Janvier, B., Marchand-Maillet, S., Melichar, M., Moenne-Loccoz, N., Popescu-Belis, A., Rajman, M., Rigamonti, M., von Rotz, D., and Wellner, P. (2005) The IM2 meeting browser family. *Technical Report*, Friborg, March 2005. 12

Lalanne, D., Nigay, L., Palanque, P., Robinson, P., Vanderdonckt, J., and Ladry, J.-F. (2009) Fusion engines for multimodal input: A Survey. *Proceedings of the 11th International Conference on Multimodal Interfaces – Machine Learning for Multimodal Interaction*, New York:ACM Press, 153–160. DOI: 10.1145/1647314.1647343. 85

Laptev, I. (2005) On space-time interest points. *International Journal of Computer Vision*, 64(2-3):107–123. DOI: 10.1007/s11263-005-1838-7. 67, 75

Larkin, J. and Simon, H. (1987) Why a diagram is (sometimes) worth ten thousand words. *Cognitive Science*, 11:65–99. DOI: 10.1111/j.1551-6708.1987.tb00863.x. 163

Latoschik, M. E. (2002) Designing transition networks for multimodal VR-interactions using a markup language. *Proceedings of the 4th International Conference on Multimodal Interfaces*, New York:IEEE Press, 411–416. DOI: 10.1109/ICMI.2002.1167030. 96

LeapFrog (2010) http://www.leapfrog.com, retrieved Nov. 24, 2010. 125

Leatherby, J. H. and Pausch, R. (1992) Voice input as a replacement for keyboard accelerators in a mouse-based graphical editor: An empirical study. *Journal of the American Voice Input/ Output Society*, 11(2). 20

Leitner, J., Powell, J., Brandl, P., Seifried, T., Haller, M., Dorsay, B., and To, P. (2009) FLUX: A tilting multi-touch and pen-based surface. *Proceedings of SIGCHI Conference on Human Factors in Computing Systems (CHI'09)*, New York: ACM Press, 3211–3216. DOI: 10.1145/1520340.1520459. 140

Lenat, D. B. and Guha, R. V. (1990) *Building Large Knowledge-Based Systems: Representation and Inference in the Cyc Project*, Boston:Addison-Wesley. 104

Lewis, M. (ed.) (2009) *Ethnologue: Languages of the World*. 16th edition, Dallas, Texas:SIL International. Online version: http://www.ethnologue.com/, (retrieved Dec. 10, 2011). 164

Lewis, M. (2014) *Flash Boys*, New York:W.W. Norton and Company. 170

Lindblom, B. (1990) Explaining phonetic variation: A sketch of the H and H theory. In *Speech Production and Speech Modeling*, Hardcastle, W. and Marchal, A. (eds.), Dordrecht:Kluwer, 403–439. DOI: 10.1007/978-94-009-2037-8_16. 28

Lisowska, A. (2007) Multimodal interface design for multimedia meeting content retrieval. Ph.D. thesis, University of Geneva, Switzerland, Sept. 2007. DOI: 10.1145/1027933.1028006. 12

Livescribe (2014) www.livescribe.com, retrieved July 15, 2014. 125, 150

Liwicki, M. and El-Neklawy, S. (2009) Enhancing a multi-touch table with write functionality. *Proceedings of the Workshop on Machine Perception and Robotics (MPR'09)*, October 4-5, Bitsumeikan University, Kyoto, Japan. 140

Lockheed Martin (2015) *The F-35 Combat Systems Fusion Engine*. http://www.sldinfo.com/whitepapers/the-f-35-combat-systems-fusion-engine/. (retrieved 2/7/2015). 63

Lockheed Martin (2015a) *The F-35 Cockpit: Enabling the Pilot as a Tactical Decision Maker*. http://www.sldinfo.com/whitepapers/the-f-35-cockpit-enabling-the-pilot-as-a-tactical-decision-maker/, accessed 3/31/2015. 108

Longcamp, M., Boucard, C., Gilhodes, J-C., Anton, J-L., Roth, M., Nazarian, B., and Velay, J-L. (2008) Learning through hand- or typewriting influences visual recognition of new graphic shapes: Behavioral and functional imaging evidence. *Journal of Cognitive Neuroscience*, 20:5, 802–815. DOI: 10.1162/jocn.2008.20504. 51

LREC (2014) The 9th edition of the Language Resources and Evaluation Conference, 26–31 May, Reykjavik, Iceland http://lrec2014.lrec-conf.org/en/ (retrieved 04/09/2015). 56

Luettin, J., Potamianos, G., and Neti, C. (2001) Asynchronous stream modeling for large vocabulary audio-visual speech recognition. *Proceedings of the IEEE International Conference on Acoustics, Speech and Signal Processing*, New York:IEEE Press, 1:169–172. DOI: 10.1109/ICASSP.2001.940794. 100

Luria, A. R. (1961) *The Role of Sspeech in the Regulation of Normal and Abnormal Behavior*. Oxford, UK: Liveright. DOI: 10.1126/science.134.3485.1063. 50, 51

Maehara, Y. and Saito, S. (2007) The relationship between processing and storage in working memory span: Not two sides of the same coin. *Journal of Memory and Language*, 56(2):212–228. DOI: 10.1016/j.jml.2006.07.009. 48

Manning, C. and Schütze, H. (2003) *Foundations of Statistical Natural Language Processing*. Cambridge, MA:MIT Press. 69

Marker, M. (2006) After the Makah whale hunt: Indigenous knowledge and limits to multicultural discourse. *Urban Education*, 41(5):1–24. DOI: 10.1177/0042085906291923. 61

Markham, J. and Greenough, W. (2004) Experience-driven brain plasticity: Beyond the synapse. *Neuron Glia Biology*, 1(4):351-363. DOI: 10.1017/S1740925X05000219. 51

Markinson, R. (1993) University of California, San Francisco, personal communication. 19

Marks, L. E., (1989) On cross-modal similarity: The perceptual structure of pitch, loudness, and brightness. *Journal of Experimental Psychology: Human Perception and Performance*, 15(3):586–602. DOI: 10.1037//0096-1523.15.3.586. 29

Martin, D., Cheyer, A., and Moran, D. B. (1999) The Open Agent Architecture: A framework for building distributed software systems. *Applied Artificial Intelligence* 13(1-2):91–128. DOI: 10.1080/088395199117504. 129, 131

Martinez, H. P. and Yannakakis, G. N. (2014) Deep multimodal fusion: Combining discrete events and continuous signals. *Proceedings of the 16th ACM International Conference on Multimodal Interaction*, New York:ACM Press, 34–41. DOI: 10.1145/2663204.2663236. 72

Massaro, D. (2004) From multisensory integration to talking heads and language learning. In G. Calvert, C. Spence and B.E. Stein (Eds.), *Handbook of Multisensory Processes*, MIT Press, 153–176. 130

Massaro, D. W. and Cohen, M. M. (1990) Perception of synthesized audible and visible speech. *Psychological Science*, 1(1):55–63. DOI: 10.1111/j.1467-9280.1990.tb00068.x. 34, 152

Massaro. D. W. and Stork, D. G. (1998) Speech recognition and sensory integration. *American Scientist*, 86(3): 236–244. DOI: 10.1511/1998.3.236. 10, 28, 40, 102

Maybury, M. (1993) *Intelligent Multimedia Interfaces*. Menlo Park:AAAI Publishers. 1

Mayer, R. and Moreno, R. (1998) A split-attention effect in multimedia learning: Evidence for dual processing systems in working memory. *Journal of Educational Psychology*, 90:312–320. DOI: 10.1037/0022-0663.90.2.312. 50

McGee, D. (2003) Augmenting environments with multimodal interaction, Oregon Health and Science University. Doctoral dissertation, June 2003. 8

McGee, D. R. and Cohen, P. R. (2001) Creating tangible interfaces by augmenting physical objects with multimodal language. *Proceedings of the 6th International Conference on Intelligent User Interfaces*, New York: ACM Press, 113–119. DOI: 10.1145/359784.360305. 114

McGee, D., Cohen, P. R., and Wu, L. (2000) Something from nothing: Augmenting a paper-based work practice via multimodal interaction. *Proceedings of the ACM Conference on Design of Augmented Reality Environments*, Copenhagen, Denmark, New York:ACM Press, 71–80. DOI: 10.1145/354666.354674. 8, 10, 114, 139

McGrath, M. and Summerfield, Q. (1985) Intermodal timing relations and audio-visual speech recognition by normal-hearing adults. *Journal of the Acoustical Society of America*, 77(2):678–685. DOI: 10.1121/1.392336. 7, 10, 28

McGurk, H. and MacDonald, J. (1976) Hearing lips and seeing voices. *Nature*, 264(5588):746–8. DOI: 10.1038/264746a0. 7, 10, 29, 33, 40

McLean, S. (2015) India's cut-price smart phones rev up telecom profits. *Wall Street Journal*, February 18, 2015. 13

McLeod, A. and Summerfield, Q. (1987) Quantifying the contribution of vision to speech perception in noise. *British Journal of Audiology*, 21:131–141. DOI: 10.3109/03005368709077786. 8, 10, 21, 28

McNeill, D. (1992) *Hand and Mind: What Gestures Reveal about Thought*. Chicago: University of Chicago Press. 11, 29, 35, 39, 40, 68, 85

MCTR (2014) Multimodal Corpora: Combining applied and basic research targets, Edlund, J., Heylen, D., Paggio, P., (eds.), Reykjavik, Iceland. http://www.multimodal-corpora.org/ mmc14.html (retrieved 4/08/2015). 56

Mehlmann, G. and André, E. (2012) Modeling multimodal integration with event logic charts. *Proceedings of the 14th ACM International Conference on Multimodal Interaction*, New York:ACM Press, 125–132. DOI: 10.1145/2388676.2388705. 95

Mehlmann, G., Endrass, B., and André, E. (2012) Modeling parallel state charts for multithreaded multimodal dialogues. *Proceedings of the 13th ACM International Conference on Multimodal Interaction*, ACM Press, New York, 385–392. DOI: 10.1145/2070481.2070555. 96

Meier, U., Hürst, W., and Duchnowski, P. (1996) Adaptive bimodal sensor fusion for automatic speechreading. *Proceedings of the International Conference on Acoustics, Speech and Signal Processing (IEEE-ICASSP)*, New York:IEEE Press, 833–836. DOI: 10.1109/ICASSP.1996.543250. 10

Meredith, M. A., Nemitz, J. W., and Stein, B. E. (1987) Determinants of multisensory integration in superior colliculus neurons. I. Temporal factors. *The Journal of Neuroscience*, 7:3215–3229. 29

Messer, S. B. (1976) Reflection-impulsivity: A review. *Psychological Bulletin*, 83(6):1026–1052. DOI: 10.1037/0033-2909.83.6.1026. 36

Microsoft (2015a) Cortana. http://www.microsoft.com/en-us/mobile/campaign-cortana/, retrieved January 16, 2015. 14

Microsoft Kinect (2015b) http://www.microsoft.com/en-us/kinectforwindows/, (retrieved Feb. 19, 2015). 125, 133, 141

Microsoft (2015c) Kinect SDK. http://www.microsoft.com/en-us/download/details.aspx?id=44561, (retrieved 2/12/2015). 57, 125, 127, 133

Microsoft (2015d) Robotics Developer Studio. https://msdn.microsoft.com/en-us/library/bb648760.aspx, retrieved (2/12/2015). 133, 154

Miller G. (1956) The magical number seven plus or minus two: Some limits on our capacity for processing information. *Psychological Review*, 63(2): 81–97. DOI: 10.1037/h0043158. 48

Miller, G. A., Galanter, E., and Pribram, K. H. (1960) *Plans and the Structure of Behavior*. New York:Holt, Rinehart and Winston. DOI: 10.1037/10039-000. 47

Minkler, M. and Wallerstein, N. (2008) *Community-Based Participatory Research for Health: From Process to Outcomes*, 2nd edition. Hoboken, NJ:John Wiley and Sons. 61

Mobile Accessibility (2014) http://mobileaccessibility.cs.washington.edu/projects/, retrieved July 15, 2014. 150

Mollon, J. D. and Perkins, A. J. (1996) Errors of judgement at Greenwich in 1796. *Nature*, 380:101–102. DOI: 10.1038/380101a0. 30

Moniri, M. M. and Müller, C. (2014) EyeVIUS: Intelligent vehicles in intelligent urban spaces. Interactive demo. *Proceedings of the 6th International Conference on Automotive User Interfaces and Interactive Vehicular Applications*, Seattle, WA, New York:ACM Press. DOI: 10.1145/2667239.2667265. 112

Moodey, H. (1942) Telautograph System, United States Patent 2,269,599, December 27, 1942. 7

Moore, G. (1999) *Crossing the Chasm: Marketing and Selling High-Tech Products to Mainstream Customers*, 2nd edition. New York:Harper Business. 134

Moran, D., Cheyer, A. Martin, D., Julia, L., and Park, S. (1997) Multimodal user interfaces in the Open Agent Architecture. *Proceedings of the 2nd International Conference on Intelligent User Interfaces*, New York:ACM Press, 61–68. DOI: 10.1145/238218.238290. 116, 129, 131

Morein-Zamir, S., Soto-Faraco S., and A. Kingstone, (2003) Auditory capture of vision: Examining temporal ventriloquism. *Cognitive Brain Research*, 17(1):154–163. DOI: 10.1016/S0926-6410(03)00089-2. 29, 33

Morency, L-P, Sidner, C., Lee, C., and Darrell, T. (2005) Contextual recognition of head gestures. *Proceedings of the 7th ACM International Conference on Multimodal Interfaces*, New York:ACM Press, 18–24. DOI: 10.1145/1088463.1088470. 11

Morimoto, C., Koons, D., Amir, A., Flickner, M., and Zhai, S. (1999) Keeping an eye for HCI. *Proceedings of SIBGRAPI'99, XII Brazilian Symposium on Computer Graphics and Image Processing*, 171–176. DOI: 10.1109/SIBGRA.1999.805722. 11

Mousavi, S. Y., R. Low, and J. Sweller (1995) Reducing cognitive load by mixing auditory and visual presentation modes. *Journal of Educational Psychology*, 87(2): 319–334. DOI: 10.1037/0022-0663.87.2.319. 23, 49, 50

Muller, M. (2007) Participatory design: the third space in *HCI, Handbook of Human-Computer Interaction* (revised 2nd edition). Sears, A. and Jacko, J., (eds.), New York:Lawrence Erlbaum Assoc: 1061–1082. DOI: 10.1201/9781410615862.ch54. 61

Müller, C., Großmann-Hutter, B., Jameson, A., Rummer, R., and Wittig, F. (2001) Recognizing time pressure and cognitive load on the basis of speech: An experimental study. *Proceedings of the 8th International Conference on User Modeling (UM'2001), Lecture Notes in Artificial Intelligence*, Bauer, M., Gmytrasiewicz, P. J., Vassileva, J. (eds.) Berlin: Springer, 24–33. DOI: 10.1007/3-540-44566-8_3. 22

Muller, C. and Weinberg, G. (2011) Multimodal input in the car, today and tomorrow. Mitsubishi Electric Research Laboratories, *Technical Report*, 2011–002. DOI: 10.1109/MMUL.2011.14.

Muncaster, J. and Turk, M. (2006) Continuous multimodal authentication using dynamic Bayesian networks. *Proceedings of the 2nd Workshop Multimodal User Authentication*, Toulouse, France. 92, 122

Murphy, R.R., (1996) Biological and cognitive foundations of intelligent sensor fusion. *IEEE Transactions on Systems, Man, and Cybernetics—Part A: Systems and Humans*, 26(1):42–51. DOI: 10.1109/3468.477859. 28

Nagajaran, U. and Goswami, A. (2015) A neutral, motion-amplifying controller for Honda Stride Management Assist (SMA) exoskeleton. *SAE International Journal of Passenger Cars— Mechanical Systems, Paper 2015-01-1400*, http://papers.sae.org/2015-01-1400/, (retrieved 2/12/2015). 120

Nakadai, K., Takahashi, T., Okuno, H. G., Nakajima, H., Hasegawa, Y., and Hiroshi Tsujino (2010) Design and implementation of robot audition system "hark"— open source software for listening to three simultaneous speakers. *Advanced Robotics* 24:739–761. DOI: 10.1163/016918610X493561. 119

Naughton, K. (1996) Spontaneous gesture and sign: A study of ASL signs co-occurring with speech. In Messing, L. (ed.). *Proceedings of the Workshop on the Integration of Gesture in Language and Speech*, Newark, DE:Univ. of Delaware, 125–134. 39

Neal, J. G. and Shapiro, S. C. (1991) Intelligent multimedia interface technology. Sullivan, J. and Tyler, S. (eds.). *Intelligent User Interfaces*, New York: ACM Press, 11–43. 9

Negroponte, N. (1978) The Media Room. *Report for ONR and DARPA*. Cambridge, MA: MIT, Architecture Machine Group, Dec. 1978. 8

Neti, C., Iyengar, G., Potamianos, G., and Senior, A. (2000) Perceptual interfaces for information interaction: Joint processing of audio and visual information for human-computer interaction, Yuan, B., Huang, T. and Tang, X., (eds.). *Proceedings of the International Conference on Spoken Language Processing (ICSLP'2000)*, Vol. 3, Beijing, China: Chinese Friendship Publishers, 11–14. 8

Ngiam, J., Khosla, A., Kim, M., Nam, J., Lee, H., and Ng, A. Y. (2011) Multimodal deep learning. *Proceedings of the 28th IEEE International Conference on Machine Learning*, Bellevue, WA, New York:IEEE. 67, 74, 75

Nicolaou, M. A., Gunes, H., and Pantic, M. (2011) Continuous prediction of spontaneous affect from multiple cues and modalities in valence–arousal space. *IEEE Transactions On Affective Computing*, 2(2):92–105. DOI: 10.1109/T-AFFC.2011.9. 76

Nicole J., Rapp V., Bailly, K., Prevost, L. ,and Chetouani, M. (2014) Audio-visual emotion recognition: A dynamic, multimodal approach. *IHM'14, 26eme Conférence Francophone sur l'Interaction Homme-Machine*, Lille, France, 44–51. 76

Niekrasz, J. and Gruenstein, E. (2006) NOMOS: A semantic web software framework for annotation of multimodal corpora. *Proceedings of the Fifth Conference on Language Resources and Evaluation (LREC 2006)*, Genoa Italy. 57

Nielsen, M. and Gould, L. (2007) Non-native scholars doing research in native american communities: A matter of respect. *The Social Science Journal*, 44:420–33. DOI: 10.1016/j.soscij.2007.07.002. 61

Nigay, L. and Coutaz, J. (1995) A generic platform for addressing the multimodal challenge. *Proceedings of SIGCHI Conference on Human Factors in Computing Systems*. ACM Press/Addison Wesley Publishing Co, 98–105. DOI: 10.1145/223904.223917. 129

Norman, D. (1988) *The Design of Everyday Things*. New York: Basic Books. 44

Nuance (2015a) Swype. http://www.nuance.com/for-individuals/mobile applications/swype/android/index.htm, (retrieved Jan. 15, 2015). 2, 107

Nuance (2015b) Dragon Drive. http://www.nuance.com/for-business/mobile-solutions/dragon-drive/index.htm, accessed 3/31/2015. 112

Nuance (2015c) Dragon Assistant. http://www.nuance.com/dragon/dragon-assistant/index.htm, accessed 3/31/2015. 133

Ochoa, X., Chiluiza, K., Méndez, G., Luzardo, G., Guamán, B., and Castells, J. (2013) Expertise estimation based on simple multimodal features. *Proceedings of the 15th ACM on International Conference on Multimodal Interaction*, New York:ACM Press, 583–590. DOI: 10.1145/2522848.2533789. 147

O'Hara, K., Gonzalez, G., Sellen, A., Penney, G., Varnavas, A., Mentis, H., Criminisi, A., Corish, R., Rouncefield, M., Dastur, N., and Carrell T. (2014) Touchless Interaction in Surgery. *Communications of the ACM* 57(1):70–77. DOI: 10.1145/2541883.2541899. 117

Okuno, H. G., Nakadai, K., Hidai, K., Mizoguchiz, H., and Kitano, H. (2001) Human-robot interaction through real-time auditory and visual multiple-talker tracking. *Proceedings of the International Conference on Intelligent Robots and Systems*, Maui, Hawaii, 1402–1409. DOI: 10.1109/IROS.2001.977177. 155

Oliver, N., Garg., A., and Horvitz, E. (2004) Layered representations for learning and inferring office activity from multiple sensory channels. *Computer Vision and Image Understanding* 96(2):163–180. DOI: 10.1016/j.cviu.2004.02.004. 73

Oliver, N. and Horvitz, E. (2005) A comparison of HMMs and dynamic Bayesian networks for recognizing office activities. *Proceedings of the 10th International Conference on User Modeling*, New York:ACM Press, 199–209. DOI: 10.1007/11527886_26. 92

Ong, S. and Ranganath, S. (2005) Automatic sign language analyses: A survey and the future beyond lexical meaning. *IEEE Transactions on Pattern Analysis and Machine Intelligence*, 27(6): 873–891. DOI: 10.1109/TPAMI.2005.112. 150

Openstream (2015) http://www.openstream.com/cueme/, (retrieved Feb. 19, 2015). 57, 133

Optalert (2015) http://www.optalert.com/, (retrieved, 2/12/2015). 111

Oviatt, S. L. (1995) Predicting spoken disfluencies during human-computer interaction. *Computer Speech and Language*, 9(1):19–35. DOI: 10.1006/csla.1995.0002. 22

Oviatt, S. L. (1996) User-centered design of spoken language and multimodal interfaces. *IEEE Multimedia*, 3(4):26–35. DOI: 10.1109/93.556458. 54, 60, 111, 116

Oviatt, S. L. (1997) Multimodal interactive maps: Designing for human performance. *Human-Computer Interaction (Special issue on Multimodal Interfaces)*, 12:93–129. DOI: 10.1207/s15327051hci1201&2_4. 17, 18, 20, 22, 23, 68, 84, 102

Oviatt, S. L. (1999a) Mutual disambiguation of recognition errors in a multimodal architecture. *Proceedings of the SIGCHI Conference on Human Factors in Computing Systems* (CHI'99), New York: ACM Press, 576–583. DOI: 10.1145/302979.303163. 20, 21

Oviatt, S. L. (1999b) Ten myths of multimodal interaction. *Communications of the ACM*, 42(11):74–81. DOI: 10.1145/319382.319398. 34, 35, 36

Oviatt, S.L. (2000a) Multimodal system processing in mobile environments. *Proceedings of the Thirteenth Annual ACM Symposium on User Interface Software Technology (UIST'2000)*, New York: ACM Press. 21–30. DOI: 10.1145/354401.354408. 20, 21

Oviatt, S. L. (2000b) Taming recognition errors with a multimodal architecture. *Communications of the ACM*, 43(9):45–51. DOI: 10.1145/348941.348979. 19

Oviatt, S. L. (2000c) Multimodal signal processing in naturalistic noisy environments. In Yuan, B. Huang, T. and Tang, X., (eds.). *Proceedings of the International Conference on Spoken Language Processing (ICSLP'2000)*, Vol. 2, Beijing:Chinese Friendship Publishers, 696–699. 19, 28

Oviatt, S. L. (2002) Breaking the robustness barrier: Recent progress in the design of robust multimodal systems. *Advances in Computers*, Zelkowitz, M. (ed.), Academic Press, 56:305–341. 20, 21, 97, 98, 100

Oviatt, S. L. (2003) Advances in robust multimodal interfaces. *IEEE Computer Graphics and Applications, (special issue on Perceptual Multimodal Interfaces)*, 23(5):62–68. DOI: 10.1109/MCG.2003.1231179. 8

Oviatt, S. L. (2006) Human-centered design meets cognitive load theory: Designing interfaces that help people think. *Proceedings of the ACM Conference on Multimedia, (special session on Human-Centered Multimedia Systems)*, New York:ACM, 871–880. DOI: 10.1145/1180639.1180831. 49, 60

Oviatt, S. L. (2012) *Multimodal Interfaces, The Human-Computer Interaction Handbook: Fundamentals, Evolving Technologies and Emerging Applications* (revised 3rd edition). chap. 18, Jacko, J. (ed.), Boca Raton, FL:CRC Press, 405–430. DOI: 10.1201/b11963-22. xxii, 4, 28, 40, 83, 84, 114, 145

Oviatt, S. (2013a) *The Design of Future Educational Interfaces*. New York:Routledge Press. xxi, 24, 27, 28, 30, 125, 157, 162, 163, 164, 166, 167

Oviatt, S. (2013b) Problem solving, domain expertise and learning: Ground-truth performance results for math data corpus. *Second Intl. Grand Challenge Workshop on Multimodal Learning Analytics, 15th International ACM Conference on Multimodal Interaction*, Sydney, Australia, New York: ACM Press, 569–574. DOI: 10.1145/2522848.2533791. 145, 148

Oviatt, S., Arthur, A., Brock, Y., and Cohen, J. (2007) Expressive pen-based interfaces for math education. *Proceedings of the 8th International Conference on Computer-Supported Collaborative Learning*, Chinn , C. A., Erkens G. and Puntambekar S., (eds.), International Society of the Learning Sciences, 573–58. DOI: 10.3115/1599600.1599708. 51

Oviatt, S., Arthur, A. ,and Cohen, J. (2006) Quiet interfaces that help students think. *UIST '06 - Proceedings of the 19th annual ACM Symposium on User Interface Software and Technology*, ACM Press: New York, 191–200. DOI: 10.1145/1166253.1166284. 50, 51

Oviatt, S. L., Bernard, J., and Levow, G. (1999) Linguistic adaptation during error resolution with spoken and multimodal systems. *Language and Speech (special issue on Prosody and Speech)*, 41(3-4):415–438. 20

Oviatt, S.L. and Cohen, A. (2010a) Supporting students' thinking marks: Designing accessible interfaces for science education. *Proceedings of the Annual Conference of the American Educational Research Association*, Denver, CO. 50, 51, 162

Oviatt, S. and Cohen, A. (2010b) Toward high-performance communication interfaces for science problem solving. *Journal of Science Educa,tion and Technology*, 19(6):515–531. DOI: 10.1007/s10956-010-9218-7. 24, 159

Oviatt, S. and Cohen, A. (2013) Written and multimodal representations as predictors of expertise and problem-solving success in mathematics. *Second Intl. Grand Challenge Workshop on Multimodal Learning Analytics, 15th International ACM Conference on Multimodal Interaction*, Sydney Australia, New York: ACM Press, 599–606. DOI: 10.1145/2522848.2533793. 146, 147

Oviatt, S. L. and Cohen, P. R. (1991) Discourse structure and performance efficiency in interactive and noninteractive spoken modalities. *Computer Speech and Language*, 5(4):297–326. DOI: 10.1016/0885-2308(91)90001-7. 18

Oviatt, S. L. and Cohen, P. R., (2000) Multimodal systems that process what comes naturally. *Communications of the ACM*, 43(3):45–53. DOI: 10.1145/330534.330538. xxi, 9, 15, 169

Oviatt, S. L., Cohen, P. R., Fong, M. W., and Frank, M. P. (1992) A rapid semi-automatic simulation technique for investigating interactive speech and handwriting. *Proceedings of the 2nd International Conference on Spoken Language Processing*, Univ. of Alberta., International Speech Communications Association, 1351–1354. 10, 53, 54

Oviatt, S. L., Cohen, A., Miller, A., Hodge, K., and Mann, A. (2012) The impact of interface affordances on human ideation, problem solving and inferential reasoning. *ACM Transactions on Computer Human Interaction*, 19(3):1–30. DOI: 10.1145/2362364.2362370. 24, 25, 44, 124, 125, 158, 159, 160, 161, 162, 163

Oviatt, S. L., Cohen, P. R., and Wang, M. Q. (1994) Toward interface design for human language technology: Modality and structure as determinants of linguistic complexity. *Speech Communication*, 15(3-4):283–300. DOI: 10.1016/0167-6393(94)90079-5. 20

Oviatt, S., Cohen, A., and Weibel, N. (2013) Multimodal learning analytics: Description of math data corpus for ICMI grand challenge workshop. *Second Intl. Grand Challenge Workshop on Multimodal Learning Analytics, 15th International ACM Conference on Multimodal Interaction*, Sydney Australia, New York: ACM Press, 563–568. DOI: 10.1145/2522848.2533790. 147

Oviatt, S. L., Cohen, P. R., Wu, L., Vergo, J., Duncan, L., Suhm, B., Bers, J., Holzman, T., Winograd, T., Landay, J., Larson, J., and Ferro, D. (2000) Designing the user interface for multimodal speech and gesture applications: State-of-the-art systems and research directions. *Human Computer Interaction*, 15(4), 263–322. (reprinted in J. Carroll (ed.) Human-Computer Interaction in the New Millennium, Boston: Addison-Wesley Press 2001). DOI: 10.1207/S15327051HCI1504_1. 8, 9, 10

Oviatt, S. L., Coulston, R. ,and Lunsford, R. (2004a) When do we interact multimodally? Cognitive load and multimodal communication patterns. *Proceedings of the 6th ACM Interna-*

tional Conference on Multimodal Interfaces (ICMI'04), New York:ACM Press, 129–136. DOI: 10.1145/1027933.1027957. 23, 28, 35, 84

Oviatt, S. L., Coulston, R., Shriver, S. Xiao, B., Wesson, R., Lunsford, R., and Carmichael, L. (2003) Toward a theory of organized multimodal integration patterns during human-computer interaction. *Proceedings of the 5th ACM International Conference on Multimodal Interfaces (ICMI'03)*, New York:ACM Press, 44–51. DOI: 10.1145/958432.958443. 29, 35, 36, 41, 42, 43

Oviatt, S. L., Darves, C., and Coulston, R. (2004b) Toward adaptive conversational interfaces: Modeling speech convergence with animated personas. *ACM Transactions on Human Computer Interaction (TOCHI)*, 11(3):300–328. DOI: 10.1145/1017494.1017498. 8, 43, 46, 152

Oviatt, S. L., DeAngeli, A., and Kuhn, K. (1997) Integration and synchronization of input modes during multimodal human-computer interaction. *Proceedings of SIGCHI Conference on Human Factors in Computing Systems (CHI'97)*, New York: ACM Press, 415–422. DOI: 10.1145/258549.258821. 17, 18, 34, 35, 40, 83, 85, 102

Oviatt, S. L, Flickner, M., and Darrell, T. (eds.) (2004) Multimodal interfaces that flex, adapt and persist. *Communications of the ACM* (special issue), 47(1):30–33. DOI: 10.1145/962081.962101.

Oviatt, S. L. and Kuhn, K. (1998) Referential features and linguistic indirection in multimodal language. *Proceedings of the 6th International Conference on Spoken Language Processing*, Sydney, Australia: ASSTA, Inc., International Speech Communications Association, 2339–2342. DOI: 10.1.1.9.8602. 20, 22, 83

Oviatt, S. L., Levow, G., Moreton, E., and MacEachern, M. (1998) Modeling global and focal hyperarticulation during human-computer error resolution. *Journal of the Acoustical Society of America*, 104(5):1–19. DOI: 10.1121/1.423888. 29

Oviatt, S. and Lunsford, R. (2005) Multimodal interfaces for cell phones and mobile technology. *International Journal of Speech Technology*, 8(2):127–132. DOI: 10.1007/s10772-005-2164-8. 8, 14

Oviatt, S. L., Lunsford, R., and Coulston, R. (2005) Individual differences in multimodal integration patterns: What are they and why do they exist? *Proceedings of the SIGCHI Conference on Human Factors in Computing Systems (CHI'05)*, CHI Letters, New York, N.Y.: ACM Press, 241–249. DOI: 10.1145/1054972.1055006. 34, 35, 36, 37, 39

Oviatt, S. L. and Olsen, E. (1994) Integration themes in multimodal human-computer interaction. Shirai, K., Furui, S. and Kakehi, K. , (eds.). *Proceedings of the 2nd International Conference on Spoken Language Processing, Acoustical Society of Japan*, 551–554 . DOI: 10.1.1.31.5485. 18, 40

Oviatt, S. L., Swindells, C., and Arthur, A. (2008) Implicit user-adaptive system engagement in speech and pen interfaces. *Conference on Human Factors in Computing Systems (CHI '08), CHI Letters*, New York: ACM, 969–978. DOI: 10.1145/1357054.1357204. 12, 55

Oviatt, S. L. and van Gent, R. (1996) Error resolution during multimodal human-computer interaction. *Proceedings of the 2nd International Conference on Spoken Language Processing*, Newark, DE:University of Delaware Press, 204–207. DOI: 10.1109/ICSLP.1996.607077. 20

Oviatt, S., Zhou, J., Hang, K., and Yu, K. (in press) Combining empirical science and machine learning to predict expertise using pen signal features, in press. DOI: 10.1145/2666633.2666638. 147

Owen, A., McMillan, K., Laird, A. et al. (2005) N-back working memory paradigm: A meta-analysis of normative functional neuroimaging studies. *Human Brain Mapping*, 25: 46–59. DOI: 10.1002/hbm.20131. 49

Paas, F., Tuovinen, J., Tabbers, H., and Van Gerven, P. (2003) Cognitive load measurement as a means to advance cognitive load theory. *Educational Psychologist*, 38(1):63–71. DOI: 10.1207/S15326985EP3801_8. 49

Pankanti, S., Bolle, R. M., and Jain, A. (Eds.), (2000) Biometrics: The future of identification. *Computer*, 33(2):46–80. DOI: 10.1109/2.820038. 8, 11

Park, S., Shim, H. S., Chatterjee, M., Sagae, K., and Morency, L. (2014) Computational analysis of persuasiveness in social multimedia: A novel dataset and multimodal prediction approach. *Proceedings of the 16th International Conference on Multimodal Interaction*, New York:ACM Press, 50–57. DOI: 10.1145/2663204.2663260. 100

Papandreou, G., Kasamanis, A., Pitsikalis, V., and Maragos, P. (2009) Adaptive multimodal fusion by uncertainty compensation with application to audiovisual speech recognition. *IEEE Transactions on Audio, Speech and Language Processing* 17(3):423–435. DOI: 10.1109/TASL.2008.2011515. 71, 100

Pavlakos, G., Theororakis, S., Pitsikalis, V., Katsamanis, A., and Maragos, P. (2014) Kinect-based multimodal gesture recognition using a two-pass fusion scheme. *Proceedings of the IEEE International Conference on Image Processing (ICIP-2014)*, Paris, France, New York:IEEE Press. DOI: 10.1109/ICIP.2014.7025299. 92

Pavlovic, V., Berry, G., and Huang, T. S. (1997) Integration of audio/visual information for use in human-computer intelligent interaction. *Proceedings of IEEE International Conference on Image Processing*, New York:IEEE Press, 121–124. DOI: 10.1109/ICIP.1997.647399. 11

Pavlovic, V., Sharma, R., and Huang, T. (1997) Visual interpretation of hand gestures for human-computer interaction: A review. *IEEE Transactions on Pattern Analysis and Machine Intelligence*, 19(7):677–695. DOI: 10.1109/34.598226. 11

Pernix Ltd., Advisory System for Tired Drivers (ASTiD) http://www.thefreelibrary.com/Wake+up+call+for+drivers-a0142306527, (retrieved 2/12/2015). 111

Perzanowski, D. Schultz, A. Adams, W. Marsh, E., and Bugajska, M.(2001) Building a multimodal human–robot interface. *IEEE Intelligent Systems* 16(1): 16–20. DOI: 10.1109/MIS.2001.1183338. 154

Petajan, E.D. (1984) Automatic Lipreading to Enhance Speech Recognition. Ph.D. thesis, University of Illinois at Urbana-Champaign. 7, 10

Pfleger, N. (2004) Context-based multimodal fusion. *Proceedings of the 6th ACM International Conference on Multimodal Interfaces*, ACM: New York, 265–272. DOI: 10.1145/1027933.1027977. 11

Pfleging, B., Schneegass, S., and Schmidt, A. (2012) Multimodal interaction in the car: Combining speech and gesture on the steering wheel. *Proceedings of the 4th International Conference on Automotive User Interfaces and Interactive Vehicular Applications*, New York: ACM Press, 155-162. DOI: 10.1145/2390256.2390282. 111

Pick, H. L. and E. Saltzman, (1978) Modes of perceiving and processing information. In *Modes of Perceiving and Processing Information*, Pick, H.L. and Saltzman, E., (eds.), New York: John Wiley and Sons, 1–20. 28

Pinker, S. and Bloom, P. (1990) Natural language and natural selection. *Behavioral and Brain Sciences*, 13(4): 707–784. DOI: 10.1017/S0140525X00081061. 27

Poddar, I., Sethi, Y., Ozyildiz, E., and Sharma, R. (1998) Toward natural gesture/speech HCI: A case study of weather narration. In M. Turk, (Ed.), *Proceedings 1998 Workshop on Perceptual User Interfaces (PUI'98)* San Francisco, CA., 1–6. 11

Popescu-Belis, A., Baudrion, P., Flynn, M., and Wellner, P. (2008) Towards an objective test for meeting browsers: The BET4TQB Pilot Experiment. *Machine Learning for Multimodal Interaction, Lecture Notes in Computer Science LNCS 4892*, Popescu-Belis, A., Renals, S., and Bourlard, H., (eds.), Berlin: Springer, 108–119. DOI: 10.1007/978-3-540-78155-4_10. 12

Popescu-Belis, A. and Georgescul, M. (2006) TQB: Accessing multimedia data using a transcript-based query and browsing interface. *Proceedings of 5th Edition of Language Resources and Evaluation Conference*, Genoa, European Language Resources Assocation, 1560 –1565. 12

Potamianos, G., Neti, C., Gravier, G., and Garg, A. (2003) Automatic recognition of audio-visual speech: Recent progress and challenges. *Proceedings of the IEEE*, 91(9), Sept. 2003. 9, 10

Potamianos, G., Neti, C., Luettin, J., and Matthews, I. (2015) Audiovisual automatic speech recognition, Audiovisual Speech Processing. Bailly, G., Perrier, P., Vatikiotis-Bateson, E. (eds.), Cambridge UK:Cambridge University Press. Price, P. (2004) Matching Technology and Application, Tutorial given at annual meeting of the American Voice I/O Society. 71, 72, 130

Price, P. (2004) Matching Technology and Application, Tutorial given at annual meeting of the *American Voice I/O Society*. 115

Promethean (2015) http://www.prometheanworld.com/us/english/education/products/interactive-whiteboard-systems/, (retrieved Jan. 26, 2015). 123

Quain, J. (2015) If a car is going to self-drive, it may as well self-park too. *New York Times*, Jan. 22, 2015; http://www.nytimes.com/2015/01/23/automobiles/if-a-car-is-going-to-self-drive-it-might-as-well-self-park-too.html?hpw&rref=automobiles&action=click&pgtype=Homepage&module=well-region&region=bottom-well&WT.nav=bottom-well&_r=0, (retrieved Jan. 26, 2015). 143

Quek, F., Shi, Y. Kirbas, C., and Wu, S. (2002) VisSTA: A tool for analyzing multimodal discourse data. *Seventh International Conference on Spoken Language Processing*, Denver, CO, September, 2002. 57

Rabiner, L. R. (1990) A tutorial on hidden Markov models and selected applications in speech recognition. *Readings in Speech Recognition*, San Francisco:Morgan Kaufmann Publishers, 267–296. DOI: 10.1016/B978-0-08-051584-7.50027-9. 69

Rabiner, L. R. and Juang, B.-H. (1993) *Fundamentals of Speech Recognition*. Upper Saddle River, NJ:Prentice-Hall, Inc. 69

Rainie, L. and Poushter, J. (2014) Emerging nations catching up to U.S. on technology adoption, especially mobile and social media use. *Pew Research Center Report*, Feb. 13, 2014. 13

Reithinger, N., Alexandersson, J., Becker, T., Blocher, A., Engel, R., Lockelt, M., Muller, J., Pfleger, N., Poller, P., Streit, S., and Tschernomas, V. (2003) Multimodal architectures and frameworks: SmartKom: adaptive and flexible multimodal access to multiple applications. *proceedings of the 5th ACM International Conference on Multimodal Interfaces*, New York: ACM,101–108. DOI: 10.1145/958432.958454. 8, 152

Recanzone, G. H., (2003) Auditory influences on visual-temporal rate perception. *Journal of Neurophysiology*, 89:1078–1093. DOI: 10.1152/jn.00706.2002. 29, 30

Reeves, L., Lai, J., Larson, J., Oviatt, S., Balaji, T., Buisine, S., Collings, P., Cohen, P., Kraal, B., Martin, J.-C., McTear, M., Raman, T.V., Stanney, K., Su, H., and Wang, Q. (2004) Guidelines for multimodal user interface design. *Communications of the ACM*, 47(1):57–59. DOI: 10.1145/962081.962106. 15

Reimer, B., Mehler, B., Dobres, J., and Coughlin, J.F. (2013) The effects of a production level "voice-command" interface on driver behavior: Reported workload, physiology, visual attention and driving performance. *MIT AgeLab Technical Report No. 2013-17A*, Cambridge, MA:MIT. 110

Reissman, C. J. (1996) *The Alert Driver: A Trucker's Guide to Sleep, Fatigue and Rest in Our 24-Hour Society*. American Trucking Associations, Transportation Research Board of the National Academy of Science, Accession Number 00728834. 111

Reithinger, N., Alexandersson, J., Becker, T., Blocher, A., Engel, R., Löckelt, M., Müller, J., Pfleger, N., Poller, P., Streit, M., and Tschernomas, V. (2003) SmartKom: Adaptive and flexible multimodal access to multiple applications. *Proceedings of the 5th ACM International Conference on Multimodal Interfaces*, New York:ACM Press, 101–108. DOI: 10.1145/958451.958454. 8

Rizzolatti, G. and Craighero, L. (2004) The mirror-neuron system. *Annual Review of Neuroscience*, 27:169–92. DOI: 10.1146/annurev.neuro.27.070203.144230. 29

Robert-Ribes, J., Schwartz, J-L., Lallouache, T., and Escudier, P. (1998) Complementarity and synergy in bimodal speech: Auditory, visual, and auditory-visual identification of French oral vowels in noise. *Journal of the Acoustical Society of America*, 103(6):3677–3689. DOI: 10.1121/1.423069. 10, 28, 40

Robokind Robots (2015) http://www.robokindrobots.com/, (retrieved 2/12/2015). 154

Rogozan, A. and Deglise, P. (1998) Adaptive fusion of acoustic and visual sources for automatic speech recognition. *Speech Communication*, 26(1-2):149–161. DOI: 10.1016/S0167-6393(98)00056-9. 10

Rohlfing, K., Loehr, D., Duncan, S., Brown, A., Franklin, A., Kimbara, I., Milde, J-T., Parrill, F., Rose, T., Schmidt, T., Sloetjes, H., Thies, A., and Wellinghoff, S. (2006) Comparison of multimodal annotation tools: Workshop report, *Gesprächsforschung*. 2006;7. 57

Ross, A. (2007) An introduction to multibiometrics. *Proceedings of the 15th European Signal Processing Conference, European Association for Signal Processing (EURASIP)*, 20–24. 121

Ross, A. and Jain, A. (2004) Multimodal biometrics: An overview. *Proceedings of the 12th European Signal Processing Conference (EUSIPCO)*, Vienna, European Association for Signal Processing (EURASIP), 1221–1224. 70

Ross, A. and Poh, N. (2009) Multibiometric systems: Overview, case studies and open issues. In *Handbook of Remote Biometrics for Surveillance and Security*, M. Tistarelli, M. , Li S. Z., and Chellappa, R., (eds.), Berlin:Springer Verlag, 273–292. DOI: 10.1007/978-1-84882-385-3_11. 3, 100, 121, 122, 123

Rosson, M. and Carroll, J. (2012) Scenario-based design. *The Human-Computer Interaction Handbook: Fundamentals, Evolving Technologies and Emerging Applications* (revised 3rd edition), Jacko, J. (ed.), Boca Raton, FL:CRC Press, 1105–1124. DOI: 10.1201/b11963-56. 53

Rubin, P., Vatikiotis-Bateson, E., and Benoit, C. (eds.) (1998) Audio-visual speech processing (Special issue). *Speech Communication*, 26:1–2. DOI: 10.1016/S0167-6393(98)00046-6. 9

Rudnicky, A. and Hauptman, A. (1992) Multimodal interactions in speech systems. In Blattner M. and Dannenberg, R., (eds.), *Multimedia Interface Design*, New York: ACM Press , 147–172. DOI: 10.1145/146022.146049. 20

Ruiz, N., Oviatt, S., and Chen, F. (2010) *Multimodal Interfaces, Multimodal Signal Processing: Theory and Applications for Human-Computer Interaction*, chap. 12. Thiran, J.P., Marques, F. and Bourlard, H., (eds.), Amsterdam:Elsevier, 231–255. DOI: 10.1016/B978-0-12-374825-6.00010-1. 40

Sainath, T. N., Kingsbury, B., Saon, G., Soltau, H., Mohamed, A-R., Dahl, G., and Ramabhadran B. (2015) Deep convolutional neural networks for large-scale speech tasks. *Neural Networks*, 64, April, 39–48. DOI: 10.1016/j.neunet.2014.08.005. 67

Salakhutdinov, R. (2014) Deep learning. *Tutorial at 20th ACM Knowledge Discovery and Data Mining Conference*, 2014. http://videolectures.net/kdd2014_salakhutdinov_deep_learning/, (retrieved 2/9/2015). 69, 93

Salber, D. and Coutasz, J. (1993) Applying the wizard of oz technique to the study of multimodal systems. *Human-Computer Interaction*, 1993, 219-230. DOI: 10.1007/3-540-57433-6_51. 53, 54

Sale, A., Berardi N., and Maffei L. (2009) Enrich the environment to empower the brain. *Trends in Neuroscience*, 32:233–9. DOI: 10.1016/j.tins.2008.12.004. 51

Salisbury, M. W., Hendrickson, J. H., Lammers, T. L., Fu, C., and Moody, S. A. (1990) Talk and draw: Bundling speech and graphics. *IEEE Computer* 23(8):59–65. DOI: 10.1109/2.56872. 8

Samsung Gear S (2015) http://www.samsung.com/us/mobile/wearable-tech/all-products, (retrieved January 26, 2015). 142

Sanchez, U. R. and Kittler, J. (2007) Fusion of talking face biometric modalities for personal identity verification. *Proceedings of International Conference on Acoustics, Speech and Sig-*

nal Processing (ICASSP), Vol 5, New York:IEEE Press, 1073–1076. DOI: 10.1109/ICASSP.2006.1661465. 122

Saund, E., Fleet, D., Larner, D., and Mahoney, J. (2003) Perceptually-supported image editing of text and graphics. *Proceedings of the 16th Annual ACM Symposium on User Interface Software Technology (UIST'2003)*, ACM Press: New York, 183–192. DOI: 10.1145/964696.964717. 43

Scherer, K. (2003) Vocal communication of emotion: A review of research paradigms. *Speech Communication*, 40:227–256. DOI: 10.1016/S0167-6393(02)00084-5. 144, 145

Scherer, K. (2000) Psychological models of emotion. In *The Neuropsychology of Emotion*, Oxford, UK:Oxford University, 137–162. 74

Scherer, S., Stratou, G., Lucas, G., Mahmoud, M., Boberg, J. Gratch, J., Rizzo, A., and Morency, L-P. (2014) Automatic audio-visual behavior descriptors for psychological disorder analysis. *Image and Vision Computing*, 32(10): 648–658. DOI: 10.1016/j.imavis.2014.06.001. 144

Schiel, F. and Turk, U. (2006) Wizard-of-Oz recordings. *SmartKom: Foundations of Multimodal Dialogue Systems*, Wahster, W. (ed.), Berlin:Springer-Verlag, 542–570. DOI: 10.1007/3-540-36678-4_34. 55

Schnelle-Walka, D., Radomski, S., and Mühlhäuser, M. (2013) JVoiceXML as a modality component in the W3C multimodal architecture. *Journal on Multimodal User Interfaces*, 7(3):183–194. DOI: 10.1007/s12193-013-0119-y. 130

Schroeder, C. and Foxe, J. (2004) Multisensory convergence in early cortical processing. *The Handbook of Multisensory Processing*, Calvert, G., Spence, C. and Stein, B., (eds.) Cambridge, MA:MIT Press, 295–309. 28

Schuller, B., Valstar, M., Eyben, F., Cowie, R., and Pantic, M. (2012) AVEC 2012—The continuous audio/visual emotion challenge. *Proceedings of the 14th International Conference on Multimodal Interaction*, New York:ACM Press, 449–456. DOI: 10.1145/2388676.2388776. 74, 145

Schutte, J. (2007) Researchers fine-tune F-35 pilot-aircraft speech system, *Air Force Print News*, http://www.speech.sri.com/press/airforce-print-news-oct15-2007.pdf. 108

Seeingmachines Corp. http://www.seeingmachines.com, (retrieved 2/12/2015). 111

Seide, F., Li, G., and Yu, D. (2011) Conversational speech transcription using context-dependent deep neural networks. *Proceedings of Interspeech 2011, Florence, Italy, International Speech Communications Association*, 437–440.

Sekiyama, K. and Tohkura, Y. (1991) McGurk effect in non-English listeners: Few visual effects for Japanese subjects hearing Japanese syllables of high auditory intelligibility. *Journal of the Acoustical Society of America*, 90(4):1797–1805. DOI: 10.1121/1.401660. 39

Seneff, S., Goddeau, D., Pao, C., and Polifroni, J. (1996) Multimodal discourse modelling in a multi-user multi-domain environment. In Bunnell, T. and Idsardi W., (eds.). *Proceedings of the International Conference on Spoken Language Processing*, Vol. 1. Newark, DE: University of Delaware and A.I. duPont Institute, 192–195. DOI: 10.1109/ICSLP.1996.607074. 9

Seneff, S., Lau R., and J. Polifroni, (1999) Organization, communication, and control in the Galaxy-II conversational system. In *Proceedings of Eurospeech '99, Budapest, Hungary, International Speech Communications Association*, 1271–1274. 129

Sense.ly (2015) http://www.sense.ly.com, (retrieved 2/12/2015). 117

Serrano, M. and Nigay, L. (2009) Temporal aspects of CARE-based multimodal fusion: From a fusion mechanism to composition components and W0Z components. *Proceedings of the 11th International Conference on Multimodal Interaction (ICMI-MLMI)*, New York:ACM Press, 177–184. DOI: 10.1145/1647314.1647346. 85

Sezgin, T. M., Davies, I., and Robinson, P. (2009) Multimodal inference for driver-vehicle interaction. *Proceedings of the 11th International Conference on Multimodal Interaction (ICMI-MLMI)*, New York: ACM Press, 193–197. DOI: 10.1145/1647314.1647348. 108

Shaer, O., Strait, M., Valdes, C., Feng, T., Lintz, M., and Wang, H. (2011) Enhancing genomic learning through tabletop interaction. *Proceedings of the SIGCHI Conference on Human Factors in Computing Systems*, New York: ACM, 2817–2826. DOI: 10.1145/1978942.1979361. 140

Sharma, R., Huang, T. S., Pavlovic, V. I., Schulten, K., Dalke, A., Phillips, J., Zeller, M., Humphrey, W., Zhao, Y., Lo, Z., and Chu, S. (1996) Speech/gesture interface to a visual computing environment for molecular biologists. *Proceedings of 13th International Conference on Pattern Recognition (ICPR 96)*, Vol. 3, 964–968. DOI: 10.1109/ICPR.1996.547311. 11

Sharma, R., Pavlovic, V. I., and Huang, T. S. (1998) Toward multimodal human-computer interface. *Proceedings IEEE (Special issue on Multimedia Signal Processing)*, 86(5):853–860. DOI: 10.1109/5.664275. 11

Shieber, S. (1986) *An Introduction to Unification-Based Approaches to Grammar*. Stanford, C: CSLI Publications, Available at: http://nrs.harvard.edu/urn-3:HUL.InstRepos:11576719, (retrieved 2/12/2015). 89, 90

Sidner, C. and Lee, C. (2007) Attentional gestures in dialogues between people and robots. *Engineering Approaches to Conversational Informatics*, Nishida, T. (ed.), Hoboken, NJ:John Wiley and Sons, 103–115. DOI: 10.1002/9780470512470.ch6. 154, 155

Sidner, C., Lee, C., Morency, L-P, and Forlines, C. (2006) The effect of head-nod recognition in human-robot conversation. *Proceedings of the ACM Conference on Human-Robot Interaction (HRI)*, New York:ACM Press, 290–296. DOI: 10.1145/1121241.1121291. 154

Silsbee, P. L. and Su, Q (1996) Audiovisual sensory intergration using Hidden Markov Models. Stork, D.G. and Hennecke, M. E., (eds.). *Speechreading by Humans and Machines: Models, Systems and Applications*, New York: Springer Verlag, 489–504. DOI: 10.1007/978-3-662-13015-5_37. 10

Singhal, A. and Brown, C. (1997) Dynamic Bayes net approach to multimodal sensor fusion. *Proceedings of the SPIE—The International Society for Optical Engineering*, 2–10. DOI: 10.1117/12.287628. 92

Siroux, J., Guyomard, M., Multon, F., and Remondeau, C. (1995) Modeling and processing of the oral and tactile activities in the Georal tactile system. *International Conference on Cooperative Multimodal Communication, Theory and Applications*, Eindhoven:Netherlands. DOI: 10.1007/BFb0052315. 9

Slevin, J. and May, R. (2011) *The Rise of Multi-Modal Warehouse Applications*. Lucas Systems, Inc., White paper, http://www.lucasware.com/_literature_140944/WP_-_The_Rise_of_Multi-Modal_Warehouse_Applications, (retrieved 2/11/2015). 129

Smart Technologies (2015) http://education.smarttech.com/?WT.ac=homepage_ed, (retrieved January 26, 2015). 123

Smith, H., Higgins, S., Wall, K., and Miller, J. (2005) Interactive whiteboards: Boon or bandwagon? A critical review of the literature, *Journal of Computer-Assisted Learning*, 21(2):91–101. DOI: 10.1111/j.1365-2729.2005.00117.x. 123

Smith, D. C., Irby, C.H., and Kimball, R. B., Harslem, E. F. (1982) The Star user interface: An overview. *Proceedings of the AFIPS National Computer Conference*, New York:ACM Press, 515–528. DOI: 10.1145/1500774.1500840. 7

Somekh, B., Haldane, M., Jones, K., Lewin, C., Steadman, S., Scrimshaw, P., Sing, S., Bird, K., Cummings, J., Downing, B., Stuart, T., Jarvis, J., Mavers, D., and Woodrow, D. (2007) Evaluation of the primary schools whiteboard expansion project. *BECTA Report*. 123

Song, Y., Morency, L.-P., and Davis, R. (2013) Learning a sparse codebook of facial and body microexpressions for emotion recognition. *Proceedings of the 15th Interna-*

tional Conference on Multimodal Interaction, New York:ACM Press, 237–244. DOI: 10.1145/2522848.2522851. 67, 71, 74, 75, 80, 100

Spence, C. and Driver, J. (1999) A new approach to the design of multimodal warning signals. In *Engineering Psychology and Cognitive Ergonomics*, Harris, D. (ed.), Hampshire, UK:Ashgate Publishing, 455–461. 33

Spence, C. and S. Squire, (2003) Multisensory integration: Maintaining the perception of synchrony. *Current Biology*, 13:R519–R521. DOI: 10.1016/S0960-9822(03)00445-7. 29

Srivastava N. and Salakhutdinov, R. (2012) Multimodal learning with Deep Boltzmann Machines. *Advances in Neural Information Processing Systems 25*, Neural Information Processing Systems (NIPS) Foundation, 2222–2230. 74, 92

Starner, T. (2001) The challenges of wearable computing: Part 2. *IEEE Micro*, 21(4):54–67. DOI: 10.1109/40.946683. 142

Stein, B. E. (ed.) (2012) *The New Handbook of Multisensory Processing*. Cambridge, MA:MIT Press. 8, 28

Stein, B. E. and Meredith, M. (1993) *The Merging of the Senses*. Cambridge , MA:MIT Press. 28, 32

Steinmetz, R. (ed.) (2015) ACM Transactions on Multimedia Computing, Communications and Applications. *ACM Society Journal*, http://tomm.acm.org, (retrieved Jan. 12, 2015). 1

Steinmetz, R. and Nahrstedt, K. (2004) *Multimedia Systems*, Berlin:Springer-Verlag. DOI: 10.1007/978-3-662-08878-4. 1

Stiefelhagen, R., Ekenel, H. K., Fügen, C., Gieselmann, P., Holzapfel, H., Kraft, F., Nickel, K., Voit, M., and Waibel. A. (2007) Enabling multimodal human–robot interaction for the Karlsruhe humanoid robot. *IEEE Transactions On Robotics*, 23(5):840–851. DOI: 10.1109/TRO.2007.907484. 154

Stone, J.V., Hunkin N. M., Porrill J., Wood, R., Keeler, V., Beanland, M., Port, M., and Porter, N. R. (2001) When is now? Perception of simultaneity. *Proceedings of The Royal Society of London. Series B: Biological Sciences*, 268(1462):31–38. DOI: 10.1098/rspb.2000.1326. 30

Stork, D. G. and Hennecke, M. E. (Eds.) (1995) *Speechreading by Humans and Machines*. New York: Springer Verlag. 7, 8, 9, 34

Stratou, G., Scherer, S., Gratch, J., and Morency, L-P. (2013) Automatic nonverbal behavior indicators of depression and PTSD: Exploring gender differences. *Proceedings of the Humaine Assoc. Conference on Affective Computing and Intelligent Interaction*, IEEE Computer Society, 147–152. DOI: 10.1109/ACII.2013.31. 144

Sugita, Y. and Suzuki, Y. (2003) Audiovisual perception: Implicit estimation of sound arrival time. *Nature*, 421(6926):911. DOI: 10.1038/421911a. 29

Suhm, B. (1998) Multimodal interactive error recovery for non-conversational speech user interfaces. Ph.D. thesis, Frederica University, Germany: Shaker Verlag. 18, 20

Sukthankar, G., Goldman, R. P., Geib, C., Pynadath, D. V., and Bui, H. H. (eds.) (2014) *Plan, Activity, and Intent Recognition*. Morgan Kaufmann Publishers/Elsevier, Waltham, MA. 117

Sumby, W. H. and Pollack, I. (1954) Visual contribution to speech intelligibility in noise. *Journal of the Acoustical Society of America*, 26:212–215. DOI: 10.1121/1.1907384. 8, 10, 28

Summerfield, A. Q. (1992) Lipreading and audio-visual speech perception. *Philosophical Transactions of the Royal Society of London. Series B: Biological Sciences*, 335(1273):71–78. DOI: 10.1098/rstb.1992.0009. 10

Sweller, J. (1988) Cognitive load during problem solving: Effects on learning. *Cognitive Science*, 12(2):257–285. DOI: 10.1207/s15516709cog1202_4. 49

Tang, A., McLachlan, P., Lowe, K., Saka, C., and MacLean, K. (2005) Perceiving ordinal data haptically under workload. *Proceedings of the 7th ACM International Conference on Multimodal Interfaces*, ACM: New York, 317–324. DOI: 10.1145/1088463.1088517. 23

Taylor, G. (2014) An overview of deep learning and its challenges for technical computing. Lecture given at *International Workshop on Technical Computing for Machine Learning and Mathematical Engineering (TCMM)*, Leuven, http://videolectures.net/tcmm2014_leuven/, (retrieved 3/3/2015). 78

TechTimes (2015) Konnichiwa! IBM Watson will learn japanese in partnership with SoftBank. http://www.techtimes.com/articles/31977/20150211/konnichiwa-ibm-watson-will-learn-japanese-in-partnership-with-softbank.htm, retrieved 2/13/2015. 154

Thacker, C.P., McCreight, E. M., Lampson, B. W., Sproull, R. F., and Boggs, D. R. (1982) Alto: A Personal Computer, in Siewioek, D., Bell, C.G., and Newell, A. (eds), *Computer Structures: Principles and Examples*. New York: McGraw Hill, 549–572. 7

Tindall-Ford, S., Chandler, P., and Sweller, J. (1997) When two sensory modes are better than one. *Journal of Experimental Psychology: Applied*, 3(4):257–287. DOI: 10.1037//1076-898X.3.4.257. 50

Tomlinson, M. J., Russell, M. J., and Brooke, N. M. (1996) Integrating audio and visual information to provide highly robust speech recognition. *Proceedings of the International Conference on Acoustics, Speech and Signal Processing (IEEE-ICASSP)*, Vol. 2, New York: IEEE Press, 821–824. DOI: 10.1109/ICASSP.1996.543247. 10, 20, 21

Touch Graphics, Inc. (2014) http://touchgraphics.com/OnlineStore/index.php/ttp-accessories/talking-tactile-pen-binder.html, (retrieved July 15, 2014). 150

Traum, D. and Morency, L-P (2010) Integration of visual perception in dialogue understanding for virtual humans in multi-party interaction. *Proceedings of Autonomous Agents and Multiagent Systems (AAMAS)*, International Workshop on Interacting with ECAs as Virtual Characters, New York:Springer. 155

Tulyakov, S., Jaeger, S., Govindaraju, V., and Doermann, D. (2006) Review of classifier combination methods. *Learning in Document Analysis and Recognition, Studies in Computational Intelligence*, Marinai, S. and Fujisawa, H. (eds.), Berlin:Springer Verlag, 361–386. DOI: 10.1007/978-3-540-76280-5_14. 63, 71

Turk, M. and Robertson, G. (Eds.), (2000) Perceptual user interfaces (Special issue). *Communications of the ACM*, 43(3):32–70. DOI: 10.1145/330534.330535. 8, 11

van Merrienboer, J. and Sweller, J. (2005) Cognitive load theory and complex learning: Recent developments and future directions. *Educational Psychology Review*, 17(2):147–177. DOI: 10.1007/s10648-005-3951-0. 49

Vatikiotis-Bateson, E., Munhall, K. G., Hirayama, M., Lee, Y. V., and Terzopoulos, D. (1996) The dynamics of audiovisual behavior of speech, Stork , D.G. and Hennecke, M.E., (eds.), *Speechreading by Humans and Machines: Models, Systems, and Applications*. Vol. 150 of NATO ASI Series. Series F: Computer and Systems Sciences, Berlin, Germany: Springler-Verlag, 221–232. 10, 34

Villaneuva, D. (2012) Voice picking not gaining traction', after 20 years, why?, http://vangardvoice.blogspot.com/2012/02/voice-picking-not-gaining-traction.html, (retrieved January, 28, 2015). 128

Vo, M.T. and Waibel, A. (1993) A multimodal human-computer interface: combination of speech and gesture recognition. *Adjunct Proceedings of Human Factors in Computing Systems (InterCHI'93)*, New York:ACM Press. 69

Vygotsky, L. (1962) *Thought and Language*. MIT Press: Cambridge Ma. (Transl. by Hanfmann, E. and Vakar, G. from 1934 original). 50, 51

Vygotsky, L. (1978) *Mind in Society: The Development of Higher Psychological Processes*. Cole, M., John-Steiner, V., Scribner, S. and Souberman, E., Cambridge MA:Harvard University Press. 50

Vygotsky, L. (1987) *The Collected Works of L. S. Vygotsky, Volume I: Problems of General Psychology*. Edited and translated by N. Minick, New York: Plenum. 50, 51

Wacom Corp. Cintiq 27QHD http://www.wacom.com/en-es/products/pen-displays/cin-tiq-27-qhd-touch#Specifications, (retrieved, 2/12/2015). 114

Wagner, J., Lingenfelser, F., Bauer, T., Damian, I., Kistler, F., and André, E. (2013) The social signal interpretation (SSI) framework: Multimodal signal processing and recognition in real-time. *MM'13: Proceedings of the 21st ACM International Conference on Multimedia*, New York:ACM Press, 831–834. DOI: 10.1145/2502081.2502223. 96

Wahlster, W. (1991) User and discourse models for multimodal communciation. Sullivan , J. W. and Tyler, S. W., (eds.), *Intelligent User Interfaces*, chap. 3, New York:ACM Press, 45–67. 9

Wahlster, W. (2001) SmartKom: multimodal dialogs with mobile web users. *Proceedings of the Cyber Assist International Symposium*, Tokyo International Forum, 33–34. 11

Wahlster, W., (2003) SmartKom: Symmetric multimodality in an adaptive and reusable dialogue shell. *Proceedings of the Human Computer Interaction Status Conference,* Krahl, R., Günther, D. (eds): Berlin (Germany): DLR, 47–62. 152

Wahlster, W. (ed.) (2006) *SmartKom: Foundations of Multimodal Dialogue Systems.* Berlin: Germany. DOI: 10.1007/3-540-36678-4. 90, 151, 152

Waibel, A., Suhm, B., Vo, M. T., and Yang, J. (1997) Multimodal interfaces for multimedia information agents. *Proceedings of the International Conference on Acoustics Speech and Signal Processing (IEEE-ICASSP) Vol. 1*, New York: IEEE Press, 167–170. DOI: 10.1109/ICASSP.1997.599587. 8, 10

Walker, R. (2012) *Freaks, Geeks and Microsoft: How Kinect Spawned a Commercial Ecosystem. New York Times*, May 31, 2012. 141

Wang FreeStyle System (1990) *PC Magazine*. 326–329. video: http://www.youtube.com/watch?v=-FRKzmFH7-cM, (retrieved 3/1/2015). 7

Waugh N. and Norman D. (1965) Primary memory. *Psychological Review* 72:89–104. DOI: 10.1037/h0021797. 48

Webster, D. and Celik, O. (2014) Systematic review of kinect applications in elderly care and stroke rehabilitation. *Journal of Neuroengineering and Rehabilitation*, 11:108. DOI: 10.1186/1743-0003-11-108. 141

Weiser, M. (1991) The computer for the 21st century. *Scientific American*, Jan.-March issue 265(3):19–25. DOI: 10.1038/scientificamerican0991-94. 139

Welch, R. B., Duttonhurt L. D., and Warren, D. H. (1986) Contributions of audition and vision to temporal rate perception. *Perception and Psychophysics*, 39: 294–300. DOI: 10.3758/BF03204939. 29, 30, 32

Welkowitz, J., Cariffe, G., and Feldstein, S. (1976) Conversational congruence as a criterion of socialization in children. *Child Development* 47:269–272. DOI: 10.2307/1128311. 46

Wertheimer, M. (1945) Productive Thinking. New York: Harper Publishers. 43

Whittaker, S., Laban, R., and Tucker, S. (2005) Analysing meeting records: An ethnographic study and technical implications. *Machine Learning for Multimodal Interaction, Lecture Notes in Computer Science 3869*, Renals, S. and Bengio, S., (eds.), New York :Springer, 101–113. DOI: 10.1007/11677482_9. 12

Wickens, C. (2002) Multiple resources and performance prediction. *Theoretical Issues in Ergonomic Science*, 3(2):159–177. DOI: 10.1080/14639220210123806. 49

Wickens, C., Sandry, D., and Vidulich, M. (1983) Compatibility and resource competition between modalities of input, central processing, and output. *Human Factors*, 25(2):227–248. DOI: 10.1177/001872088302500209. 40, 49

Winzenried, A., Dalgarno, B., and Tinkler, J. (2010) The interactive whiteboard: A transitional technology supporting diverse teaching practices. *Australasian Journal of Educational Technology, (Special Issue)*, 26(4):534–552. 123

Wittenburg, K., Weitzman, L., and Talley, J. (1991) Unification-based grammars and tabular parsing for graphical languages. *Journal of Visual Languages and Computing* 2(4): 347–370. DOI: 10.1016/S1045-926X(05)80004-7. 90

Woods, W. (1970) Transition network grammars for natural language analysis. *Communications of the ACM*, 13(10):591–606. DOI: 10.1145/355598.362773. 96

Woolf, B., Burleson, W., Arroyo, I., Dragon, T., Cooper, D., and Picard, R. (2009) Affect aware tutors: Recognizing and responding to student affect. *International Journal of Learning Technology*, 4(3/4):129–164. DOI: 10.1504/IJLT.2009.028804. 144

World Wide Web Consortium (2014) State Chart XML. http://www.w3.org/TR/scxml/, (retrieved 2/11/2015). 96, 129, 130

Worsley, M. and Blikstein, P. (2010) Toward the development of learning analytics: Student speech as an automatic and natural form of assessment. *Proceedings of the Annual Meeting of the American Educational Research Association (AERA) Conference.* 145

Wu, L., Oviatt, S., and. Cohen, P. (1999) Multimodal integration—A statistical view. *IEEE Transactions on Multimedia*, 1(4):334–341. DOI: 10.1109/6046.807953. 11, 92

Wu, L., Oviatt, S. L., and Cohen, P. R. (2002) From members to teams to committee—A robust approach to gestural and multimodal recognition. *Proceedings of IEEE Transactions on Neural Networks*, 13(4):72–982. DOI: 10.1109/TNN.2002.1021897. 73, 92

Xiao, B., Girand, C., and Oviatt, S. (2002) Multimodal integration patterns in children. *Proceedings of the International Conference on Spoken Language Processing (ICSLP'02)*, Hansen J. and Pellom, B. (eds.) International Speech Communication Association, 629–632. 35, 36

Xiao, B., Lunsford, R., Coulston, R., Wesson, R., and Oviatt, S. L. (2003) Modeling multimodal integration patterns and performance in seniors: Toward adaptive processing of individual differences. *Proceedings of the 3rd ACM International Conference on Multimodal Interfaces (ICMI/PUI'03)*, New York:ACM Press, 265–272. DOI: 10.1145/958432.958480. 35, 36, 50, 51

Xu, T., Yu, X., Perlik, A., Tobin, W., Zweig, J., Tennant, K., Jones, T., Zuo, Y. (2009) Rapid formation and selective stabilization of synapses for enduring motor memories. *Nature*, 462, 915–19. DOI: 10.1038/nature08389. 51

Yang, G., Pan, F., and Gan, W. B. (2009) Stably maintained dendritic spines are associated with lifelong memories. *Nature*, 462:920–24. DOI: 10.1038/nature08577. 51

Yu, D. and Deng, L. (2015) *Automatic Speech Recognition: A Deep Learning Approach*. Berlin:Springer Verlag. DOI: 10.1007/978-1-4471-5779-3. 116

Zakharov, K. (2007) Affect recognition and support in intelligent tutoring systems. Ph.D. Dissertation, Dept. of Computer Science and Engineering, University of Canterbury, New Zealand. 144

Zeng, Z., Pantic, M., Roisman, G., and Huang, T. (2009) A survey of affect recognition methods: audio, visual, and spontaneous expressions. *IEEE Trans. Pattern Analysis and Machine Intelligence*, 31(1):39–58. DOI: 10.1109/TPAMI.2008.52. 76, 143, 145

Zetes (2009) (R)Evolution of the Market for Voice Solutions in Europe: A White Paper. http://www.retail-systems.com/rs/whitepapers/WP_%28r%29evolution_of_the_market_for_voice.pdf, retrieved 2/12/2015. 129

Zhai, S., Morimoto, C., and Ihde, S. (1999) Manual and gaze input cascaded (MAGIC) pointing. *Proceedings of the SIGCHI Conference on Human Factors in Computing Systems (CHI'99)*, New York: ACM Press, 246–253. DOI: 10.1145/302979.303053. 8, 11

Zhang, J. and Patel, V. (2006) Distributed cognition, representation, and affordance. In *Cognition Distributed: How Cognitive Technology Extends Our Mind*, Dror, I. and Harnad S., (eds.), Amsterdam: John Benjamins,137–144. DOI: 10.1075/pc.14.2.12zha. 44

Zipf, G. (1935) *The Psycho-Biology of Language: An Introduction to Dynamic Philology*. Boston, MA.: Houghton Mifflin. DOI: 10.1525/aa.1936.38.3.02a00270. 28

Zoltan-Ford, E. (1991) How to get people to say and type what computers can understand. *International Journal of Man-Machine Studies*, 34:527–547. DOI: 10.1016/0020-7373(91)90034-5. 46

Author Biographies

Dr. Sharon Oviatt is well known for her extensive work in multimodal and mobile interfaces, human-centered interface design, educational interfaces, and communications interfaces. She was the recipient of the Inaugural ACM ICMI Sustained Accomplishment Award and a National Science Foundation Special Creativity Award for her pioneering research on mobile multimodal interfaces. She is also a member of CHI Academy. Dr. Oviatt has published over 150 scientific articles in a multidisciplinary range of venues, including computer science, learning and cognitive sciences, and linguistic sciences. She is an Associate Editor of the main journals and edited book collections in the field of human interfaces, and authored the chapter on "Multimodal Interfaces" in *The Human-Computer Interaction Handbook* (3rd edition). She was a founder of the International Conference on Multimodal Interfaces (ICMI), which became an annual ACM-sponsored international conference series under her guidance.

Dr. Philip R Cohen is internationally known for his work in multimodal systems and artificial intelligence (intelligent agents and natural language processing). He is a Fellow of the Association for the Advancement of Artificial Intelligence, and past President of the Association for *Computational Linguistics*. He has over 120 refereed publications in a wide range of venues, and is the recipient (with Prof. Hector Levesque) of an inaugural Influential Paper award by the International Foundation for Autonomous Agents and Multi-Agent Systems. Cohen is currently Vice President, Advanced Technologies at VoiceBox Technologis, Inc. His prior positions include being Founder and Executive Vice President of Research at Adapx Inc., professor and co-director of the Center for Human-Computer Communication in the Department of Computer Science and Engineering at the Oregon Health and Science University, and a Senior Computer Scientist and Director of the Natural Language Program in the Artificial Intelligence Center of SRI International.

Printed in the United States
by Baker & Taylor Publisher Services